CW01512822

NO OTHER PLACE

GEORGE
NORTH

NO OTHER PLACE
MY AUTOBIOGRAPHY

HarperCollins*Publishers*

HarperCollins*Publishers*
1 London Bridge Street
London SE1 9GF

www.harpercollins.co.uk

HarperCollins*Publishers*
Macken House, 39/40 Mayor Street Upper
Dublin 1, D01 C9W8, Ireland

First published by HarperCollins*Publishers* 2025

1 3 5 7 9 10 8 6 4 2

© George North 2025
Map illustrations © Nicolette Caven 2025

George North asserts the moral right to
be identified as the author of this work

A catalogue record of this book is
available from the British Library

HB 978-0-00-873590-6
Waterstones ISBN 978-0-00-879431-6

Printed and bound in the UK using 100%
renewable electricity at CPI Group (UK) Ltd

To Becky, Jac and Tomi, and my whole family.
Thanks for all the love and support.
It's been a hell of a ride.

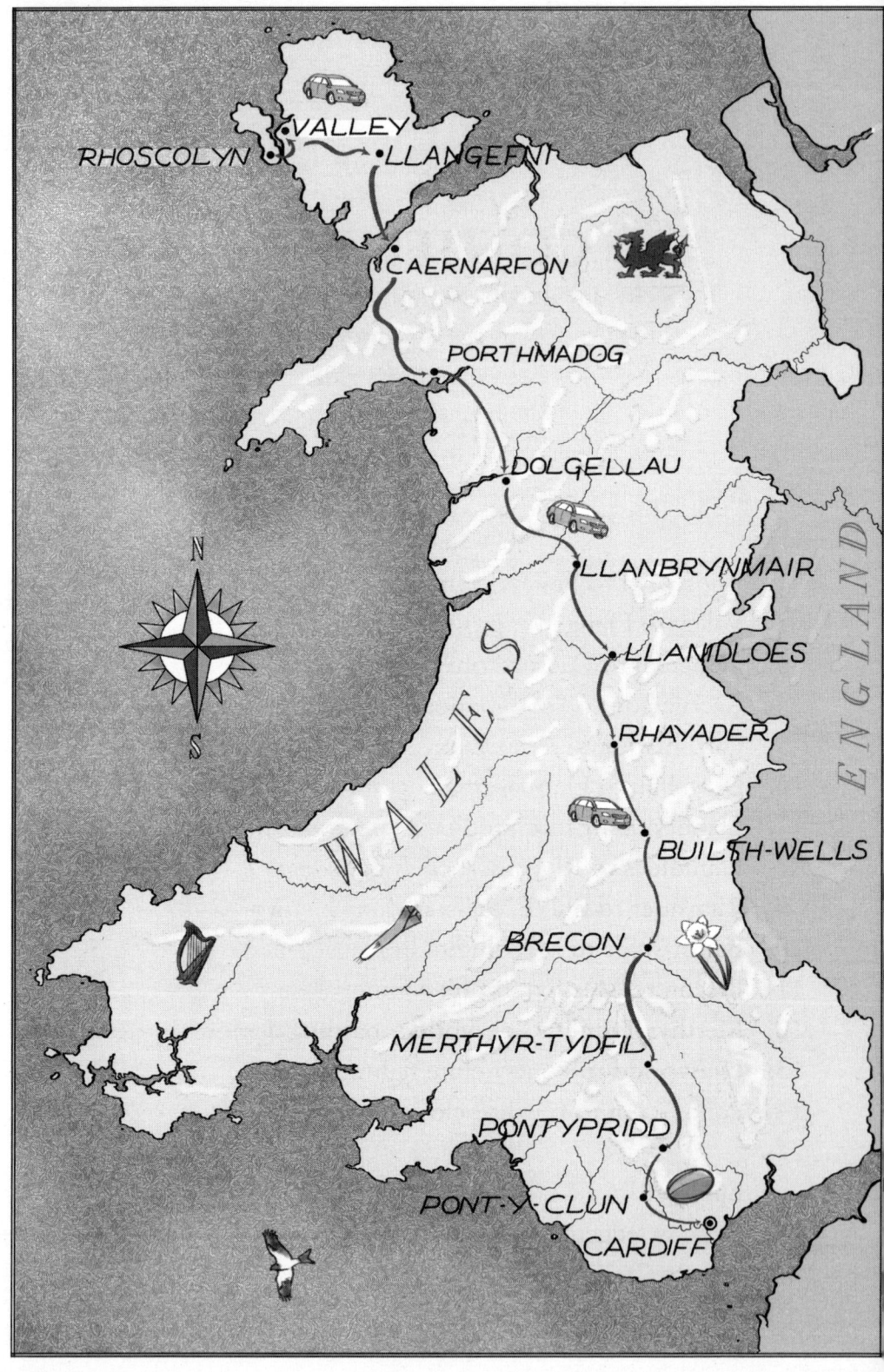

CONTENTS

PROLOGUE

Hello, my name is George.

Here's what you need to know about me, at this point. I'll shake your hand, when we first meet. I'll ask you how you are. I'll bring the energy and I'll bring the positive vibes.

Sapping is contagious. So too is being positive and bouncing around, which means I decided long ago that my cup would always be half full. It's a new day, let's get on with it.

Here's something else I have to tell you. I fell in love with this game for the open spaces. For the feeling of running as fast as I could, and those spaces opening up, and hearing everyone else dropping away far behind me.

I fell in love with what it did to those who might be watching. How me running free and clear seemed to make the people I cared about happy. How it made them jump around.

I learned my trade in the grassroots. Where you trained hard, and the pitches were heavy with mud and you might not have enough players, but you kept going. When it rained and you lost feeling in your fingertips and people wanted to smash you backwards just as much as you wanted to glide and step past them. Those qualities stay with you, when it goes from being a game to a career.

It's hard, sometimes, this life of triumph and despair. A lot of the time you wake up hurting and throw yourself back into it and you go to bed hurting more. A lot of your days you feel like you're in a deep hole.

You get used to living with big periods of crap, with doom and gloom coming for the unwary. Living in a constant state of, this is super hard, but I can't give in now. As Rob Howley – great player, great coach – told me once: George, you have to learn to be comfortable being uncomfortable.

Ah, but if you can weather the storm, if you can carry all this on your shoulders – it's all there for you. All the thrills you could ever dream of, the team-mates who will fight for you until the end, just as you would for them; the ecstatic, ear-splitting moments, those days in the sunshine and nights under the lights where you think: I wouldn't want to be anywhere else in the world.

Rugby picks you up from the place you were born and carries you along with it. It teaches you about hard work and big emotions, about coping with crisis and coming back when others might falter instead. It takes you away from your family but it binds you tight to them, too.

I grew up a long way from the heartlands of the Welsh game. Everything can feel like a battle, when you're far from the big clubs and academies and gyms. When there's so much talent available that no-one need bother looking in the back of the cupboard.

That journey from Rhoscolyn in Anglesey to the Principality Stadium in Cardiff is the story of my time. Sometimes the destination seemed an impossible distance away. A dream far beyond in the mists and imagination. Other times it was a slog, like my dad and I driving in his battered Vauxhall Cavalier through snowstorms and frozen mornings, so many hours behind the wheel, too many miles ahead.

It's also my inspiration. When you play rugby for Wales, you don't do it just for yourself. You do it for your family and your coaches, but you also do it for every village and town you pass on the way. When times are hard you look around and take fresh motivation from knowing what it means to them. When it comes good, your own pleasure is multiplied a hundred thousand times.

Every time I start that long journey, from the far north of my country to the far south, it fills my heart. It reminds me why I did it all, and who I did it for.

This is the story of how I got from there to here. Never a straight line, never a dull day. No other place I'd rather have begun; no other place I ever wanted to reach.

ONE

RHOSCOLYN TO VALLEY: GETTING STARTED

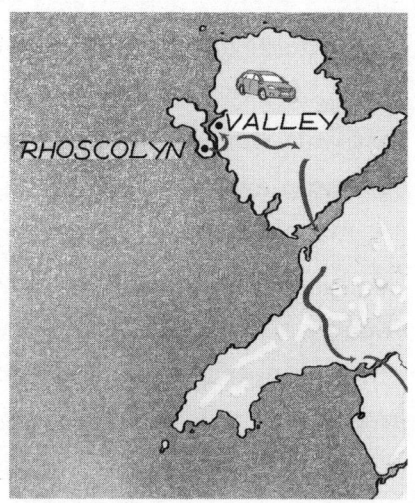

IN WHICH WE TALK ABOUT:

climbing trees/Daf Robs/Mollie the collie/a fantastic beach/
jumping off cliffs/a sit-on lawnmower/dangerous trampolines/
Ysgol Gymuned Y Fali/Little Josh/The Bonc/the single best day
of the year/red rugby jerseys/wild excitement/bale bach/
three-legged races/Dawnsio Gwerin/bunk beds/
Tom and Georgie

Do you ever truly know the place where you grow up, until you're far away?

Maybe you've been to Anglesey on holiday. Maybe you've raced through it to catch the ferry at Holyhead and get over to Ireland. Maybe to you it's just the lump sticking out at the top of the map of Wales, joined to the mainland only by a pair of bridges.

I didn't think of it as small when I was a kid. The beaches and the farms and the fields never felt cramped or crowded. I could ride my bike all day and never run out of roads. You never got lost, but that was a good thing. You were never a stranger, because everyone knew you and you knew everyone.

Here's how it works. You have uncles and aunts who aren't actually your real uncle and aunt, but are so familiar they are referred to as such. You know people by their first name and their house. Quite early on you become accustomed to your mum casually mentioning John Ty Coed, and you'll know exactly who she means. Someone else will drop in a story about Iyfor Ty Capel, and no-one bats an eyelid.

You walk home and every car beeps at you. You see some-one walking the other way and they're waving while still in the near distance.

It's like a safety-net and a benign surveillance system at the same time.

'Oh, your Uncle Eddie saw you climbing a tree on the way home from school – no wonder your trousers are ripped.'

It's a way of feeling part of everything around you, in a way that baffles those from elsewhere. People become places.

Auntie Dawn will also be known as Dawn Ty Coed. Places also become people; the farm belonging to the Parry family, where you might spend most of your summer messing about, becomes Parry Plas – Parry's Place.

Conversations develop between your mum and your aunt-who-isn't-an-aunt which only make sense from the inside.

'You remember Sally's daughter, right?'

'Oh yes.'

'Well, Sally, her best friend's Diana, and obviously Diana's sister used to be my cousin's friend.'

'Ah, do you mean Debbie?'

'Yes, Debbie. Anyway, have you heard she's getting married?'

'Yes, I have.'

When marriages come they cause havoc for the one from the mainland. A wedding where everyone has to be invited, and your baffled partner can't make sense of any of it.

'Bloody hell, you've got a lot of aunties and uncles.'

'Well, they're not really my auntie or my uncle.'

'But you've written Auntie Bev and Uncle Glyn and Uncle Eddie and Auntie Ange.'

'Yeah, but they're just like really, really good friends of my mum and dad. Like extended family. And I've always known them as Uncle Ed and Auntie Ange.'

Everyone has their name, and everyone knows them. Sometimes it's based on a former job. Like Major, who was in the Army long ago but now dog-sits for you every now and again and feeds the cats when you're away on holiday. Sometimes you're defined by your parents – 'Ah, that's Dave and Meg's boy.' Sometimes it's a contraction of your full name: Dafydd Roberts becomes Daf Robs. Sometimes it's both – 'Ah, that's Dave and Meg's Daf Robs …'

Some people love city-living, because of the anonymity of it. You can bowl about and no-one knows who you are and no-one cares where you're going. But when everyone knows everyone, you're looked after. It's not even an obvious looking after. There aren't that many people around. You can get up to more mischief and there are more places to explore and more dangers to go with them. But there's always someone who is keeping an eye out for you because they know who you are.

I liked that feeling of there being no strangers. I loved how low-key it was. You weren't getting a lift every time you want one, because there's farms to be run and always jobs to be done. So you jumped on your bike and you pedalled to the next house over or the next village, and you saw what might be going on over there, and when you caught up with that person who knew exactly who you were and how you were related-not-related, you made minimum fuss out of it. 'Alright there, what's happening?'

We ended up in Anglesey because my English-born dad was an engineer in the RAF and got posted to the air base at Valley, on the far south-west edge of the island. At a party he met my mother, and sensibly decided to ask his bosses if he could stay.

He settled fast. When I was getting out of bed in my pre-school days Dad would be going for a run before work with our dog Mollie, who was a collie, hence the name. When he rode his bike to the air base just down the road, Mollie would run with him. Then, when he left the air force, he set himself up as a blacksmith. Anything metal you saw on your bike escapades round the island could quite possibly be made by him: gates, railings, balconies.

Rhoscolyn is a small place, even by Anglesey standards. A fantastic beach, definitely better than Rhosneigr down the coast, with cliffs and inlets, open to all the weather the Irish Sea can throw at you, which is a lot of weather. Our house was on a direct line with the runway at RAF Valley. The smaller planes would come in to land over us, and the bigger ones come out our way. You'd see the Red Arrows and the Hawks screaming over, your eyes and your ears filled with their noise and speed.

This was the set-up in my family. My elder sister Natalie, who is a Hadingham these days, married her husband Ed, who is a farmer from Suffolk way, and had four kids. Then Hayley, who is now a Cushing, in Northampton, with three kids. Then there's my brother, Gau, who is now married with two kids. When I was 15 weeks old, Dad got posted to Kathmandu, Singapore and Hong Kong. Hayley was head girl at her school in Hong Kong; Gau was head boy. His father was in the Nepalese Gurkhas. Gau wanted to come back and study in the UK, so we basically took him in, and he never left. Next comes my brother Josh, 18 months older than me. Then there's me, the last but the largest, the biggest baby the family had yet seen. All of us always having big family Christmases, big birthdays, big summer holidays.

As a kid I was a jack of all trades. As long as the suggested adventure didn't involve being sat inside on my backside, I was up for it. Which, since most of my neighbours were farmers, and all our neighbours my mates, was straightforward to achieve.

Summer was always busy. People would arrive to stay in the holiday caravans and surf on the beaches. When the tourists went home, you made your own fun in their absence. Plans were hatched with Daf Robs for the next day while the current one was still in progress.

'Ah, should we go on the mountain bikes?'

'Yeah, yeah, we'll go on the mountain bikes.'

'I'll meet you at this place at 4.30 p.m.'

'Yeah, okay, cool, cool, cool.'

We'd meet and go for a bike ride. On the days when it was sunny – which wasn't every week in Anglesey – the question would change. 'Ah, do you want to go jumping?'

Jumping would mean we'd lob ourselves off Four Mile Bridge into the sea. Or we'd ride our bikes south instead of north, throw them down behind a hedge and spend hours jumping in off the cliffs, climbing back out a hundred yards further along and then doing it all again. Usually in knackered old wetsuits, because North Wales is not Barbados. The key piece of equipment was wetsuit shoes with a good rubber sole. There's a lot of scratchy old rocks in Anglesey. There's a lot of barnacles.

Our house was not huge. A bungalow we all happily crammed into. We didn't have as much as some other families, but it was fine. We had a roof over our heads, the house was always warm, and every night we had a bellyful of food. You trimmed your sails according to the season. When we needed trainers, we'd go to the market next to my dad's work in Valley, and we'd buy them from this fellow selling stuff out of the back of his lorry. My eyes were inevitably drawn to the Adidas ones. My parents were drawn to the more competitively priced Hi-Tec. You knew that the laces on the Hi-Tec ones would split and fail within a couple of weeks. You dreamed of the day when Adidas on your feet were a genuine possibility. But you didn't stress, and you didn't worry about it. Mum and Dad grafted for us. We had everything we wanted. You just sometimes had to get to it in a roundabout way.

My dad's years of training as an engineer was the usual way in. Rhoscolyn was a place of quadbikes and motorbikes and bashed-up old cars, reflecting the farming background of most people there. The openings for us would usually come when my mum was away. That's when we'd jump in Dad's wheezing Cavalier, zoom across to Liverpool to pick up a knackered motorbike or up and over to Wrexham to look at a rusty quadbike being flogged by a farmer outside the town, and then spend the next week taking it apart and trying to fix it up. All around Dad's workshop would be scattered these carcasses and innards of various formerly useless machines, parts and components cannibalised to form new Frankenstein bikes that won few prizes for aesthetics but worked an absolute treat.

You could always find a way, if you put your mind to it. At one stage Josh and I really fancied a trampoline. This was the era when they started popping up in everyone's gardens rather than just down the hall at the local leisure centre. We were desperate to have one, but a sparkling new one was out of the question. So when Dad returned home one day with one which didn't have a safety net around the outside, my mum lost her head.

'Dave, why have you bought the kids a trampoline with no net?'

'Well, it was cheaper, wasn't it?'

Dad: always the Yorkshireman. Mum: away working late the following week. Daf Robs was over at ours. We'd worked out that a fine addition to jumping off Four Mile Bridge and jumping off the cliffs near the beach would be jumping on the trampoline – softer landing, more repeat jumps per minute of effort.

We'd been bouncing for a few hours when I looked back at the bungalow and had a brainwave.

'Wouldn't it be cool if we could jump off the house onto the trampoline? Imagine how high we could get!'

Dad was the responsible adult in the house. I went inside and flagged it to him. Immediately he was on board.

'Yeah, yeah, that would be amazing …'

He was the one who helped Daf Robs and me push the trampoline up against the side of the house. The exact moment Mum arrived home was the first time both Daf and I jumped off the roof onto the unguarded springs. The exact moment we both bounced sideways to amazing new heights was when we saw the true Welsh mother emerge.

Everywhere you looked was potential fun and willing accomplices. Rhoscolyn is the middle of nowhere by Anglesey standards, Anglesey is the far corner of North Wales and

North Wales is the Arctic Circle if you're from Cardiff. But it felt like the centre of everything to me, especially in the summer months. Opposite our house was a field of static caravans. The same families would come every holiday, and because their kids were the same age as us, we'd be best friends with Tom and Georgie every time they stayed. No-one seemed to worry too much about what you were up to, as long as there was a few of you. One to get in trouble, one to stay with them, one to sound the alarm and go for help.

My dad was always keen on motorised kicks. That's why he bought a second-hand sit-on lawnmower for us, one day. It had nothing to do with the quality of our grass, and much more to do with the fact that my mum would never have allowed us near a quadbike at this age. First he fixed it up so it moved. Then he took off the cutting blades, so what we had left was fundamentally a very, very small tractor. He made a trailer from odd wheels and bits of metal, stuck two old car seats in the back of that, and then set us off. We would go up and down the drive at three miles an hour, taking it in turns to steer, giving our mates Tom and Georgie rides. Up and down, up and down, for hours at a time.

School was initially up in Valley, when we lived closer to Dad's work. Even though we lived round the corner at that point, we were always late. In the same way that the sun rises and the sun sets, my mother is late. We reached a point where all the clocks in our house were set 10 minutes fast, but that just seemed to give her the illusion of a buffer that didn't really exist. So most mornings would be a blind panic as she belatedly realised we once again were not going to make it.

'Get your shoes on! We've got to go! We've got to go!'

On dry days it would be a sprint round the corner to the school gates. If it was hammering down, which was a daily possibility, the wording might change but the vibe would stay the same.

'Quick, get in the car! I'm late for work!'

One of my best friends at primary school was Little Josh, so named to differentiate him from my brother, who was both older and larger. Little Josh lived a similar distance away on the other side of the school. But whereas you could set a clock by our inability to stick to a clock, Little Josh had the discipline of Major and his old army pals. We would arrive laughing our heads off, half-dressed, sprinting up to the entrance, and Little Josh would always be waiting, nicely turned out, ready to go.

The school itself, Ysgol Gymuned Y Fali, was a series of grey one-storey buildings. There was a nice old brick part and then various bits which had been bolted on down the years. One of the classrooms was a static caravan with the wheels taken off, used as the meithrinfa, the nursery. More thrilling was something we called the Bonc, which at the time felt like a large hill in the playground, but in retrospect was actually more a mild incline. The Bonc was the basis for pretty much every game you wanted to run. Hold the Bonc when the bell went for the end of breaktime and you were pretty much the king or queen of Ysgol Gymuned Y Fali.

The playground similarly shrank in size when I returned in future years. What felt like an enormous expanse to five-year-old George was revealed to my adult self as two netball courts with multi-coloured lines painted on it for multiple sports. These also provided excellent imaginary roads on bike safety day, which was always hotly anticipated. Could you cycle down the tramlines of a tennis court no-one ever played tennis on while extending your right arm out to the side? For the experienced bike adventurers among us, this was tame stuff, but still significantly better than sitting inside.

We were thrilled with what we had. Out the back was a full-size football pitch with a pronounced slope from one goal to the other. When sports day was on – the single best day of the entire year – you would run down the hill, which made you feel like a legend. When you played football on it, you had the classic conditions conundrum: take the uphill first, and then capitalise in the second period, or establish a first-half lead with the assistance of the slope and then defend it for all you were worth? 'Park the bus, boys, we're 2–1 up! No-one leaves our box!' I tended to the optimistic approach: soak up your downhill, then back yourself second half. Let your superior fitness come into play.

There weren't that many of us in the school. Somewhere between 12 and 15 kids per class, only five years in total. The lessons didn't have a huge impact on me; I coloured in, and I did spelling tests, and I paid attention when the nice lady came round and showed us how to brush our teeth in the dental hygiene class, or look out for nits. I'm in my early thirties now, and I still follow her advice each morning and night: 'If you can lick your teeth and they feel they're not smooth, you've missed a bit.' I've never had nits. Her job is done.

I was more drawn to what would happen when school ended. If Mum couldn't pick us up because she was working late or simply running late, Josh and I would walk over to Dad's yard. It should have taken us 10 minutes or so. It never did, because there were always stones or conkers to kick down the road, or trees to climb. I was less about focus on the job in hand and more about losing myself in any sort of distraction that ended in scuffed shoes.

My favourite day of all, beyond even the annual sports day or cycling proficiency? When our collie Mollie escaped from her kennel at the back of our house, heard the noise of a hundred kids running around in a nearby field and jumped enough fences that she could join in. Oh, the giddy thrill of her arrival.

'There's a dog in the school! There's a dog in the school!'

Running outside to have a look. All the other kids screaming.

'Oh my God, there's a dog!'

The sudden shock of recognition. 'Oh my God, that's my dog! Get away from my dog!'

Oh, the magic of being able to play the hero. 'Mollie, get back! Here, Mollie ...'

Sport was always around us. Rugby was always there. My dad would casually mention that he had played a bit, but he was never over the top about it. He didn't encourage us to support a particular club or region. What you couldn't miss was the excitement in the air whenever Wales played. Everyone cared. Everyone watched.

For a kid tuned in to the people around him, you couldn't miss it. Early on in primary school, Wales were playing a Six Nations match just before St David's Day. We all piled into one of the classrooms and crowded around a little TV to watch. All the kids from across the different age groups were in their own outfits – some of them in red rugby jerseys, others in traditional costume, bonnets borrowed from dressing-up boxes or dance classes, quite a few with a daffodil or leek pinned to their chests.

I had no idea what was going on. The rules seemed impenetrable. The game stopped a lot. But the colours were intense and the energy tangible. There was a raw excitement in not knowing what was going to happen next. It wasn't like watching a film where you knew there was a guaranteed happy ending, or reading a book where you could cheat and jump to the last few pages. With rugby, no-one seemed to have any idea. I loved what that did to everyone around me. I wanted more. As soon as possible.

As other matches came along, it was seldom about who they were against and never about the competition. It didn't matter if it was a Six Nations game or the autumn internationals or a summer tour. It was just that same wild excitement in everyone around you – the aunties, the uncles, the parents of friends, the big brothers and the people in the shops and in the fields. I still didn't really know what was going on, but it was like the whole of Christmas time squashed down into one day, the sporting equivalent of running home from school at the end of the winter term: 'Santa's coming! Oh wow, Santa's coming!'

Rugby took longer to become something I played. Were the things I did transferable to my future career? Riding my bike with Daf Robs must have helped build an engine. Jumping off cliffs requires a certain kamikaze bravery. Climbing trees is good for upper body strength.

Then there was the baling work, or what we called bale bach – small bales of hay, just about small enough for us to lift. My friends Rhodri and Meilir lived on a farm called Parry Plas on the other side of the village, and went to the same school. It was an unwritten rule among all the farmers that everyone helped each other out when help was needed. When it was time to get all the bales in, we would all get a call, and they would let us ride round the field on the quad-bike and the motorbikes and fill their tractor trailers with bales. At the peak of the season, in late summer, you'd be heaving these bales about all day. Your hands would be prickly from the hay and torn up from the coarse string that bound them. When the bales were stacked high and the other lads could no longer throw them up on top of the trailer, I'd be the last one at the bottom, flinging them up, going along behind the tractor and grabbing all the ones the farmer couldn't pick up with the mechanical claw at the front of his tractor. When you had to go back to the farm to unload, you had to do the reverse and chuck the bales from the trailer into the barn. You'd end up with heat rash, and you'd end up starving hungry, but you also got strong, fast – without even noticing you were training.

So lots of things I did would end up helping with my rugby. But I think that's looking at it the wrong way round. The reason I would fall for rugby, when it eventually arrived, is that it came from the same place as all those adventures. It fitted into all the things I naturally wanted to do, and all the things that gave me a thrill: being outside, moving fast, messing about with my mates.

And, of course, the sense of competition. My three key events on sports day each summer were all classics: egg and spoon, beanbag-on-head race and the three-legged race. The balancing ones were not my strong point. The finesse of the beanbag was not for me; I would have to concentrate so hard that my tongue would stick out the side of my mouth. Egg and spoon I would sometimes let myself down. If I was behind coming into the closing stages and in desperate need of making up places, it wasn't unknown for my thumb to pop out onto the egg and secure it in place as I picked up speed. Not all the time, of course, just when I was lagging and needed to get back in the mixer.

The three-legged race was the one for me. My advantage came in my size and speed. I could drag people with me when others would find themselves anchored. With the passing years I like to think that the communication skills I had to develop in elite sport were my point of difference; a successful three-legged pairing thrives on simple, clear instructions. 'Left! Right! Left! Right!' But if I'm brutally honest, that came later. At primary school I was almost entirely a dragger.

It's a technique game, the three-legged. Arm around your partner's shoulder, rather than their waist. It's a superior binding. Never attempting to run without the lock, maybe the weaker of the two competitors getting to choose their preferred side. The outside arm driving hard, the inside arm the grip. Timing is critical, because this is not an event you can raw-dog. Embrace its complexities. It's a lifestyle, not a phase.

I wanted to win, of course I did. But sports day brought so much. No lessons, sitting outside, loads of cheering and jumping around. It could have been specifically designed for the young G. North. Plenty of cheat food – teachers selling ice-creams for 50p, bags of sweets being knocked out that quite clearly say on the packaging, 'MULTIPACK: do not sell individually' and the teachers selling them anyway.

But I wasn't a natural performer, in other ways. Not one to seek the limelight nor the chance to take centre stage. When December came around and casting for the nativity play took place, I had no interest in a leading role – Joseph, Herod, any of the big hitters. I would set my sights on Shepherd Number Five and let no-one else get close. The only line of dialogue I would want would be one said in unison with four other kids: 'Lo, it is baby Jesus …'

Which made my experience with Dawnsio Gwerin all the more painful. Dawnsio Gwerin, for non-Welsh natives, is traditional folk dancing. A boy and a girl in historic costume, paired together and then dancing a formal routine with three other couples.

It was never going to be my first choice of activity. But somehow I raised my hand at the wrong time, or took the wrong letter back to my parents, or gambled that they would take one look at my moves and sack me off before it began. Because the other choices were even worse: writing a poem, growing an impressively large leek, or performing a traditional Welsh song. Little Josh and I thus allowed our names to go forward in some confidence, and then suddenly we found ourselves selected and the whole awful process in motion.

Worst still, the standard of competition we were up against had taken a nosedive that term. Quite by accident, we found ourselves moving up the rankings until we were somehow selected for the final of the Urdd. Don't know what the Urdd is? It's a celebration of Welsh culture, with competitions in poetry recitals, singing, art … and traditional folk dancing.

That year it was held in Cardiff. So Little Josh and I were sent down with our dance partners, our mothers as chaperones/transport logistics, wearing the itchiest of costumes which had been used by multiple children across multiple decades and had spent the previous 11 months in a bin bag in someone's dusty attic. Smart black school shoes on, buffed furiously by my dad to make sure they looked half tidy, the worst thing of all having to hold a girl's hand in public and in front of one of your best mates. A truly disgusting idea to a young boy.

At this stage I was a strong boy, but I wasn't the biggest kid in school. I was stocky but stayed average height until puberty kicked in, at which point I became gangly until puberty got a second wind and I had a rapid growth spurt. My brother was the one who grew early. He was the one the elders in the family predicted would be the tall one, the one who would match my dad's 6' 3", or catch up with his 6' 2" when he had a disc removed from his spine.

It was Josh and me, as the two youngest in the family, who shared a bedroom. We had two sets of bunk beds, one each, mainly because we had so many in the family we frequently needed spare beds for relatives and stragglers. Variety being the spice of life, I would mix it up between top and bottom. I had a PlayStation 2 stashed down below, but it barely got a look-in. There were too many interesting things to get up to outside.

Our garden was relatively small. That didn't matter, not when you had the rugby field down the road, and the beaches, and your mates' farms. If the sun was shining, we would go bodyboarding on the big waves at Rhosneigr, or my sister Hayley would drive Josh and me over to Trearddur Bay in her Fiat Uno for ice-creams. If it rained, there was Tom and Georgie in the caravan park over the road, with their Super Nintendo *Mario Kart* and *Streetfighter*. When it rains on a caravan, it sounds like the end of the world. Maybe that's why we'd often fail to hear Mum shouting out the window to come home because dinner was ready. It became a loose arrangement: if your mates were at your house at teatime, they'd get fed there. If I was at Tom and Georgie's and missed the maternal signal through the drumming of rain on tin roof, I'd get my feed with them.

Once a term, you'd accept being inside at school after usual hours, because it was school disco time. There was a strict gender divide in place: the girls standing around talking politely, or dancing on the makeshift dancefloor, us boys banging back a blue Panda Pop and a handful of Skittles and then spending the rest of the evening sliding around on our knees, getting sweaty and clammy. Watch out, ladies.

We had no interest in talking to them. They considered us below them, quite rightly. I was into sliding about on my knees at the best of times, but under the flashing lights of the mobile disco it was like some glorious new level of endeavour. This being Anglesey, there was only one DJ, and he had also DJed at the school discos of most people's parents, as well as many of their weddings and landmark birthday parties.

That was our way of seeing things, of doing things. That was our world.

TWO

VALLEY TO LLANGEFNI: GROWING UP

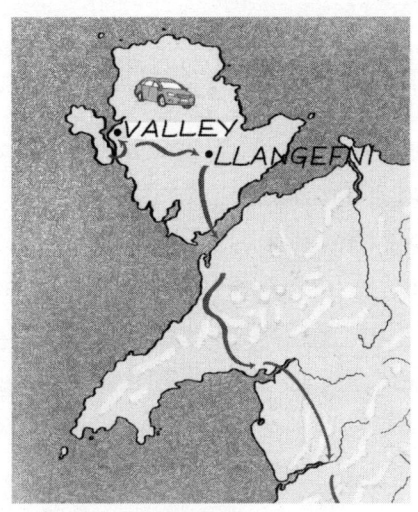

IN WHICH WE TALK ABOUT:

Llangefni RFC/Klinsmann dives/Romania in Wrexham/'Let me rip!'/an instinct deep inside/Aberystwyth's premier nightclub/ Iori Hughes and Martin Williams/Ysgol Uwchradd Bodedern/'George, what did you do that for?'/Rhodri and Meilir/Clarks – black, bog-standard/Josh the exam machine/ Pwllheli or Rhyl or Ruthin/compartmentalising the shittier aspects/the dancing feet of Shane Williams/going full-fat milk/'You stop when you're done ...'

So while it was inevitable that I would end up at the rugby club, there wasn't a rush. Josh was the first one to go down to Llangefni RFC, and when he came back with glowing reports, my fraternal jealousy and our natural competitiveness kicked in.

'Ah, it was good was it?'

'Yeah, yeah, really good.'

'Well, I want to go, then.'

'No, it's my thing.'

'No it's not.'

When I went down for the first time, aged 11, I immediately understood what he meant. 'Bloody hell, this is nuts …'

It didn't matter that it was smashing down with rain. This was not an unusual scenario for the Rhoscolyn crew, and as part of my commitment to the outdoors lifestyle I was comfortable operating in all conditions. It didn't matter that we weren't allowed on the main pitch and instead were sent to the cabbage patch right down at the bottom. It was actually better: there was more mud, you had no choice but to slide around, and if you put your mind to it, you could slide for miles and end up in even more mud.

Even in those first couple of weeks, rugby began to mean something to me. An attitude of: things are a bit crap, the weather's not great, pitch isn't the best and there's not enough of us to really do anything properly, but we may as well make the most of it as we're here. A togetherness, between all of you getting stuck in.

Rain? Bring it on. I found I actually played better when it was wet, purely because it was more fun. I loved larking about with the other boys, doing Klinsmann dives, nice long ones on our chests. At Llangefni the cabbage patch was right down the far end of the club. Your mum and dad would start watching you, and then after about 10 minutes they'd go back to the clubhouse for a cup of tea in a polystyrene cup. They couldn't see us from up there, so we could crack on even more. By the time we got back to the clubhouse they would be outside waiting for us, shaking their heads, muttering among themselves.

'Look at the state of this …'

Many was the time I had to travel back home in my pants because I'd had to strip off my ruined kit in the boot of the car. I had no real interest in hanging about to watch the seniors, or see the older age groups train. There was no fun in watching. The fun was in the doing.

Dad had taken me to Twickenham when I was nine to watch England play Italy. My main takeaway had been how impressive it was to witness fellow spectators whistling with two fingers in their mouth. This was the sort of skill I wanted to learn. To my dad's great regret he taught me. It was all he heard the entire journey back home to Anglesey.

I was 11 years old when I went to my first Wales game – playing Romania in Wrexham, one of the warm-up games before the 2003 Rugby World Cup. A couple of my friends from the farm across the way from us were going; I played rugby with their two brothers. I can remember almost nothing of the match itself, certainly none of the 24 points Gavin Henson scored, although Mike Phillips later informed me he made his Wales debut that day and scored a try. It was the atmosphere that stayed with me. That same sense that every-one around me was more alive than at any other time. There may not have been much two-fingered whistling, but there was noise and shouting and joy everywhere you looked. That and the drive from Rhoscolyn to Wrexham, which felt like it took four days.

So Dad never said to me, fancy going to watch this club game today, or shall we see who the seniors have got this weekend? I played, and I only stayed if it was the end of season awards or if my mum was late to pick me up. Mum being Mum, the lateness was a regular thing, but even then the club and the community were there like an invisible safety net around you. One of the other mums would be waiting instead: 'Don't worry, George, she's rung me. Come have a cup of tea.' Maybe on those days you'd be less keen on trav-elling back home in only your pants, but it wasn't the end of the world if you did. Everyone knew most things about you anyway. What was there to hide?

Always outside over inside, always bouncing around the place. It made my daily decision-making a simple process.

'Do you want to go for a bike ride?'

'Yeah, that sounds good.'

'Do you want to go for a run?'

'Okay, cool.'

'Do you want to go jump off this bridge?'

'Yeah, screw it, we'll give it a go ...'

It wasn't the physical contact that worked for me when rugby came along. Some kids can't wait to smash other kids. My younger son Tomi was still shy of his third birthday when we took him down to Rugbytots for the first time. This is normal in Wales. When we moved to Provence my fear was that he was more of an outlier. His elder brother Jac had been ambivalent about the tackling drills he had done. Tomi would be like a tornado. He would want to join in. I could imagine exactly what was going to happen: he was going to crunch some poor kid, and I wouldn't have enough French words to apologise.

What ramped up my excitement was when our age group changed and we were allowed to go from playing on half a pitch to a bigger one. Suddenly there was so much more room for fun. Suddenly there was so much more space to run. My vibe was a simple one: 'Watch out, let me rip!'

Space was freedom. Running was escaping. Being chased by my mates was the purest type of fun, even better than chasing them. I was a hare rather than the hound. I'd get a giddy laugh on, swerving to get away from one, accelerating away from another. All the time thinking, you can't catch me …

When we were allowed to score tries – now that felt special. As a kid in Wales, you don't speak about how many tackles you've made. I hadn't met Shaun Edwards at that point. You talk about how many tries you scored. Same with football: it was always, 'I scored three goals today,' never 'I shut down three promising attacking opportunities with two solid tackles and an interception.' You were trying to make your mum and dad happy, you were trying to make them proud about what you were doing and them taking you there. It didn't matter that tries only counted for a single point, if at all. You didn't care that no-one could remember the score at the end, or any specific details. I would run back up to the clubhouse to tell my mum and dad, and just as parents do when their child presents them with a drawing and they can't work out what the hell it's supposed to be, their reaction spoke of their own pleasure in my enjoyment.

'Oh wow, that's amazing!'

There were never any financial inducements on offer. I was used to having to earn my pocket money by doing jobs around the house – washing the car, mowing the lawn. But it didn't work the same way with rugby – a lolly for every try or a quid for every five. I was never motivated that way. You could have offered me a bag of chips for every 10 tries I scored, and it wouldn't have made me want to score 10 tries any more than I did already.

It was pure pleasure. An instinct deep inside just looking for the right excuse to get out. When as an adult you're drunk and you're running, you feel like you can run as fast as you can and still never get tired. It was the same when I was a kid, except rather than being drunk it was giggling. I could run and run, and when I was laughing my socks off at the fun of it all, it was like fuel kept pouring into my tank. I could keep going as long as I wanted to.

Years later, when I was breaking into the Welsh side and I had an operation on my labrum (my shoulder) my mates and I went away camping in Aberystwyth for one of the boys' birthdays. I was only just out of my sling, but we were drinking, and spirits were high. We were in Aberystwyth's premier nightclub when my mates started asking how my shoulder felt. High on life, I windmilled my arm with delight. Half an hour later, I ran to Aberystwyth's second-best nightclub with my arm flinging about all over the place. I felt fine. I felt incredible. I told the boys so.

When I woke up a few hours later in a soggy tent, the magic potion had well and truly worn off. Nothing felt incredible now. It felt catastrophic. 'Oh my fucking God, what have I done?'

There is no pain as a kid. There's no need to warm up. You just go. No child ever says they don't want to play because they'll get sweaty. It's raw enjoyment, and if it changes as you get older and your messaround with your mates becomes a career, if you can hold onto some of those old feelings and tap into them when times get darker and more serious, then that's a magic potion of its own too.

And, of course, you need the right people around you. At Llangefni we had Iori Hughes and Martin Williams, coaches who taught you about fun, but also about punctuality. Who could gently help you build your skills and understanding of this complex game but do it in a way that all felt natural and enjoyable rather than finger-wagging or tedious. Both were very welcoming, very North Walian – giving instructions first in Welsh, and then translating afterwards. Iori was a former front row, and you could tell from the moment you laid eyes on him. Passionate about his rugby. Martin was a former back row forward, a few seasons having passed since his own playing days. They were the ones who taught me that it was about enjoyment first, but that part of the enjoyment was getting stuck in. You didn't stand around and watch everyone else, with Iori and Martin.

At around the same time there was Keith Withers, my PE teacher at the secondary school I had started at, Ysgol Uwchradd Bodedern. There had been no rugby at the school until Keith had started a team, converting footballers, coaxing reluctant others to give it a try. He was one of those teachers who helped you with your rugby, and your other sports, but also kept an eye out for you in everything else you did. He was your typical PE teacher, always in a polo shirt, looked older than he was but unreal on a badminton court. He taught me all those wonderful rugby basics; working together, understanding what all your team-mates did, bringing people together. He could get the best from the disparate talents at his disposal. He could keep even the reluctant coming back for more.

At Bodedern no longer was it a two-minute walk to the school gates. Now there were the joys of the school bus – a dash down the lanes to the pick-up point, us the first on board on the outward leg and the last drop-off on the way back. It felt like we had to get up at the crack of dawn, and the bus had seen better days and more exciting trips. A double-decker on an island that otherwise had no call for mass public transport, the sort of heavy aroma that spoke of years of misuse and minimal interior valeting. But it was worth being first men in to get the prize seats – lower deck, far back, two sets facing forward, two facing back for maximum conversational opportunities.

These were the seats on a raised section, which allowed you to run the rule over those getting on board at subsequent stops. It was a false kind of superiority, because we were the sort of kids who could talk a good game but were actually scared of their own shadows. No seatbelts, so always the temptation to have a wander around, and always with the same result: getting shouted at by a driver who had not envisaged his driving days encompassing mobile childcare. Because the double-decker had seen service on a long-ago proper route, it still had the push-button bell built into the ceiling and poles. All of us knew we weren't supposed to ring it, which meant we all rang it every chance we could. When we did, the blame had to be shifted with immediate effect. 'Oh George, what did you do that for?'

It probably took us 25 minutes, although it felt like at least an hour. Little Josh had gone to a different school now, a bigger one up Menai Bridge way. But Daf Robs would jump on board, either in Four Mile Bridge when he was staying at his grandmother's, his Nain's, or from Valley, near his house. Daf was a year older than me, pretty much between me and my brother, but our shared interests kept us together.

In this pre-mobile phone age, the bus conversation was key to your social diary.

'What are you doing now?'

'Nothing. What are you doing now?'

'Nothing.'

'Should we go out on the bikes?'

'Yeah, yeah, yeah, I'll meet you there.'

We had quite the group building around us. The boys at the rugby club; the lads, like Rhodri and Meilir, from the farms all around; more and more from school. Socialising on bikes, off cliffs, on quadbikes. We got ourselves into trouble, often. I got told off a fair few times, which was my own doing. There were different levels to it: entry – coming home covered in shit; medium – riding home with no lights, and having to launch yourself into a hedge to avoid a car coming the other way; elite – being spotted on a quadbike on the main road by one of your mum's friends.

It usually began with optimism – 'I'll just pop out for an hour' – and then a misjudgement. I found it almost impossible to accurately judge when it would get dark, and how much time I had to get home before it did. I'd take a glance at the sky, make a calculation and seldom get it right. There would come a lurching realisation that I had to be home in 10 minutes but was still 10 miles away, because other more exciting ideas had presented themselves to me: 'What's down this way?' 'What's over this lane? 'Ah, I wonder where this comes out ...'

Inevitably, I would get home in total darkness. When the telling off came, my mum was the hairdryer and my dad the much scarier quiet, disappointed voice. Was it a fraction rich of my mother to take offence at someone else being home late? It's not for me to say. What she deserves credit for is her accuracy with a missile. You know that Angelina Jolie film, *Wanted*, where she bends bullets? My mum could do that with shoes. She once hit me down the hall round the corner. It was a different era. I probably deserved it. I was genuinely impressed.

You couldn't be scruffy leaving our house, not with my father's military background. The uniform at Ysgol Uwchradd Bodedern was an unusual one: black trousers, red shirt, black and red tie, navy jumper. This red shirt was not a polo shirt. It was a shirt shirt. The tie, as befitted the era, was worn short and fat. A big square knot, the little skinny end of the tie tucked inside the red shirt shirt.

This style was never going to cut it with my dad. There was much talk of not going to school looking like that – absolute shambles … no son of mine … you know the sort of thing. He taught me the classic old Royal Air Force double Windsor, which was never going to work for me, so we compromised and met in the middle at the half Windsor.

The cool kids would wear black trainers. A Nike black on black, an Adidas all-black Stan Smith. The teachers could tell they were trainers, which was against the rules, but because of the sober colour, they could exist somewhere near the margins – a grey area for black shoes, if you will. It's the sort of thing you can get away with now with a trendy suit, but in Anglesey in the early 2000s it marked you out as an edgy maverick. The coolest kids of all would go for big old fat Timberlands, possibly an Etnies or a DC. But these were both over the top and overly expensive, so it was a brave kid who persevered.

Mine? Clarks. Black, bog-standard. If they came home dirty, perhaps after a game of football in the field, my dad would spot it and make us polish them. Worse was the suggestion that, as our feet grew, we should play rugby in his old eight-stud Gilbert boots. In a world where you dreamed of Predators, an antique boot that came up to your ankles was a heavy blow indeed. When I arrived in Provence for my professional swansong, almost 20 years later, the announcer at the ground turned out to be called Gilbert. He was a lovely fellow, but every time I saw him all I could see were these horrendous daps I was forced to wear as a kid.

I was never a massive rebel. The way we were dragged up gave you too much of a conscience. I wasn't the kid in school who would chew toilet roll and spit it at fellow pupils through a straw. I wouldn't bite hard sugary sweets in half and launch them across the classroom, as the Timberland crew would. I would push things to the point of almost doing them and then go full Code Brown. I couldn't push myself further because I was always wary of the hairdryer when I got home.

My crimes were more sociable, more red collar. Getting sent out of the classroom for talking. Failing to pick up on clear instructions first time around. My timing was generally a fraction off. Someone else would be talking during lessons and get shouted at, but I would then forget this and start talking myself, and since the teacher had already lost their head and I was the next cab off the rank, I would be the one who got sent out.

Even as an adult the same malaise dogs me. If I need to get some admin done I have to take myself to a part of the house where there's no-one to talk to. I have to ask others not to find me and engage me in conversation, or I'll find my attention wandering and my admin untouched. Since this wasn't a feasible option at school, where leaving the classroom was the sentence not the plea bargain, the same scenario would often repeat.

Me, enthusiastic and bouncy like a labrador: 'How you getting on?'

'Shh, teacher says we can't talk.'

'What you up to?'

No reply.

Me, persisting: 'What do you reckon this is going to be like?'

From the front: 'George! Stop talking!'

'Sorry, sorry …'

I was always 'George', never 'North'. In my year I think I was the only one. If there were two of us Georges, I spent the whole of secondary school ignoring him. I did keep an eye out for the other North in town, my brother Josh, although this brought its own complications. If I got into a scrap defending his good name, he would then get into a fight with me for assuming he needed my help to protect him. I got it, but he was my brother. I wasn't going to stand around while some idiot who didn't know him tried to ruin his bus journey home.

Because Josh was the intelligent one. Josh was the exam machine. Maybe it turned out to be horses for courses, in its own way: he became an osteopath, I ran around in the mud for a living. I would always just get my study plans the wrong way round. Josh would do three hours' work and then make sure he took an hour's break. I would do an hour's work and then reward myself with three hours elsewhere.

All the time, rugby was giving me its own complementary education. We were playing bigger games now, travelling beyond the island, making regular trips across the bridge to the mainland, along the coast or deeper into the country. We were setting off on epic journeys to Pwllheli or Rhyl or

Ruthin or Dolgellau. All of them felt a million miles away. All of them gave you a slightly different perspective on where you came from and what other people thought of it.

That was the geography and maybe some of the economics. Rugby was subtly giving us much more. The manners to shake someone's hand, to say please and thank you. The ability to communicate, not only with lads your own age but lads you didn't know or parents and coaches. There was working together, when a game needed winning, and there was dealing with adversity, when it ended up taking a different turn. I can keep going: respect, discipline, focus, drive. An honesty, when things needed to be done – okay, let's just do it, and not whinge and complain. Maybe you had to be open to it for it to go in. Maybe it was just building layers upon the things you'd been taught at home.

It worked both ways, too. Like any family, we had tough times, and we had crises. Sometimes things happened that were hard to make sense of, or left you feeling powerless, or deeply upset. From these other times I seemed to quite quickly develop an ability to process difficult stuff, to compartmentalise the shittier aspects. I found I could take information that wasn't fun or nice, or big emotions I couldn't understand in the moment, and put them somewhere to deal with while I cracked on. I wouldn't say anything, but I would sit there and work my way through it my own way. When I was ready, I would talk about it.

In rugby, either in the heat of matches or in the aftermath of great disappointments, this would turn out to be an incredibly useful tool. I didn't overthink the emotions before a game. I learned I could cope with making a mistake. The wheels didn't come off if we lost a critical game.

It all strengthened the bond between me and this sport which meant so much to the people and places all around me. I was growing now, not in heft but in height. Catching up with Josh, going past lots of the kids at school. I could run away from tacklers but I could run over a few too. As rugby became more intense, I rode that wave. Even in the summer holidays I would drag myself away from the beach or having a wild old time on the bikes to go and train, because the internal monologue always made sense.

'Ah, the waves are big today, I might just leave it ...'

'But I really enjoy training.'

'Also I'm having a great time here ...'

'Yeah, and training will be exactly the same. Let's go ...'

I never felt tired. I always felt hungry. Both Josh and I were endless holes for food. Huge breakfast, biggest lunch possible at school, straight into the fridge when we got home. Yoghurts and custard creams on the sofa, flipping open kitchen cupboards to see what delights might be stashed inside.

There was never a defining single moment when I realised I might be good at rugby. No look from a coach or comment from a parent or morning when the sky opened and a beam of light hit me and I felt chosen for a particular path. But there was one day when we were playing in the schools' cup for Bodedern, as the unfancied team, and I scored a try where I just ran away from everyone. I put the ball down and turned around and was hit by the realisation that all my team-mates, and all the parents watching, and the teachers – every one of them was bouncing around with joy and excitement. The strangest thought popping into my head: 'Holy flip, I've just done something that's made a lot of people happy, and it's something I don't think everyone could do.' Then the next one: 'That was actually really good fun.' Never blowing smoke up myself, not thinking, well done me. Simply: I loved doing that. Everyone else seemed to love it too.

You have those momentary little miracles and you gradually come to the realisation that this could mean something significant for you going forward. I started training with my dad most days, every week. Somewhere in the middle of a hard physical session he'd pass on a tip from his own playing days, which sometimes made sense and sometimes drove me mad. 'Wear different coloured socks in a trial match, so you stand out' – well, I could get on board with that, because if a military man is up for breaking dress codes, you know it must be for a good reason. As for shinpads – I was playing back row at times, but my dad's tales of having to wear them because opposition players kept booting him in the leg at rucks were several decades too distant. His obvious lack of pace already raised questions in my mind about his abilities as an openside; his passing did little more to convince me of his credentials.

Family, community, club and school. Those coaches at Llangefni and Bodedern, Iori Hughes, Martin Williams and Keith Withers, knew I was a sponge and kept soaking me. Anglesey was also deep in my bones. You couldn't grow up here and not realise that people here didn't get given many chances. To make something good happen, you had to make sure you worked on everything and anything. And that was good with me. I never had a problem with hard work. It all made sense to me: you love doing this thing, you want to do more of it, so let's do this stuff.

You had your rewards when you did. As I added elements to my game, I started to move slowly through a creaking representative system. You'd start to notice the same kids cropping up in other good sides – the fast ones, the ones with a side-step you fancied adding to your own game, the mysterious ones who seemed to make it all look much easier than it was for you. Then there were the big lads, the ones who had a full beard at 14 and were starting to lose their hair at 15. It was astonishing looking at these giants, these men up against us skinny boys. 'What the hell have they got in the water in Powys?'

I got into a sevens tournament for North Wales. My jersey was six sizes too big, and my shorts looked like they'd been passed down from a prop in the late 1970s. But I loved pulling that ropey old kit on, because it represented not just my region but all the work I had been putting in. It even had a sponsor's name on the front, and if the sponsor was one of the other players' fathers, that was fine too.

Rugby was wrapping itself around every part of my life. I'd wear my Llangefni jersey out and about with jeans or shorts just to show people where I played and what I liked doing. I'd watch Wales matches on TV, spot the blatant similarities between Adam Jones and Duncan Jones, the Hair Bear Bunch, and assume they were brothers. I'd notice the dancing feet of Shane Williams and the beautiful way Eddie

Butler would describe them. When Shane accelerated and Eddie went with him, the whole thing would just light up. At this stage in Wales's rollercoaster rugby history, we were probably getting hammered by 40 points at the time. Shane and Eddie made you feel like you were going to win the World Cup.

Weirdly, as a kid so soaked in all this Cymru cosmology, the only rugby poster I had on my wall was of Jonny Wilkinson. Even with an English father this was considered a rogue move in Anglesey. But I had this instinctive respect for the way he went about his work, and the standards he set himself. I'd heard the stories of how, if he missed one kick in a set of 10 in training, he would have to start again from zero. I watched the clips of him with his mentor Steve Black, and I admired his mad search for perfection, because it sort of made sense to me too. If he was English – well, someone's got to be, haven't they?

I got to see him play once in the flesh, when Dad took me to that England–Italy game at Twickenham, my big sister Hayley living locally with her husband Cush and managing to bag us some tickets. I couldn't have cared less about what was happening in other areas of the pitch. I kept my entire focus on Jonny and the 10-metre circle around him. It was like going to see a world-famous band and just staring at the lead guitarist and all the things he was doing on his fretboard. Who cared about the bass player? I was looking at the real heart of it all.

About 15 years later, I actually had the chance to meet him, at Dylan's Hartley's testimonial at the Grosvenor House hotel in London. I wasn't expecting to spot him, and went a bit shaky at the knees when I did. I actually texted my mum.

'Oh my God, Jonny Wilkinson's here!'

'George, make sure you go and say hello and speak to him.'

It took me a while to build up the confidence. To work out what I was going to say to him. I would play it cool, that was the plan. Congratulate him on his career. Probably not mention the poster.

As I walked towards the table, I was good to go. Then I noticed he was in deep conversation with someone else. No problem, I'm the sociable sort. I'll say hello to this other fellow and then give him the brush-off and crack on with Jonny.

That was the point when the other bloke looked up at me, and I realised it was Prince Harry.

'Oh shit …'

'Hello George!'

I ended up having a really cool chat with Harry. He loves his rugby. We went deep. Except, once the official royalty had finished, the rugby royalty had disappeared. It took me a good half-hour of increasingly frantic searching and barging other guests out of the way until I found my own prince again.

The thing about never meeting your heroes? It didn't apply with Jonny. He told me I was doing really well. He was very open about his own mistakes, and what I could learn from them. He told me you had to have something to take your mind off rugby, which wasn't what I was expecting. I was able to text my mum again when he left for a second time, and give her a glowing endorsement with an unexpected House of Windsor kicker.

Even with my Wilkinson love, and a dad from Yorkshire, there was never any question over which nation I would support in the Six Nations. Technically I could have played for England, but all I ever wanted to wear was the red jersey. When you're a kid, you have your dreams – 'I want to be a fireman,' or, 'I want to be an astronaut.' The process that takes you there doesn't matter, and neither does the fact you have no idea how hard it's going to be to make it happen. It was the same with the idea of becoming a professional rugby player. As I grew up and started getting picked for teams beyond my corner of Anglesey and then the island itself, this thing became less of a dream and more something that might be tangible one day. Not real, not yet, but something that was no longer impossible. Something where I did realise how hard it was going to be, but was happy to put that relentless work in. 'Imagine if I could …'

What was still in the dream stage was playing for Wales. Not because I doubted how much I wanted to, or how dedicated our coaches were. It was pretty much logic. No-one from North Wales had played for the national side since Robin McBryde had started winning caps at hooker in the mid-1990s. He was held up as such a rarity that when we had a presentation night for our region, he actually came. There's a photo somewhere of Muccers handing me an award. But while he hailed from Bangor, he'd had to move to south Wales to get his career going. No-one really turned professional from Anglesey, let alone thought about going all the way to the top. Even when seasoned rugby watchers were telling me I had half a chance, I tried not to set my goals too high. I knew I had some of the right attributes. I knew I had a good mindset. Would it result in something? I just had to keep trying. Keep hitting all the training sessions, keep doing my private extra ones. Keep getting picked for this side, keep getting asked to play for the next representative team up. Keep finding enjoyment in all of it.

In sport there is a clear pathway, if you can keep moving along it. It's not like trying to be the best guitar player in Wales, or the best writer. It's not based on personal taste. If you're good enough, in sport, you'll get picked eventually, even if other kids from other regions are more visible and get spotted first. You can make a pretty relentless case for your inclusion, if you keep coming up against those kids and beating them.

And I was never going to moan. Okay, it was so much harder to make it from Anglesey than Cardiff. But I was still getting more opportunities than many had before me, and many were around me. My dad didn't ever complain when we had to drive for hours after his work to get to a training session or trial. He would drink his coffee, still in his dirty overalls, and he'd jump in the car and off we'd go. We were all half-full people, because you had to be. What was the point of being any other way?

When I pulled on those jerseys, whether they were too big or tatty or had been worn and washed multiple times before, they still felt like they fitted me. Because I wasn't just wearing them for me. They were for everyone else around me – my family, my friends, our coaches, our teachers. The farmers up the lane, the kids with the caravans. The aunties and uncles who were never actual aunts and uncles. When we travelled the roads from Anglesey – when we went over the bridge, and we wound our way east along the coast, or south into the mountains, or west to the peninsulas – I had multiple threads unspooling behind me, connecting me to all those people and all those places.

You commit to sport when you're young, and you're saying no to a lot of other things. You don't do the nights out, you don't do the illicit drinking in someone else's empty house. You miss birthday parties and bargain holidays to hot islands. You do all that because you understand the opportunity ahead of you. You understand that all these people you grew up with would rip an arm off to have the chances you are having.

You can't help but absorb all this stuff. Dad had a favourite phrase he'd like to bring out on regular occasions: 'You stop when you're done, not when anyone else tells you.' I watched him graft all day and he lived it. He'd come in from work, and I'd say, 'Dad, do you want to go for a run?' And he would nod and say, 'Yeah, yeah, let me have a cup of tea first and we'll go.' He taught me how to lift properly. At times it drove me mad; my mates at school seemed to be lifting more than me. His answer was that they weren't doing it right. 'George, build your foundations strong, get the technique, and then the weights will come.'

First thing in the morning we'd do weights together before school. If he'd left early, I'd get the bus home after school, and I'd have to show him that I'd done my homework, and then we'd go to the gym together. On the weekend, if there was no game because they didn't have enough numbers, we'd do a bike race between me and him instead. It wouldn't start as a bike race, but five minutes in it would generally become one.

It's a precarious balance for some parents to find. What's pushing to a beneficial point, and what's pushing too hard? My dad would always ask. That was the difference. His tone would change. 'Do you want to go?' It was never, 'You need to go.' He would ask me, and if I hinted I was too tired or too sore or not feeling well, he would support me. That was liberation to me. 'Whatever answer comes out of my mouth, I've just got to speak true, and he will back me all day long.'

The corollary of this was that when you said, 'yeah, I'm good,' you went hard. You didn't go half-arsed. You gave it everything.

Maybe this was always going to happen, growing up surrounded by so many farms and so many fields of cows. But it gave me a phrase, for this attitude: 'I'm going to go full-fat milk.' Not semi-skimmed sort of trying, and absolutely never red-top skimmed cat pee. Full-fat milk. In those pre-school weights sessions, in training at school, in bike rides that became bike races, in matches at weekends and on the long drives to fresh challenges. If you're going to do something, you do it properly.

What you don't realise yet, because you're not at that level, is that there's a little group of you, spread around the country, who are all doing the same thing, and one day are all going to come together. In the ordinary world, the idea of moderation is a good thing. Just do things in moderation – it's much better, you don't get hurt, you don't get damaged. Most elite sports people have the opposite perspective. They've got the ability to fuck off moderation, to say, I'm going to absolutely hammer myself today. They drink full-fat milk.

When I'd made it to where I dreamed of being, when I'd been in the Wales team for a few years, I'd look around the training barn at the Vale or the gym, and I'd see it in the other lads all around me. You trained with Sam Warburton, and everything was full-fat milk. If he missed out on a rep, or came up a couple of seconds short on a Wattbike rep, he would abuse himself. Talk to himself in the punchiest possible terms. Say things you could never say to someone else. You did whatever you needed to get it done, because that's elite sport. The ones who make it have an unbelievable ability to put themselves in a place where they're super uncomfortable, and actually be happier there than anywhere else.

Now it takes you a while to learn that the same attitude doesn't always translate to the real world. You can't go full-fat milk at people every day in your personal life, or in business. If you think you can, you still can't go as point-blank as you do in rugby. People get offended. They take it personally. They want to go green-top.

But you never lose it entirely, if you've had it. Years after he retired, Sam and I were due to make an appearance for Breitling together in London. The text conversation went like this:

'Are you at this gig in London?'

'Yeah, yeah. Are you in this hotel?'

'Yeah, yeah. It's got a decent gym.'

'Do you want to bring some gear?'

'Mate, yeah, I'm there.'

So we trained before this appearance. A hard upper body session, into a SkiErg finisher. Pretty full-on. And he pulled up with a couple of seconds left on the set, and he said it again – the same thing I used to hear him say when were at the Vale and in our pomp and full-fat milking everything.

'You little bitch, Warbs. You little bitch …'

THREE

LLANGEFNI TO CAERNARFON: LEARNING FAST

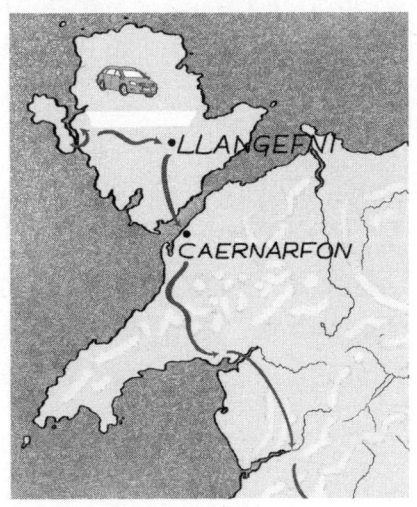

IN WHICH WE TALK ABOUT:

Welsh rugby's nowherelands/Llandovery College/George, you can't complain here/Ceitho and Sister Anne/the list on my bedroom door/non carborundum Illegitimi/Rusga/Cereal Club/ doing my extras/tying shoelaces/Barry Banks/an unfortunate phone call/cutting hedges/leggy enthusiasm/North Dock, Llanelli/Benetton away in Treviso/'Let's fucking go!'/ 5,127 prototypes

I was glad I was from Anglesey. But when people said it was a long way from anywhere else, it was difficult to argue, even if your instinct was to say, it depends where you're going. Everything significant that happened in Welsh rugby seemed to be along the M4 corridor. If it wasn't motorway-adjacent, it was certainly far south of where we were. So lowly were expectations of North Wales age-group teams that we weren't even usually allowed to play the big boys from the regions unless handed a special invite – which made the game arranged against Scarlets Under-16s in August 2007 quite the occasion.

We weren't just the outsiders that day. It was like we had travelled back in time. They rocked up in a lush, fitted Scarlets kit that looked the nuts. We turned up in shirts from the late 1970s – loose in the arm, looser round the middle, as heavy as a pair of your grandma's curtains. They were new to us, but they were as ancient in rugby fashion chronology as my dad's ankle-high boots.

We played on neutral territory, a little town on the A470 in mid-Wales called Llanidloes. Neutral, but much quicker for them to get to than us, although we were getting used to that by now. It was the ultimate underdog story; a North Wales age-group team had never beaten one of the big boys, and no-one expected it to change this time.

That sort of suited me. I was aware I was on Scarlets' radar, like my team-mates Rhodri Jones, Ben Taylor and Jack Roberts, but it was more than that. This was the first time I felt I had something tangible to show for all the work I'd been putting in. It made things seem more straightforward than they had before for a kid from Welsh rugby's nowhere-lands: if you put the hard yards in, did your basics and then the extras on top, people who mattered might begin to notice. It informed our attitude before kick-off. 'Boys, we've got to be in it to fight, we've got to show them what North Wales can do.'

Remarkably, we beat them. Jack fed me to send Ben over for our first try. Rhodri tackled everything. At 5–5 and with 20 minutes to go, Jack intercepted a loose pass to go over in the corner, and then banged over the conversion for 12–5. Watching it all was a man called Mostyn Richards, the elite performance manager at the Welsh Rugby Union. Not only did the win make some of us individuals bigger blips on his country-wide radar, but afterwards he declared that North Wales could join the other academies in the Reebok League and play against them all.

I genuinely think it was one of my greatest days in rugby. Even now, all these years later, when Becky and I drive north from Cardiff to Anglesey and pass through Llanidloes, I point the rugby ground out to her and tell the story. And on each re-telling she says, 'George, I know. You say it every time.'

We beat Cardiff Blues North 14–10 a few months later. A second scalp from the big league that apparently we weren't good enough for. And it led to places in the Wales Under-16 training squad for those four of us: Ben Taylor, Jack Roberts, Rhodri Jones and me.

Oh, the way this made you feel … You get picked for North Wales Under-16s, you feel like you're doing something right. You get picked for Wales Under-16s and you can genuinely see a path ahead of you that leads directly to your dreams. It doesn't mean you're going to get there, and I was never one to focus too far ahead. There were too many hits to make and lines to break in this moment. But you can suddenly see how the system works. Play well here. Get noticed. Play well at the next stage. Stay on the magic escalator.

The only downside was the photo of me in my Wales kit that the school took to put on a prominent wall – with a goofy grin on my face, Gilbert rugby ball held to my chest, long white tassels of my red velvet cap hanging down over my left ear like the earring of an exotic dancer. There is grey breeze-block in the background, which must mean it was taken in the bowels of a stadium somewhere, and it's genuinely horrendous. It keeps doing the rounds on social media, and I feel a bit sick every time it pops up.

But it kept opening doors. Kevin George was in charge of the Scarlets academy. Scarlets had tie-ins with two schools, for promising young players: Coleg Sir Gâr, in Llanelli itself, and Llandovery College, 30-odd miles further north. Llandovery was steeped in rugby; it had produced at least three Welsh captains and a heap of British and Irish Lions, including Cliff Jones and, just a few years before, Alun Wyn Jones. It was a fee-paying school, which would rule it out for my family, although there was a chance of a scholarship, which might rule it back in. Mum and Dad would do everything they could to make it happen.

The bigger issue was me. I was growing fast now, constantly mistaken for a flanker rather than a centre or winger, and I was starting to get used to looking down at the top of team-mate's heads, rather than meeting them eye to eye. But while I had the height of a grown man, I had the self-confidence of a boy. Actually, that's not quite true; I knew what I was doing on a rugby field, and if you gave me space and a ball to run into it with, I was certain I could make it worth your while. I was just shy. I liked being at home, and I was fine there, I could talk both the back and front legs off any nearby livestock. With my mates from Anglesey I loved nothing better than a very basic practical joke. But put me in front of a stranger and I could force a hello out and that would be it. The idea of going to a school three or four hours' drive away where I would have to stay for weeks at a time was horrendous.

But that's the other side to growing up in a place like Anglesey. You understand that if you want to move up, you might have to move on. I had seen it all around me. Kids going to faraway schools, adults going to distant jobs. You could still come back. You just had to loosen some of the ties.

So we took the plunge. The autumn of 2008, scholarship secured, I began at Llandovery. And, at the start, I hated it.

It was all too much for me. I didn't want to be away from home. I could just about make beans on toast, but didn't have the nose to tell whether a pint of milk had gone off. I didn't know how to wash my clothes; I'd certainly never ironed any. The only thing I could do really well was tie a double Windsor knot. Everything else was a shock to the system: the roll call each morning, the inspection to see if your shirt was ironed and your top button done up. They even checked your top lip for stubble, at a point where I would have loved the ability to produce a wisp of bum-fluff.

I was lonely, I was out of my depth. And I was stuck. I remember thinking, George, you can't complain here. You can't say you don't want to stay because Mum and Dad have forked out this cash we can't really afford.

And yet I was still there. I had rugby, and that was sort of my sanctuary, but I even started to question that a little bit. 'Is this too much? Maybe it's not for me …' Because my schedule was full-on. When I wasn't doing school work I was training. When I wasn't training I was failing to make palatable post-training food. I was beginning to question everything I'd held true in my life so far. They were right. Anglesey was a long way from everywhere.

I survived because I went full-on practical. That ability to compartmentalise coming through. 'Well George, we'll have to deal with this week and then see where we're at next week. We can deal with today before we worry about tomorrow. We can get through the next hour before we think about the day.'

I was beginning to navigate this foreign world at 16. There were others who had been in the Llandovery system for much longer. We called them lifers. And gradually I became friends with one of them, Ceitho, whose mother was the school matron. They actually lived in the town. They knew everyone, everyone knew them.

It changed things for me. Ceitho's mother Sister Anne was a lovely lady, although she could put the fear of God into you at times. But he and his brothers and his mum were all lifers. They knew how things worked, and they could answer the questions of a kid who did not. They knew another lad,

Rhodri James, RJ, who lived in London but had family roots Carmarthen way, so I was picked up by him too. And then there were my fellow North Wales rugby *émigrés*, Jack Roberts and Rhodri Jones. Sometime deep into a cold November, I looked around and thought, maybe I can stick this out until Christmas now.

I also had to remind myself why I was there. So I started drawing up a list of all the things I wanted to achieve. I stuck it up on the back of my bedroom door, and every morning, before I walked out for roll call, fastening my top button and optimistically running a finger over my upper lip in the hope of meeting some friction, I'd read the list out to myself:

1. Beat Dad in the bike race
2. Get Brecon socks
3. Run 10 metres in under 1.6 s
4. Run 40 metres in under 5 s
5. PDT 5.4
6. Play for Llandovery in the Principality League
7. Play in the Millennium Stadium
8. Bench 120 kg
9. Squat 200 kg
10. Play for Wales
11. Score a try for Wales

The Brecon socks one – this was a tradition at the college, where the big game each year was against Christ's College, Brecon. It's one of the oldest school fixtures in the country, running unbroken for more than 140 years. When you played for the college, you played in a white jersey, navy shorts and navy socks. If you played the Brecon match, you were awarded special red socks. The tradition carried on each year; in any given match for the Llandovery 1st XV, you would see some boys in navy socks, and the chosen few in red. Hence the prominence of Brecon socks on the list on my door.

PDT 5.4? PDT was the phosphate dec test. A 40-metre sprint, 10 times, flat-out, with a walk recovery in between. The test measures your drop-off from first sprint to last. It's about keeping your times as consistent as possible. As for the 5.4 bit – at the time, my best clocking for 40 metres was 4.88 s. 5.4 was the average I wanted across the ten sprints. In other words, I wanted to be fast, and I wanted to keep being fast.

Every third weekend you were allowed to go home, from the Friday late afternoon after lessons to the Sunday evening. It was hard for me to escape; I was always either training or playing. I barely went back to Anglesey at all until Christmas. When I got there, I was shattered – physically, emotionally. I just wanted to eat and sleep.

But something had changed in me, without me noticing. My parents could see it, so too my brother. The way I was holding myself, the way I was starting to look after myself. A way of talking to people I didn't know so well, as well as those on the sofa next to me.

And when I went back to Llandovery after Christmas, I was like a pig in wet muck. I absolutely loved it.

I'd subconsciously soaked up a lesson that would serve me well in the years ahead. When the shit's flying, you can't see where you're going. You have to get out of there to really appreciate what's been happening. Going back to Anglesey had cleared the air for me. I could see now I'd been exactly where I'd wanted to be, doing exactly what I wanted to be doing. It was also like being on one massive sleepover, which was a winner every way you looked at it.

It was probably weird, for a young kid, but I'd always had a determination in me, an ability to focus on a goal. 'I want to do this, so let's do it.' That can take you a long way when things get hard. My dad used to enjoy quoting a Latin phrase at me: *non carborundum Illegitimi*. Don't let the bastards grind you down, in his telling of it. Now it turns out it wasn't a true Latin phrase, and for 32 years he'd been getting it back to front. It should have been *Illegitimi non carborundum*. But it still became my first tattoo, as an adult, and I still went for his version, rather than the correct one, because it meant more to me.

That January, returning to Llandovery, I added another line to the list on the back of my door. 'Every day is a battle.' If that sounds overly dramatic for a 16-year-old at a fee-paying school, it was a good daily reminder that the journey I was on, from where I'd come from to where I wanted to be, was never going to be simple. You just had to keep moving forward. If it was easy, everyone would be doing it.

The tougher stuff I'd seen as a kid seemed to have come with a silver lining. I could experience something difficult, compartmentalise it, and move on. Now I was living this weird life of pain and enjoyment I wasn't getting lost on the side roads. I could actually see it in pretty simple terms.

No-one's going to give me this.

I'm going to have to fight for it.

Each day I'm going to be better than the day before.

Over the following years I'd meet quite a few high-level athletes. And the good ones all had the same innate ability to squash any sort of real pain or emotion that took away from their focus or drive. Was it healthy? In this world I wanted to succeed in, yes. When I was tired in the mornings, when my body would be sore and aching, I'd never say I wasn't feeling great. I would have to be in the arsehole's arsehole to complain. Every day was, yeah, I'm good to go, because it felt like a pleasure and an honour to be where I was.

I didn't share all these emotions with my parents, or with Little Josh or Dav Robs. I processed it myself, and I formed alliances with those who could help. Tom Rusga was far too clever to be my friend. I should never really have mixed with him. But luckily for me he loved rugby, and he had the same sort of focus I did. Some sessions I would do on my own – get up at 5.45 a.m., be in the gym for 6 a.m., then be back and showered and pointlessly shaved for roll call. Other mornings Rusga would come with me and train, and we'd barely speak to each other, but we'd communicate in other ways, and we got ourselves through it. It's an underappreciated skill, the ability to share stuff without really speaking. Even when we were non-verbal, we would still be processing stuff, and when we did speak, we would both drop into it, and it would all be wrapped up in three sentences and that was enough for him and enough for me.

In those early morning gym sessions with Rusga, we both understood what we were doing for each other. I needed to know that what I was doing was hard. I also needed confirmation that I had to do this to get to where I wanted to be. There could be no success without sacrifice.

'You good?'

'Yeah.'

'How's it going?'

'It's tough, but ...'

You watched and you learned. When it was hard, it showed you the standard you needed to be at. If you couldn't do it, you thought about what you should add to your sessions so you could.

Exactly the same as when I was home and with my dad. I needed him to stand there at the end of a session and catch the 50 passes I was going to make off each hand. We didn't need to talk. We both knew why we were doing it and that it took us both to make it happen. It's like Bradley Cooper in the film *Aloha*. His character used to date a girl, then he left because he's a dickhead and everyone hates him, but everyone really loves him, then she's got married and he comes back. I'm paraphrasing a little, to be fair, but anyway. There's a scene where he's in the kitchen with the husband, and they just look at each other and nod and not one word is spoken, but they say all the things they need to say.

That was me and Rusga. That was me and my dad. Years later, it would be me and Scott Williams.

So this is not me claiming to have done it all on my own. We had a South African boarding master in Tŷ Dewi, the house I was in for my first year. Barry Banks was sympathetic and hard, focused and compassionate. Not a hair to be seen on his upper lip, but always some dense sprigs trying to make their way through his shirt buttons or over his collar. He was brilliant for me. Whenever I needed a tap on the back or a little shake-up, he would notice and deliver.

In Tŷ Dewi I was lucky. I had a big room. I'd come out, turn left and Ceitho's was the first on the right. We used to do film nights in his room, or Cereal Club, or a ground-breaking combination where you'd watch films while eating cereal. Barry Banks would let us do it because he knew we both needed it.

Here are the rules of Cereal Club:

1. Don't talk about Cereal Club
2. Bring your own to eat
3. Host every other Cereal Club
4. Host to provide cold milk

One night I was particularly tired from training. I was in Ceitho's room, eating cereal in his chair, duvet pulled up under my nose, watching a film. Ceitho was lying on his bed. We both fell asleep. We both stayed asleep. Only when the bell rang in the morning did we wake up.

Barry had clearly been to my room and found it empty. When he walked into Ceitho's he saw the two of us appearing to be enjoying an illicit sleepover, cold cereal stuck to our pyjama tops. Everything was in place for a royal bollocking. Instead he raised his eyebrows, held up a hand and said, 'Boys, I don't want to know.'

In that first term I didn't really have a balance. It was all rugby, rugby, rugby, which meant I got shouted at for school, school, school. Barry understood what I was doing and where I wanted to be. And from him, and Ceitho, and Rusga and this unfamiliar world of a boarding school, I absorbed a mindset and a routine that would help me all the way through. Up early. Gym. Iron my shirt, tuck it in. Be on time. No, be five minutes early. Solve your own problems. When you can't get your laptop to work on the school Wi-Fi, go and knock on the geeky kid's door to bribe them with food and get on their personal network. Doing a full day of school, and then more training afterwards, and walking back in the pitch-black and seeing all your mates in the common room having a laugh and a joke when you've just completed your fifth session of the day, and this time with big hairy men, not just college students, and not complaining about it but feeling good.

Because the training load was getting heavier. On top of the school work, the college training, the college games, the Scarlets academy training and the Scarlets Under-18s games, I was also now training with the first team squad at Llandovery RFC. It was all to push me, and for bigger people to push back against me, and if I looked like a baby giraffe up against these semi-pro real men with real hair on their upper lips, I could feel all the good stuff it was doing for me.

Wales Under-18 selection seemed slightly arbitrary. Sometimes I was in and sometimes I was out. If you were from the south of the country and had been in the picture since you were 14 years old, you seemed to have a better chance of regularly being picked now than you did if you were an outsider from the north. I wasn't bitter about it; I'm not a bitter sort of guy. I used it as a reality check – 'Okay George, you've made it this far, but you haven't made it anywhere yet …' – and a motivation. I would have to be disciplined every single day. There could be no shortcuts. No-one was going to hand me any of it.

The school liked its sporting successes, but it didn't just want a load of rugby mutants. It wanted us to emerge as rounded individuals. So me and Rhodri Jones and Jack Roberts were enrolled in the Duke of Edinburgh gold scheme, and we were encouraged to develop the sides of our characters that might otherwise have held us back. I was being picked as an outside centre at this point, and while you can't be quiet anywhere on the rugby pitch, my natural shyness was becoming a problem the higher up the ladder I went.

I was a listener and a doer because I didn't feel like I had earned the right to speak at that point. I thought it was all about keeping quiet and learning, soaking it all up like a spotty sponge. The more experienced ones would get into me. 'You've got to speak, George. You've got to speak.' I didn't transform myself overnight. I still thought it was sometimes better not to speak in certain situations because there were enough voices going on and enough being said. Me piping up just to echo a point wasn't going to carry the same weight. When I felt strongly I would say something, but I also felt safe that the players around me would drive the standards to where they needed to be. But I got the message. At international level I wasn't going to be able to survive by just getting by. I would have to add weight, have to help, have to voice my opinion, whether I was right or wrong. You have to be part of the journey. You can't just be there for the ride.

I wanted to never give anyone an excuse not to pick me. That was always my mindset, really. I've worked far too hard, I've had to leave home, where these guys live round the corner. This doesn't sit well with me. I'm here for a reason and I'm not going to dance around it.

It seemed you were at a disadvantage if you came from North Wales. If they didn't know your face, they could only judge you on your performances. So if I could always do my job all the time to the right standard, then I would never give them a reason to ignore me. And fighting like this made being vocal a little easier. I was honest about my own prep and my displays. So if they came to me and said, 'Ah, G, you missed a tackle,' I could say, 'Well, no. I know I didn't. You show me which one I missed.'

I'd argue the point.

'You haven't done your extras.'

'Well, I have. If you look back, I've been out there doing my defence work, doing my attack work, my aerial skills.'

'Your body can't take the load of high-speed metres.'

'Well, actually, I've been through my GPS and I fucking can.'

Not because I was chopsy or arrogant, but because I was eliminating the excuses around me. That same lovely simplicity: if I do all these things, I can make it. I can do all these things.

It was a massive help having Rhodri and Jack there as well. A familiar face when you'd done a full day of school and training, someone else who was going through it and not complaining. Because it was pretty full-gas, as we settled into it. Monday morning doing weights with Tom Rusga at 5.30 a.m., full day of school, then off to our various regions to train – a van to pick us up outside the school and drop us off, a couple at Dragons, a couple at Scarlets. A full evening of training, back just before 9 p.m. for a quick shower and a bit more school work. Tuesday up early for weights, the full school day, then training with the Llandovery men's team in the evening. Wednesday was a half-day for us, so I would do my school work in the morning, our college rugby training in the afternoon and then go down to Parc y Scarlets to do my own weights and running down there. Thursday was a full day of school then I'd do my weights in the evening and my skills work. Friday was spent preparing with the college for our game on the weekend or, as I progressed, a match for Scarlets Under-18s. With that kind of schedule I was quite quickly racking up a lot of volume and a lot of mileage just because of the nature of your week. A match at the weekend, squeeze in your recovery and then crack on and do it all over again the following week.

You do that for two school years, for two seasons, and it doesn't half give you a robustness in your body. You become accustomed to the volume and to delivering your best even when you're exhausted and want to watch films under your duvet while eating cereal.

Up, go, donk. Up, go, donk. That's what it felt like at times. That level of repetition. It was like being a 100-metre freestyle swimmer. They will do thousands of metres in the pool every week but they're still a sprinter.

I had become robust mentally and now I was becoming tough physically. I was still in my teens but I felt close to being ready for senior rugby. I was also eating like a horse.

I wasn't cooking myself fantastic meals. But I'd become friendly with the dinner ladies, and they fell into the excellent habit of giving me slightly bigger portions than everyone else on the sly. Other times I just went illegal; when they weren't looking, I'd put one yoghurt on my tray and then stick another in my pocket to take back to my room. I thought of it as borrowing, rather than stealing. Pick the moral bones out of that one.

Any part of the day I was not in a classroom or on a rugby pitch I would spend eating. After a while I developed the ability and menu to eat in those environments too. Protein shakes became the big winner. Cereal was the other go-to. You could fill a bowl with half a packet and half a cow's daily output and just get the calories down you and go off again.

Wednesdays became peak hunger day because they were halfway through the week. After college training, after our half day in school, we'd all pile down to the local Chinese and order half the takeaway menu. I was doing so much physical work there was no time to overthink it. While I enjoyed an egg fried rice, it was no longer about food as an aesthetic experience. It was just fuel. I had to get it in me because I knew the next session was coming along quickly, and I had to be ready for it.

Then there was the other side to it. Sleep. There would frequently be evenings when I would walk into the common room, sit down with the intention of conversing and then realise I was tired and I physically couldn't speak. I'd sit there for a while, contributing nothing, and then think: well okay, I may as well just go to bed.

But that was fine. I had found my groove. I had found a way of living that worked for me. I was quite at ease with a succession of early nights as my school mates stayed up having fun. 'Well, if this is what I've got to give up to get my dream, then so be it.'

We weren't a wealthy family. We've never gone without; my dad would always find a way. I'm not a sob story. But without the Scarlets scholarship I could never have gone to Llandovery, and without all the extra work my parents were doing to keep me there, I was going back to Rhoscolyn. So whenever it would all get too much, I'd use that to re-stock my reserves. 'Well, you wanted this. You put yourself here. How many people have not had this opportunity from North Wales?'

I was still a teenager. And at that age you can be as disciplined as you like, but there will always be the natural inclination to balance it up with letting off some steam. Oh, I could be an arse at times. I was an instinctive and incessant wind-up merchant. I loved a basic prank then, and I love them now. I've wound people up throughout my professional career, and I do it at home. Some of my funniest moments with Becky have been jumping out on her from behind a door. Bear with me, it'll make sense later.

I needed some sort of mental release, because it was a constant pressure between the eyes, the way I was trying to be. I'd be nodding off at quarter to ten at night and then remember I'd forgotten to do a piece of homework. I'd need to be up at 5.30 a.m. to do my weights. And even as I'd be thinking, ah, shit-balls, George, you had to find a way. I had to keep making the sacrifices or it would all fall down.

Hence the pranks. There are sportsmen who love cutting a tie in half or chopping the toes off a pair of socks so your foot goes straight through and keeps going. I was always a scarer. I was a jumper-outer. I was a tie-shoes-togetherer.

A boarding school provided textbook conditions for the last of these, because there were so many boys in one place and so many shoes. I would sneak into a room and tie every lace I could find to all the other laces, to a level of evil complexity where it would take them hours to successfully extricate a shoe. Whack in a little opened tin of tuna on the radiator in some boys' rooms so they could smell them but not find them. Hide in a wardrobe and spring out with a rebel yell as someone opened the door to access a clean shirt.

Classics of the genre, each and every one. And once you'd done each one a few times, you were on top. You had them guessing. Even when you weren't inside someone's wardrobe, they'd think you might be. Even when they didn't need their rugby boots until the afternoon there'd be a panicked search before breakfast to make sure they weren't inextricably linked to someone's school shoes.

Did I get whacked? All is fair in love and war at a boarding school. There would always be a few bust-ups, simply because of all the hormonal teenage boys cramped together in one space. All of us had our ups and downs. But if you were struggling – if you were too high, or too low, or buzzing up and down between the two – Barry Banks would spot it. Strong enough to hold you accountable, warm enough that you could always go to him. So many young men at quite a crucial point in their life when their fathers weren't there to help them, and Barry was able to subtly guide you each and every day.

I remember coming back from training late one evening because the M4 was closed. By the time I got back to my room all the lights were out and the boys asleep. He was still up, waiting for me. No dramas, just a, 'Get a shake, get yourself showered, get to bed.' When I was up early in the morning, he was there waiting to let me out to go to the gym. Go to the gym, come back, rushing around, get my shirt, get my blazer on, shoes are polished, tie done up, top button done. Running downstairs for roll call thinking I've cracked it, and him standing there shaking his head.

'George, get rid of that fluff on your top lip.'

I'd made no further progress in growing anything on my face except the occasional spot. But I knew the rules weren't going to bend for me. So you sprint upstairs, take out a Gillette razor that's not had a single blade change because you haven't needed to, do one quick sweep of the top lip and you're back downstairs. Only then did I get the nod. 'Okay, go on then.'

Now that might all seem a bit petty or unnecessarily authoritarian. Some of the boys certainly didn't like it. But it all reinforced in me that you had to hold yourself to these standards every single day. It wasn't a pick and choose. And when you're 17, and you're starting to think about alcohol and girls and combining the two in a Llandovery hostelry ready to accept your unusual height as proof of age, it's a world of easy temptations out there. It's a lot easier giving in than giving stuff up. It's easy to listen to the voice saying, 'Do you know what? I'm not going to go to class today' or 'I'm not going to go to that session today' or 'I'm not going to do my passing today.' I needed the constant reminder that you couldn't hit the standards only when it suited you. You were either 100 per cent in or you were out.

And it worked for me. As I came towards my A-Levels, Scarlets told me they were going to offer me a development contract. A more experienced player would have described it as a chance to get paid bugger all money to do a full-time job. I saw it as a reward for those long crazy days and exhausted weeks at Llandovery. I would get the chance to train around the senior team – to hold the pads in contact sessions, to be the defensive line when they were practising set plays. You could come in early to do your weights around the big boys.

My last A-Level exam was on a Monday morning. But there was a problem. It was the same Monday morning that my first pre-season as a proper Scarlet on this development contract was supposed to begin. I remember looking at the schedule and realising. It seemed catastrophic. Either I missed my last exam – a no-goer with the school – or I risked going awol on my first day as a sort of senior player.

I spoke to the academy manager Kevin George in something of a panic. He seemed unexpectedly relaxed.

'Look, just ring the head coach. Explain it and he'll be completely okay.'

He might have been relaxed. I wasn't. The idea of phoning Nigel Davies to tell him I was going to miss the first day of pre-season was the pits. The absolute pits.

I dialled the number Kevin had texted me.

'Hi Nigel, it's George North.'

'Who?'

Oh shit …

'Er, George North? I'm with the senior academy.'

'Hello George.'

'Thing is, I've got my last exam next Monday, but it's the same Monday that pre-season starts. Am I okay to come after? Like, I can be there Monday afternoon …'

'Oh, don't worry about that. Just come in on the Tuesday.'

That's how he ended the call. Immediately I started analysing his manner and response. Oh God. He didn't know who I was, he wasn't bothered whether I turned up or not. This really was the pits.

I did the exam on Monday morning. Everyone went to the pub afterwards. They'd come of age, they could drink. I nursed a Diet Coke. By the time they were on their third pints and giddy I was almost sobbing into my ice-cubes. I wanted to be here, with these boys. But I also wanted to be with Stephen Jones and Tavis Knoyle and Regan King and Matthew Rees and Morgan Stoddart, even if none of them knew who I was and none of them gave a flying one whether some shy gangly teenager was there gawking at them or not.

I had another issue. Term was over. I couldn't stay at Llandovery College, even under the benign tutelage of Barry Banks. I couldn't go home to Anglesey, because I was supposed to be training with Scarlets each day. The club would eventually help me find a cheap flat-share with Rhodri Jones in North Dock in Llanelli, but that would take a couple of months. Where was I supposed to live until then?

Once again it was Ceitho to the rescue.

'Ah, just stay with us.'

'I can't just stay with you. Ask your mum.'

So he asked Sister Anne, and she phoned my parents, and within about a day it was happening. And with Sister, very much like my mum and dad, there was no such thing as a free bed. You had to earn your keep. Quite quickly a routine formed: I would go training with Scarlets each morning, commuting from Llandovery town to Llanelli, haemorrhaging money on petrol, nominally now a professional rugby player yet, on the development contract, unable to afford the fuel. Ceitho would go out to his summer holiday job. When we came back we'd be set to work cutting the hedges. The next evening we'd be cutting the grass, the next cleaning all the windows.

Between the two of us we would somehow get all these jobs done. And, once again, it was exactly what I needed. It kept up my routine of work, focus, work. There was no time to worry about anything; you were either training, working, eating or sleeping. Ceitho was like a brother by now. Sis became a surrogate mother. I had been well tutored. So even in the miniscule gap between eating and wanting to go to sleep, I'd be jumping up from the table. 'Thank you, thank you, can I do the dishes?'

Training with Scarlets, development programme or not, was some mad new level of intensity. I was exhausted at the end of every day. My body was sore. It had been faster and harder going from school sessions to Llandovery RFC in the Principality League. This was an acceleration on a non-linear scale.

Every day I learned something about myself or the game. It could have been humbling, if you'd mistakenly fancied your-self as a big fish after having some success with the Under-18s. On the training pitches at Parc y Scarlets you were reborn as a minnow. But while I took a battering, and it took me a while to keep the weight on that I needed, I found I was able to adjust to the intensity and stay there.

The hard graft of the past few years had given me a robust-ness in my body. My top two inches were also getting stronger. I never found myself double-guessing myself – 'Ah, if I do this, I'm going to be screwed for tomorrow ...' My mindset was more, 'Well, I know I can do this.' And then: 'Well, today was a tough day. But I got through it, so bril-liant. Next day I can push again, see what happens.'

On the field, all those senior players were good with me. I was all leggy enthusiasm. I thought I had to be wherever the ball was. I thought I had to chase everything, or else I wasn't trying hard enough.

Pretty quickly they started filing away at those rough edges.

'George, you're running around like a headless chicken. Give yourself a moment to breathe and pick and choose.'

'What do you mean pick and choose?'

They would demonstrate on the training pitch and then show me a video clip. We'd work at it on the laptop.

'See here, you don't need to go. You don't need to go.'

'Why?'

'Go back to where you've come from, because knowing the play we've called here, it's going back to you.'

My mentality began to change. I'd thought before that if I chased the ball, I had the best chance of getting my hands on it. But I was actually burning myself out. Gradually I realised that if I did go, I had to make sure I got the ball. And in the meantime, I had to be patient. Effort wasn't running after everything. It was holding your position and kicking until it could deliver the most.

Session after session, clip after clip.

'Take a breath, George. Let's sit down. Let's review that. Why are you here? What justifies you being in this position right now? Where should you be?'

Senior rugby taking form in front of my eyes, its shapes and patterns and subtlety. An education at Llandovery, a university course now. My instincts moved on every week. 'Where am I most likely to get my next touch? It's not there, is it? It's back where I should be ...'

It all came at you. You could be fast but you had to know when to deploy that speed. You could be committed but you had to understand where to commit. You could work your socks off, but you had to learn how to fuel it all.

In these warm summer months, from having most of my meals prepared for me by school, to Sister Anne's ample helpings, and now, in the North Dock flat with Rhodri Jones, having to cook for myself was a real challenge. You quite quickly realise that there's a lot more planning involved; if you went to the fridge after training, no-one had magically filled it for you. You either ate badly – the stub of a block of cheese, a handful of dry cereal – or you didn't eat when your body needed it most.

So I began to work it out. If I had training on Monday and Tuesday, Monday could be the classic spag bol day, and Tuesday could be chicken. That would mean Sunday at the shops. Into that plan then had to come all the other elements of recovery that were now available – soft-tissue massage, ice-baths. It wasn't actually like going to the university of rugby. It was taking a full-time job.

There was never an easy day. Each session meant something, in the grand scheme of things. Each block in training was held to a certain standard. You were exposed to this rawness and pace and just had to hold on for dear life.

Maybe that was the biggest shock of all. I'd come through a tough system. I'd survived it and then flourished. But these boys went hard every single day. The first-team regulars attacked each session like their jobs were on the line. The ones who weren't picked for that weekend were still working flat-out in case there was a drop-out and they got called up. And if you really weren't involved, you were expected to sacrifice yourself for those who were. To ask yourself, okay, what can I do to help the lads get better?

It rubbed off on you, the attitude and the ability. And the fact I was there, with all these great players I'd looked up to for so long, helped clear my view of the path ahead. I was on the same training pitch as Stephen Jones, using the same gym. I was nowhere near his league, but we were doing the same things on the same days. Surely this gave me a chance. I looked at Sean Lamont, a big winger, Scottish international, and I thought, well, he's a big winger, I'm a big winger, maybe I could do what he's doing.

It wasn't that I wanted to impress anyone or felt I had to. It was more about the example they were setting for me. They were at the same club as me and had achieved everything I ever wanted to. Well, maybe this was exactly where I needed to be and what I needed to be doing to one day achieve the same.

I never thought about my tender age. It wasn't holding me back; it was the opposite. Everything was all so new and exciting and challenging that I would come home from training and be absolutely buzzing. I was sore, and later on in the evening I would be absolutely shattered, so tired I could barely stand. But I always bounced back. It changes as you get older, all this stuff. The buzz changes frequency. You carry fatigue from day to day. At 18 years old I was still awash with the elixir of youth. I didn't even need a warm-up, or so it felt. I could run straight off the team coach onto the pitch and play 80 minutes, and nothing twanged or pulled. Not indestructible, but totally confident that my body could instantly deliver what I wanted it to.

Something else became apparent, as that first pre-season started shedding its prefix. Morgan Stoddart, who could play at full-back or on the wing, had been away with the Wales squad on the summer tour and come back injured. The same was true of Sean Lamont on Scotland duty. The way the Scarlets squad was structured before the season proper began meant that, for those initial pre-season friendlies, I might have to play because I was the only one in that position who was fit.

I mentioned it on the phone to my mum. 'There's a chance I'll get a run-out.' I spoke to my dad. 'You know what? I might actually get a game here because there's … not to do myself a misjustice, but there's no-one else.' I talked to myself, as I drove back to the little flat in North Dock. 'Well George, if you can keep yourself in one piece, do what you're told and learn your job inside out so if that point comes where there is no-one they can pick apart from you – well, you've got a chance.'

And so it came to pass. I got picked for a warm-up game. It went okay. I went back to the list I'd had on the back of my door at school and crossed one of the ambitions off. They picked me for the next one too. That also went fine.

When the opening game of the season came round, Sean was still out. We were due to play Benetton away in Treviso in the Magners League. Players were now coming in and out of the squad as the real stuff came around – some older boys propping up the squad where we had injuries, and younger boys they brought in and out to have a look at. I was still the man in possession. So it was both a shock and sort of what I expected when Nigel Davies told me I was playing.

Another one to cross off the list. First a senior appearance for Scarlets, now a competitive one. I was a professional rugby player now. One part of my brain might have been screaming, 'Jesus Christ, George ...' But the other part was calm. 'This is exactly what I want to do, and exactly where I want to be.'

Later on in my career, I'd work with sports psychologist Andy McCann at the WRU to find a way to cope with all the adrenaline and nervous energy I would feel before a big game. We put a countback system in place, a marker and a tool for each time. Three hours until kick-off, you're putting your bags on the coach, remind yourself you've packed them well. Two hours to go, approaching the stadium: tell yourself you've done all the prep you needed to do. Coming out of the changing-room, running onto the pitch? Bending down to touch the whitewash of the touchline. Thinking: I'm ready for this. All the cogs are aligned.

I'd keep doing that whitewash one until the very end. It might sound a bit weird, it might sound unnecessary. But it wasn't a superstition, a lucky omen. It was about perform-ance. There are other aromas in a rugby stadium as you run out that you might get elsewhere: beer on breaths, massage oil, sweat on clothing. Only running onto a pitch could I get the distinctive smell of whitewash. That was the marker, and the thought I tied to it was stark: 'The work's been done. It's go-time.'

For now, I was in the moment. It was a sticky afternoon in the north-east of Italy. One thing I hadn't anticipated was the clouds of midges that swarmed all round your face as soon as I took my position for kick-off. Me waving my hands around, snorting out of my nose to keep them away, thinking, 'Jesus

Christ, please just leave me alone, stop buzzing around my bastard ears …'

Looking back, I don't think anyone or anything can really prepare you at that age for how quickly shit happens in serious sport. Not the psychology stuff we'd done, not the months of increasingly intense physical work. One minute the ref was looking at his watch and blowing his whistle, the next it was everything on warp speed all around me.

Thoughts coming at me fast too.

'Fuck, we're in it now …'

'Don't chase, not yet …'

'Come on George, you're here now. May as well go and give it full gas …'

I was on the right wing. We went wide from the left. Gareth Maule threw a long pass. Suddenly I was free on the inside, and the pass came timed for me to run onto at speed.

I almost stopped running. It seemed to go so suddenly quiet as I stepped the cover defence into open space that I wondered if the referee had called it back for a forward pass. It was too easy. I was in so much room it just had to be wrong.

And as quickly as that thought came in, another overtook it.

'Well, there's no noise. Let's fucking go.'

You can see my speed change, if you watch the clip back on YouTube. You can see this tiny fraction of a moment where I'm umming and ahhing, and you can see the fraction where I'm not thinking any more. I'm just going as hard as I can. You can see it on my face. I'm not looking around, I'm not checking for support. I'm just running as hard as I can for the corner flag.

There's a big smile on Nigel Davies' face when I tumble over the try line. I only noticed that later when we watched it back as a team. I was trying to play it cool, although my heart was trying to punch its way out of my chest. It did the same when I scored my second professional try, crashing over off a short pass, dragging the tackler over the line with me.

I was in the flat in Llanelli the next evening when I got a phone call from my mum.

'George! Put on the TV! Warren Gatland's talking about you!'

It was *Scrum V*. I don't know why I wasn't watching; I always watched it in those days. Maybe it was exhaustion. I was good for nothing but the sofa and staring at the ceiling.

Gats was still talking.

'I've heard a lot about him already and he was impressive. If he keeps playing every week and keeps performing like that, he's definitely going to catch the eye, which he has already started to do. So it's about taking these opportunities and being consistent.'

Of course it was thrilling to hear that. I was one proper senior game in. I was 18. The hair on my head still looked like the hair on a more hidden part of my body. But it didn't take much to remind myself that they were just words. They didn't mean I was going to get picked to play for Wales. That would be insane. I still fitted into my school blazer, I still had a smoothish upper lip. Being talked about meant nothing; loads of players got talked about. Loads of people still talked about being talked about – 'Oh, I would have made it, had I not blown my knee out …' The only thing that counted was if you did get selected, and then played, and then played well enough to get selected again. There was a reason why I hadn't written a line on my door list that said, 'Get mentioned in passing by Warren Gatland as part of a longer interview on a Sunday evening rugby programme shown mainly for Welsh viewers.'

It's only when you do make it that you can look back and see the footprints you left behind you. Wales is a small nation. It has only four professional teams, and that's been under stress for as long as I can remember. The likelihood is that if you're good, you'll get a chance. If you're good enough and then you survive, you'll probably get another chance. And at that time, two years into the first Gatland regime, one Grand Slam already on board, the bulk of the squad's experienced players experiencing a rebirth under the coach – well, they could take a few more risks on young lads to see if they could sink or swim. The coaching group knew that 98 per cent of the group was settled and could deliver when needed.

I kept my place in the Scarlets side. Six matches in a short period of time. That's not much of an education, in some ways. I didn't score two tries in every game. That was fine. The thing I'd noticed was that it wasn't the two-try games that mattered. Well, they did, but not if you were invisible the week after. The players who'd been first choice for five years, for seven or nine – it wasn't that they were always outstanding, or never had a bad game, but they were consistent.

Stephen Jones explained it to me after one training session in the early autumn rain. He told me to think about two lines on a graph, where the x axis is time and the y is level of performance. The top line represents an outstanding individual performance – man of the match, champagne in the showers afterwards. The bottom line is a bad display – not doing your basics, not helping the team, not putting a shift in.

No-one was ever all top or all bottom. No-one was ever a straight line. Instead the really good players had a line that went up and down. Some games they'd be right up high; others down low. The secret was to stay between the lines. To never drop onto the bottom line. If you're always between man of the match and okay, you'll be performing consistently. As you become more experienced and better equipped to cope with the demands of that level, those two lines will naturally get closer and closer. Then your personal graph goes from champagne in the showers to a pretty solid game, rather than just an okay one.

It resonated with me, when Jonesy told me that, and not only because he was the living embodiment of it. I'd understood from all I'd seen in age-group rugby and at school that you had to be consistent. But until you see it day to day, what the real athletes do at this level, you don't really fully appreciate it.

People outside elite sport sometimes think it's all about natural talent. It's about genius. Same with musicians or writers – the muse just whispers in your ear, and you produce this perfect song or story. Most of the time it's not. It's about a musician trying to write a song and then comparing it to better songs, about writing loads more songs and keeping on writing songs, even when they're not that good, and then practising writing songs when everyone else is down the pub. Some days a writer will produce something beautiful and the words will flow, and other times it's clunky and each word can feel like they've carved it out of their own flesh. It's still fundamentally about practice and consistency. If you want to write well, keep writing.

I listened to a podcast once with James Dyson. He said it took him 5,127 prototypes to create the world's first bagless vacuum cleaner. It's a berserk number. Most of us would have given up by 100. But it makes absolute sense when you've been around elite sport. Obsession gets a very bad rap in lots of ways. But there's something about obsession, if it's channelled properly, that's very useful for success, whether you're doing sport or business or something cultural or anything else.

Where elite sport differs from music or writing is that it is purely based on ability. It's not about a well-run marketing campaign or appearing on the right radio shows. It's just if you are good enough and you're prepared to do what they want you to do. Once the senior players and the coaches at Scarlets could see how I went about my work and that I was into it 100 per cent from the first minute of each day, I think they started accepting me. I knew I was big and getting stronger and had the acceleration of someone smaller. I understood now too that those attributes would not take me all the way.

And then, if there were any danger at all I might be taking it all for granted, I got a stress fracture in my ankle.

Maybe I'd done too much too soon. I don't know. Maybe I was just unlucky. Maybe it would have happened even if I'd still been playing age-group. I just remember my ankle screaming, and while I didn't really want to tell the physios, it was screaming in a way that didn't really give me a choice.

I had a scan. That confirmed it. A stress fracture isn't the worse injury, but it's niggly. Royally niggly. Lesson number one: this game doesn't care who you are or what age you are. Lesson number two: I would have to look after my body. The elixir of youth was not as potent as you imagine. I couldn't just climb off the coach and play 80 minutes. I would have to listen to my body, understand how it feels, realise that I was still a young man in a big man's environment.

It was probably also my first blob of doubt.

'Well, oh shit. Maybe my body isn't quite ready for this level yet.'

A slightly more optimistic version: 'Oh shit. Where does this put me now?'

I had hoped to discover I was a good rehabber. I wasn't. I was impatient. I didn't like sitting down at the best of times. I found out early that when the physios tell you to do something, you do it, even when it's three things every hour every day for 10 days. You have to bite your tongue when you think you're ready and they think you're not.

I'm sort of glad it happened, looking back at it. It wasn't an ACL or an Achilles. As importantly, I figured out another layer of what it would take to complete my door list. If they told me to hop on one leg 150 times every hour, then that's what I was prepared to do to be in that position. If I wanted to be at this level, these were the sacrifices I would have to make.

I'd watched the older boys go about their work when various parts of their bodies were aching or creaking or strapped up. Every one of them had their own little things to do every day to keep themselves in working order. I'd have to get ahead of the curve and get on top of this before it started happening more frequently – work out what I needed and when I needed it. Staying at the club an extra two hours doing recovery and treatment when all the boys have finished? Yep. Staying in each night with my foot and my ankle in an ice bucket four times a day? If it's got to be done then I'm doing it.

It was an easy choice, really. I still found myself getting giddy with the excitement of it all. Professional rugby was turning out to be everything I wanted to be doing, and I was getting to do it every day. Learning a new skill, enjoying a familiar one like taking someone on the outside and beating them for pace. Putting in good work with people I trusted and players I looked up to.

I felt like I was riding a wave. And as I did so, I was shouting at the top of my voice. 'Holy shit-balls, this is incredible ...'

FOUR

CAERNARFON TO PORTHMADOG: BREAKING THROUGH

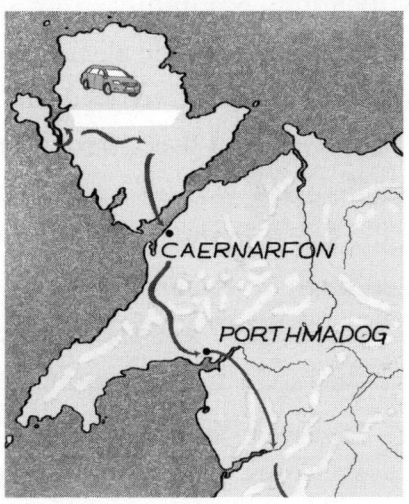

IN WHICH WE TALK ABOUT:

*a second hand Fiat Stilo/'Don't take the piss now, George'/
actual Shane Williams/Keanu in* The Matrix/*Jesus Christ it's
Mike Phillips/'Shouting at you is a good thing'/traffic on the
A483/the Welsh Jonah Lomu/Bryan Habana knows who I am/
all of Anglesey/a carrier bag of Dairy Milk and Haribo/
Colosseum level shit/'Smash it, pal'/don't let it bounce/
singing 'Mr Brightside'*

So I'd played those games for Scarlets, and I was beginning to find my feet in the senior world. I'd played at centre in three of Wales Under-18s' Five Nations matches earlier in the year. But as autumn 2010 rolled round, and with proper big clashes for the national side against Australia and South Africa, Fiji and New Zealand, the thought had never come into my head up to that point that I might somehow be involved in a capacity that wasn't just trying to blag some tickets for the Millennium Stadium.

When the thought did pop in there, during the week of the squad announcement, it only arrived because naturally, being part of another rugby squad, I was surrounded by piss-takers and wind-up merchants. I was also coming back from the stress fracture in my ankle, midway through what at Provence they would call *le stage de recuperation*. As my team-mates were piling in – 'Oh, G, you've got a chance.' 'Yeah, you've definitely got a chance …' I found myself too hyped up. My interior dialogue instinctively tried to present the opposite point of view: 'Look George, there's no fucking chance. You're only 18, there's no way he's going to pick you. He's got people he trusts, players he leans on. Don't let them get to you.'

The squad announcement was on a Wednesday towards the end of October. I was heading into Scarlets for physio, parking up outside, when I got a text message. It said it was from a Caroline Morgan at the WRU. It said I had been picked in the Wales squad for the autumn internationals.

Now I didn't know Caroline Morgan at this point. I didn't know she was PA to the national team. I didn't know she was the most organised, hard-working and trustworthy woman in the northern hemisphere. I simply feared she was one of the Scarlets boys in disguise.

Internal dialogue part two: 'The boys were taking the piss yesterday, weren't they? This message coming today, it's obviously a piss-take. What a fucking sick joke, isn't it?'

At the same time, there was enough doubt creeping in to make me twitchy. I didn't want to reply and find myself in a text conversation that would be forwarded in real time round the rest of the Scarlets squad. At the same time, what if Caroline Morgan were an actual woman, rather than a hairy prop, and what if she genuinely worked at the WRU, and what if I really had been called up to train with Wales?

Now the internal dialogue was panicking. 'What the hell do I do here?' Thinking back and forward, back and forward. 'Who do I call? What do I say?'

I decided to ring my agent, Christian.

George: 'Christian, how you getting on?'

Christian: 'Well, thank you George, What do you know?'

George: 'I've had this text about Wales, but I think it's the boys taking the piss.'

Christian: 'Okay, George …'

George: 'Can you just ring this number and find out?'

Christian: 'Yeah, yeah. I get it, I get it. No worries. Send it through.'

I forwarded the number. I sat in the car and waited. It was now really close to my physio appointment. 'Oh my God, I'll be late here, come on …'

Incoming call, Christian Abt. 'Nah, G, congratulations. It's true, boy!'

Incoming thought, George North: 'Well, stone me …'

What do you do, when you're 18 years old and you're sitting in a secondhand Fiat Stilo, the poor man's VW Golf, in a car-park in Llanelli, and you've just been called up by your country? You phone your Welsh mother.

'Alright Mam?'

'Yeah, good. How you getting on? How's your day?'

'Yeah, fine.'

Normal chit-chat in the least normal of moments. Mums can pick up on this kind of thing.

'Oh, what's wrong?'

'Nothing's wrong. Nothing's wrong. Nothing's wrong.'

I can't work out how I tell my own mother.

'You'll never guess what, Mam.'

'I knew something was wrong.'

'I've been picked for Wales.'

'Oh, don't take the piss now, George …'

Luckily for me, I wasn't on my own, the first day in camp. From Scarlets there was Stephen Jones, Jonathan Davies and Tavis Knoyle. This opened up the possibility of lift-sharing along the M4 from Llanelli to the Wales team hotel at the Vale. All three of my regional team-mates had far better cars than my Fiat Stilo. It wasn't even a nice colour. It was a sort of dark purple, despite my claim at the time that it was racing black. It also had a name, Eric. No-one ever names a good car. You don't hear Jaguars referred to as Dave or Aston Martins called The Lovebox. It's only the bad ones.

The first day we went in, Jonesy offered. 'I'll drive today, George.' I thought I had to show willing. 'Oh no, I'll drive.'

They were familiar with the Stilo by now. 'No, no, honestly George, I'll drive.'

Jonesy the first day, then Foxy, then Tavis. Inexorably my turn came around. All of them jumped in the Stilo, squashing themselves in. I turned the key in the ignition. Pretty much every light on the dashboard came on. It was like a cramped mobile disco.

Jonesy was very nice about it. 'Are you sure this car … are you sure you don't want me to drive?'

I'd backed myself into a corner, even as I was reversing out of the parking space.

'No, no, I'll drive, don't worry. It's only fair, isn't it?'

That was the only time that autumn I ever took us in. There seemed to be a firm consensus among the other three after that. 'Don't worry, George, we'll drive from now on …'

I had a strategy worked out for training sessions, when my ankle rehab allowed. I knew I wouldn't be fit for the opening game against the Wallabies, but that was fine. I was looking at this month purely as an opportunity to be the biggest sponge in South Wales. It was a squad packed with players who had won the Grand Slam in 2008 – Mike Phillips, Gethin Jenkins, Alun Wyn Jones, Lee Byrne. It had quite a few players who'd also been part of the Grand Slam winning team of 2005: Martyn Williams, Ryan Jones, Tom Shanklin. It had Shane Williams in it. Actual Shane Williams!

It made my approach very simple. Work as hard as I could. Learn as much as possible. That way, if I never won a cap, I could leave the Vale with a couple of free meals and a ton of knowledge. Learn, understand, take it away.

What I hadn't expected was that these big characters were also solid blokes. This was the era of rugby players discovering good coffee, unless you were an 18-year-old from Rhoscolyn, in which case you'd tried a Nescafé once and not really fancied another one. Mike Phillips would come and find me in the team room along with Shane.

'George, we're going to go for a coffee. Do you want to come?'

I was a kid. I could move fast on my feet but not always think on them. I was honest.

'I don't really drink coffee …'

'Don't worry, just come for a cup of tea.'

Me still in the wrong headspace. 'I don't really fancy a cup of tea – it's minging.'

'Don't worry, they do milkshakes.'

'Right you are, I'll come for a milkshake then.'

These were the small but important gestures from the first day. To me, all of it was astonishing. I had Shane Williams, Mike Phillips and Stephen Jones asking if I wanted to go for a coffee. To them it may well have been, the poor fucker will be sat on his own otherwise, so we may as well just ask him. And I certainly didn't say much in those conversations in the coffee shop. I was just sort of there. But they still all looked after me. Jonesy would always come up to me before a session or in the middle of one and say, okay George, this is what we're running today, you got it? After the session, he'd come up to me again and say, George, you know we ran the five-man option, then the 96 option – just your timing was a little bit off, okay?

It was never done in a bad way. He wasn't telling me off, and he'd never shout at me so I felt like a bag of shit. It would be little details that I could soak up.

'George, just come half a second later …'

He seemed to have an innate ability to see all these tiny things while going full gas. Training would be flat-out, and he'd be looking at Mike Phillips and scanning the defensive line while also managing to communicate with me. 'G! G! Come here! Come here! Inside me. Stay inside.' Me trying so hard not to be away with the fairies, to not listen to the voice in my head yelling, oh my God, this is incredible, where the hell am I, what am I doing here? Everything Jonesy did was making my job easier. That's the moment, seeing all this stuff up close, when you realise how good some players are and how underrated they might be.

That's only Stephen Jones. In those first few sessions I couldn't stop looking at Shane. I'd grown up thinking of him as a genius, which made it very hard not to just stare and think, fuck, what a guy. And then you saw how he thought about the game and how he talked about it, and you began to understand more about what he was looking for from the rest of us, how he could create what would be good for him. Every bit of it moved my thinking on. Okay, if Shane is thinking like that but it's a team game, where do I need to be? What do I need to change about me?

Then there was James Hook. He could play anywhere – step it up at 10, step it up at 12, do a job at 13, do a job at 15. He had the skillset and the rugby nous to do pretty much everything. I watched him in those training sessions and how he was in and out of the line seamlessly and all I could think was: that is class.

People appreciated Shane. They didn't always seem to appreciate Hooky enough. You would hear punters in the pub flying into him. And I would listen to the critics and think, hang on, how many players do you know who can catch a ball going away from them, step two blokes, bounce on the outside and play a 25-metre pass off their left hand to put someone else away?

You trained with James and it was like he was seeing the game as Keanu in *The Matrix*. Everything was in slow motion for him. It was like when I got to know Brian O'Driscoll on the Lions tour three years later. The way Drico saw things made you realise you were in black and white and he was in HD.

It's a gift, when you're this age, to have players of this beautiful ability around you. I'd had it, briefly so far, at Scarlets with our Kiwi centre Regan King. I'd have it again when I got back to Llanelli. There'd be a set-piece call, and Kingy would spot among all the other things going on that I was running around like a headless chicken, and he would look at me and just put his hand out, and I knew that meant calm down and slow up. And as I was running, he would be talking to me around the corner, saying, 'Come late on my outside shoulder. Just slow down. Outside shoulder.' The move would kick in, everything frantic, and still he was somehow talking to me – 'G, the call is this. But listen, I'm going to bounce at the 12 and then I'll get 12 and 10 to bite and you come late on my outside shoulder.' Then he would step and basically I was just flying through holes all the time.

That detail and the way he thought about the game was how I scored so many tries so early in my career. Because I had people like him and Jonesy going to me: 'George, your timing's just a little bit off. If you come a little bit later on this play, I'll get on the outside shoulder, then you've just got to go, you've got the wheels, I'll put you away.'

Maybe you'd expect all that from Jonesy, from Shane. People liked them. They expected the hard work. Maybe you wouldn't from Mike Phillips. He had a reputation, even then, and he didn't mind playing up to it at times. But to me, from that first shy nervous day, he was class. He didn't just keep an eye on me. He went out of his way to make sure I was okay. Later on, I'd be sitting having a cup of tea with my mum and dad, and he'd come over to say hello. He'd take the time to introduce himself to my parents and ask them questions, even as I could see from the expression on my dad's face that one of his answers was, 'JESUS CHRIST, IT'S MIKE PHILLIPS.'

In training you could not miss his dedication. His preparation, his focus, his drive ... my eyes were already open, but he was the instructional video in front of them. Right George, you knew these players are the best we've got, now you're seeing why. You're here, and that's mental on its own, but now you're going to have to work every single day like they do to make sure you stay here. You're never getting a game unless there's some mad injury crisis, but you've got to be ready. Their level has to be your level.

They were never easy on me. That's not the same thing. I was the new kid, so I was the lackey. And I wouldn't say boo to a goose, let alone no.

'George, get the bags.'

Me, externally: 'Sure.' Me, internally: 'Fucking right I will.'

'George, do the laundry drop off. Then the pick up later.'

External: 'No problem.' Internal: 'I will take every dirty garment you have.'

They could sometimes be loose, that group of senior players. When the right moment came they could enjoy themselves. But they worked so fucking hard. And they protected each other, and as I began to find my feet at this new level, I became a lot more aware of how important that was. When you're under the spotlight in club rugby it feels bright and harsh. Then you're thrown into international rugby, and suddenly it's, 'Holy shit-balls, there are now 73,000 people shouting at me …' That's when you have to keep it tight. That's when you have to look after each other. Because when it gets loud and nasty and the light is so bright that there's nowhere to hide, you still have to deliver. You still have to play better than anyone else in the country.

I wasn't scared of the players. I was scared of not matching their standards. And if it was an intense feeling with my sort of team-mates, it was off the scale with Shaun Edwards.

Shaun was probably one of the best people I've ever been coached by. Actually, you can scrub out the probably. The standards he demanded of you, even as an 18-year-old in your first season of senior rugby, were insane – the knowledge of the game he expected, the clarity within everything you did. No-one ever wants to cock up in training. With Wales in that mad month, I was shit-scared of cocking up because I would have Shaun screaming at me. Subsequently, as I began to earn my place in the side, and did some good stuff, as well as some bad, it made no difference. He shouted at me anyway.

Except, in Shaun's own words, 'Shouting at you is a good thing. It means I think you've got potential. If I don't shout at you, it's because I think you're useless.' Once I worked that out, it simplified things for me. 'Well George, just keep pushing. That's all you can do.'

He was never cruel to you, even when you weren't entirely sure he could remember your name. I was 'Kid' in this first autumn campaign, which was at least better than Hallam Amos, when he came in as the next youngster on the wing a few autumns later. Shaun must have misheard his name in the first session, because for years afterwards he would call him Alan. Someone else would say, do you mean Alun Wyn? And he would look puzzled, and say, no, Alan Amos.

But he was always on you. At the start of the session, one question: 'Are you ready?' You'd say, yeah, definitely. Then the next question: 'Do you know your stuff?' And even if you were certain you did, there was something about his delivery and the way he looked at you that made you think, oh no, do I really?

You dreaded his wrath. I had Lee Byrne at full-back in one of those early sessions. Lee had many attributes as a player, but you wouldn't have put him forward to represent the squad on *Mastermind*. We had a move to run in training, and Lee gave me a shout just before.

'Don't worry, G, I'll take last.'

I was 18 years old. He'd won a Grand Slam. So I did exactly what I'd been told, and hit last-but-one.

Shaun lost his head.

'Are you fucking stupid, lad?'

Me frozen on the spot, guts going. Thinking, I was just doing what I was told, and now I'm getting shouted at.

'You said you know your job ...'

Lee Byrne chirping up. 'Oh, my bad ...'

Us running it again. Lee can't remember. Lee does the same thing again. So does Shaun.

'KID! Are you fucking stupid?'

So he would ride me like banshee, but he was really good with me, too. If you don't know Shaun you don't see the reflective side, the religious side, the empathetic one. The first game of that autumn was against Australia. I wasn't fit enough to be considered for selection, not that I imagined anyone was doing any considering. But at the start of the second week, which would build towards the Test match against South Africa on the Saturday, he showed me glimpses of the other part of him. Jogging over to walk off the training pitch alongside me one lunchtime for a quick word in my ear.

'Kid, I know what it's like.'

I didn't look up. It took me a while to be ready for full eye contact with Shaun. I just thought, this is different, something's not right here if he's talking to me like this.

Then the second quick word.

'I played for Great Britain at 18 years old. Just know your role, do your detail and go do your thing.'

It still scared the life out of me. I still didn't know what was going on. Christ alive, George, he's either going to kiss you or punch you ...

Tuesday came. I trained as part of what felt suspiciously close to a 1st XV. Mike Phillips and Stephen Jones were the half-backs. The centre pairing was James Hook and Tom Shanklin. Shane was on the right wing. I was on the left. Lee Byrne was at full-back.

I wasn't in denial, because I didn't let myself think the thing I could then deny. So when the team was announced and the team we had been running in training was the team that was going to face the world champion Springboks on Saturday afternoon, I was astonished to the point of not quite knowing what to do. Which is once again the point when you instinctively call your mum.

'Now you won't believe it this time, Mam ...'

'Oh, what now?'

'Nah Mam, I mean it.'

'No George, stop it ...'

'Mam, they've picked me.'

'No, stop it now, don't take the piss ...'

I kept saying it. She kept sounding annoyed. She kept calling me an idiot. Then she seemed suddenly concerned that I was going to get hurt. Mothers in Anglesey instinctively understand how big and fierce South African rugby players actually are. By the time she settled on a more positive emotion – 'Oh, that's amazing news, congratulations ...' – I was moving to the next stage. 'Mum, I best ring my father ...'

His reaction was less nuanced. It was quite clear from his tone of voice that he was bouncing off the walls. He was at work, although that made no difference to the bouncing.

'Oh my God, this is incredible. Have you told your mother?'

'Yeah, I've told my mother.'

'Ah, brilliant, brilliant, brilliant.'

'I think she's worried.'

'She'll be fine. Now, we'll definitely come down for it.'

'Great.'

'How many tickets can you get?'

In the next few hours it became apparent that half of Anglesey was up for a day out south. I'd never had to source a single ticket for an international match at the Millennium Stadium. Suddenly I needed 500. Aunties who were aunties. Aunties who weren't actual aunties but may as well have been. All sorts of uncles, legit or otherwise. Traffic on the A483 was going to be the stuff of nightmares.

You try not to read the newspapers or look at your phone too much. I just wanted to get to Saturday in one piece and cross the white line so I had definitely played for Wales. To get there and size myself up against whatever the challenge was going to be. The Wales media team probably made the right call in not putting me forward at the team's press conference; the nice generic statement they made up on my behalf – 'I have just got to control myself and look forward to the game ... I will be nervous but I will give it my all' – realistically better than me opening my mouth and all manner of giddy excitement spilling out.

However, it did mean I missed what Warren Gatland told the press that Thursday lunchtime, and what Shane Williams said a few minutes later.

Gats: 'Someone has written about George that he is the Welsh Jonah Lomu. That's the last thing he needs and I have to protect him.'

Shane: 'I was asked whether I would compare George to Jonah Lomu. Physically, I probably would.'

All I got out of Gats in person was one word: 'Congratulations.' That was it, plus a good firm handshake. I didn't know it then, but this would actually be Gats in quite a talkative mood. As you got to know him, he wouldn't say much more, but you were fine with it, because he didn't need to. That week he just let me crack on. No need to overcomplicate it. Understanding you had his trust was enough.

There's another quote from that day that I've only found out about recently. It's from Matthew Rees, who was my captain at Scarlets, when he was asked, like Gats and Shane, about me being picked.

'He's the strongest player in the Scarlets squad in terms of power output in the gym and lifting weights. But he has speed as well as power and never shows any fear.'

Reading that now makes me smile, even as I struggle to discuss it without feeling like a massive bellend. But to me I wasn't doing anything special. I never thought, look at me, I'm the strongest here, or, I'm doing the best at this, this and this. It never popped into my brain because that's not me as an individual. But I was also a mix of obsession and awe. Everything I was experiencing was all I'd ever dreamed of. I was enjoying every aspect of it, and I instinctively understood that if I wanted to stay here for a long time, I had to sacrifice more than I had done to get here in the first place. I would do all the things I saw I needed to do to be in contention for that jersey, as automatically as I would brush my teeth or tie my bootlaces. After a while, it would shift ever so slightly. 'Well, now I'm here, some other bugger wants my shirt, how do I keep it from him?' For now, it was easy. Never a question of why would you, only why not?

The Springbok starting XV was announced later that day. It had experience, a track record and a reputation for aggression. It was most of the team that had beaten the British and Irish Lions the year before. It was a decent chunk of the team that had won the last World Cup in France, a tournament I'd watched in my parents' lounge, aged 15. Up front was The Beast, Tendai Mtawarira. In the second row was Victor Matfield and Bakkies Botha. It was a good job at this point that I didn't foresee the hit Bakkies would put in on me later on Saturday afternoon. How he would line me up and batter me, the big bastard. In the back line there was Ruan Pienaar, there was Morne Steyn. There was also Juan Smith and Jean de Villiers.

And there was Bryan Habana. First Shane, now Habana. Maybe my two biggest heroes growing up, and now I was lining up with one and playing opposite the other. My considered thoughts: 'Fucking hell.' There is no other way of saying it without swearing.

Return of the internal monologue. 'George, just don't give him the outside. This guy has raced a cheetah and won. So whatever you do, don't give him the flipping outside ...'

And yet ... after these past couple of weeks of training, after the milkshakes with Jonesy and Mike Phillips and

Shane, after training shoulder to shoulder with these lads …
I had this lovely sense of confidence from knowing they were
next to me. As much as I knew what was coming would be
absolutely brutal and at times total carnage, I had heroes of
mine alongside me. They had treated me like one of them. I
wasn't one of them, not yet, but for the first time, I could
imagine a time when I might be. I wasn't in a safe space. I
was playing against Bryan Habana. But of all the places I
could be, this was the side I wanted to be on.

Maybe it was naivety. The foolishness of youth and the
unknown unknowns. Habana was asked about me in one of
the South African press conferences. He said: 'We've done
some analysis on him this week. I know he's bigger than
Shane.' If I'd been thinking about it I might have reflected
that they can't have done that much analysis, because everyone's bigger than Shane. But I wasn't. I was looking at these
new team-mates of mine, and remembering all I had
watched them do on my parents' TV, and everything I
had witnessed them doing in training, and being consoled
by rather an uplifting thought: well, these buggers don't
seem scared, so maybe I should have more confidence in
myself.

It was only later, looking back with enough experience to
know the difference, that I could see my benign delusions for
what they really were. 'George, that was a really stupid thing
to think, because they had done it before, and you hadn't.'
But, at the same time, all of them had started somewhere.
Everyone had a first cap. Everyone had a first training session
where imposter syndrome had them round the ankles and

brought them down. So what else can you do other than decide to crack on?

It seems strange to me now, when they open up that stadium to all manner of games and corporate events and live concerts. But I'd never actually been on the pitch at the Millennium Stadium until our captain's run on the Friday morning. The serious training is done by this point. It's just a chance for you to feel the grass under your studs, to take a few high balls and to remind yourself of the sightlines and the way the roof looms over you when it's closed. But I remember looking around, as the other players walked off, and getting a tangible sense of a calm before the storm. Hearing the pigeons flapping under the steel struts, the workmen shouting, the security staff flipping back seats. The voices and the echoing.

In future years it would become my favourite part of international week. By the time of the captain's run you were there. You had been selected, you were fit. The comparative peace and quiet gave you a window to think, allowed you to remember why you did it, who you did it for. I would always take a moment before walking off the pitch to suck in as much of that calm as possible, because you knew when you fast-forwarded 24 hours, some fucker would be trying to rip your head off.

Meanwhile there were the various formalities of matchday minus one to learn. The ticket scenario was getting no easier. Lesson no. 16, for the debutant that week: if you're playing, you'll be given four free tickets and no more. Doesn't matter if you're an only child or one of eight; the WRU lives in a world of nuclear families. To get merely my direct relatives in we would need at least three of them to also be selected and granted a seat allocation. There could be some horse-trading among the players, with spares passed around between you all, but that came with a tax of serious piss-taking. 'You want 30 tickets? That's all of Anglesey!' they kept saying to me. I considered my response carefully: 'Yeah, it probably is, to be honest.'

I had to hand responsibility to my dad in the end. Get him everything I could, let him coordinate the text messages and the car-share options and the scramble for hotel beds. I got the sense of much topping and tailing being planned. Jump in with your auntie and uncle, lad, it's what they expect from us lot in Anglesey anyway …

The protocols, the pecking order. The Friday evening, hanging round the team room, and some of the older boys playing cards. Paul James calling me over.

'Oh, George, we just fancy a bit of chocolate and stuff.'

'Ah right, okay. Do I just go and ask reception or something?'

'No, no. There's a garage down the road at Talbot Green.'

So that was the early part of my evening, borrowing a car to get up there and fill a carrier bag with Dairy Milk and Haribo. A rite of passage for the youngest member of the squad, sorting the senior boys out with their contraband, not hanging around when you got back to see who took what but dropping and running before Shaun Edwards stuck his head round the door. Being the youngest one for quite a time,

I would get on pretty familiar terms with the lads behind the till up at Talbot Green.

Next issue was sleep. Everything in my head had suddenly sped up to 100 miles an hour. All I wanted to do was get a solid seven hours' in. That's what I normally had before big games, if you could call a handful of games in regional rugby normal. But then I started overthinking it. George, this might be your one and only cap. Even if it's not, you only ever get one first cap. You don't want to cock this up, do you?

Within minutes I was petrified. 'Holy shit the bed, it's now like 10 o'clock. So if I fall asleep at, say, half past 10, then seven hours is going to be like … half past 11, half past 12, half past one, half past two, half past three, half past four, half past five, half past six … But then no-one wakes up at half past six for a game. So maybe I should go to bed a little bit later. But then what if I don't sleep straight away? Then I'm only getting six hours' sleep. Could easily be five. And if it's five, why wouldn't it become four?'

That's when I asked the team doctor for a sleeping tablet. It felt like a better idea than staring at the ceiling all night. It felt like I was less likely to wake up groggy that way than if I stayed awake until the terrified pre-dawn and only managed to squeeze in a few hours before my arse went again.

I'm better at understanding myself now. Of course I was going to struggle to settle into my matchday routine. I was 18 years old. I was still to establish one. It wasn't a complete unknown, but there was enough that was unfamiliar to leave me feeling both enormously excited and absolutely terrified.

I was tiptoeing around the older players so I didn't upset their routines while also thinking that I should be focusing on what I needed to do. I tried going through the things that had worked for me at Llandovery and Scarlets, and then began watching other players, thinking, well, these men are the crème de la crème, actually do I need to be doing what they're doing?, and then coming back again with, no, let's do what I know and what I feel. This constant back and forth, this relentless anxious churn.

I slept until about 7.30 a.m. in the end. Not the best un-broken night, but enough not to feel minging. Looked around my room, at the alarm clock, at the piles of kit on the carpet. Okay. This was it.

I couldn't eat huge amounts that morning. I reconciled myself with being a grazer. I could nibble constantly so I felt I had enough food inside me for energy without having so much I felt heavy and lethargic. A pre-match meal of pushing small items around a big plate, a walk through the lobby past the supporters who have come out to the hotel, a climb up onto the bus.

I didn't have time to look around. Everything was acceler-ating. Thoughts coming in uninvited. 'This player who likes being the last one off the bus, that's a weird one, because there are so many things at play here – if someone drops their headphones and they go everywhere and they spend 10 minutes trying to find them and untangle them, does this mean the last man is then compromised because he can't leave until the clumsy one sorts himself out?' Other thoughts popping up as a counterpoint. 'George, why are you even worrying about this? Get on with it. Focus back on your job, like Shaun Edwards said.'

When the bus comes off the M4 and into the eastern suburbs of Cardiff, you see all the supporters piling into town. Coming off trains, out of cars, out of buses, rosettes on, scarves, cans on the go, cheers and fists waving as they spot the team coach. It's awesome, and it's better than anywhere else in world rugby – better than south-west London, the northern suburbs of Paris, the south of Auckland. Naturally it makes your backside go again. Okay, this is real, this is happening. I've got two hours, take a breath, remind myself I know what I'm doing ...

Nothing can prepare you for the changing-rooms at the stadium. I get goosebumps thinking about that place even now. Club rugby has an atmosphere. There's bounce there. Going into the Millennium Stadium is like Colosseum-level shit. The noise, the tension, the chanting, the songs. You soak it all up, or rather it hits you like a wave and tumbles over and over you. Suddenly you can't wait. You walk out onto the pitch to warm up and it's a physical impact on your chest and ears and heart. It's love at first sight. 'Holy fuck-balls, this is a slice of me. This is what I want. There's no other place I ever want to be ...'

The number 14 shirt hung by my locker. Lee Byrne's to one side, Tom Shanklin's to the other. Every player in their own groove, some getting strapped up, Adam Beard, strength and conditioning coach, shouting the timings, telling us how long we had before last man out. The sound of men slapping their shoulders, psyching themselves up. The smell of Deep Heat, of Vicks. That smell will stay with me until my last breath. The noise of Neil Jenkins vomiting in the toilets. He'd done it as a player, and now he was doing it as kicking coach. Me with all these men, these legends of Welsh rugby, up on a pedestal. 'Jesus, if Jenksy's being sick, should I be sick?'

You find out a lot, in those split seconds before a big game. How people react under intense pressure, where the cracks show. Where we pull together so they don't.

I didn't want to say anything at all, for fear of saying the wrong thing. Not screaming, like some; not shouting, like others. Just thinking about my job. About how many of my family were out there in the stands and how long their journey had been. Sometimes a simple negative: don't cock up. Talking back to myself, even as I said it. 'Well, no. I'm not going to cock up. I'm here to do a job. The first line-out is this. The first scrum's going to be this. I've practised it, I know it. I know my role.' And then you bring yourself back to that clear, simple focus. There's a point where, even on your first cap, you're pig-sick of waiting. An excitement, cutting through it all. 'Yeah, yeah, this is good. Yeah, yeah, yeah, yeah. Get me the fuck out of here now. Get me into the arena.'

In the last few moments before we walked into the tunnel, it was all taps on the back and good luck to each other. No going back. No time for much else. That was when Shane Williams came up to me, punched me on the arm and looked into my eyes.

'Smash it, pal. You know you're here for a reason.'

I nodded. I wasn't good for much else. Then he gave me a big smile.

'Trust me, it's easy. Just go out there and enjoy it.'

It's quite the thing, when the greatest try-scorer in your nation's history comes up to you and says that. It completely threw me, in a good way.

'What? What did he just say? It's easy?'

Competing internal narratives again. 'It's easy for you, who's played 80-odd times, scored all these tries. Of course it's easy.' 'Well, if Shane says it's easy, then maybe it's not as bad as you think. How hard can it be?'

I floated into the anthem. I sang the first few lines with everything I had. Then, just for the briefest of seconds, I stopped. This intense wave of noise hit me with a force I'd never experienced anywhere else – a power, a closeness, a life force. It felt like the ultimate justification of all the hard work and all the things I'd done and all the things I wished I had. All of it was suddenly worth it, because I was here.

There was something I had done all the way through my fast-forward career to that point. A little mental trick I used on myself. It came from asking myself a question: 'What can I do to get myself ready for this game?' You never know when your first action is going to come, as a winger. You might have to wait long minutes for your first touch of the ball or first tackle. I always looked for early hits or early touches, but you could never guarantee it. So on the first kick-off, I would say to myself, as the whistle sounded and boot hit ball, 'Let's go.' A signal to myself that the hard work had been done, the heavy weights lifted, the skills ticked off. 'Let's go. Now it's time to work.'

So I said it again, as Steve Walsh blew his whistle, and that great gale of noise swept down from the stands, and the green shirts of the Springboks came thundering towards us. The early touches came. Morne Steyn launched some Morne Steyn long-range penalty shots. And I scored a try.

The move was called Block Tune. Something we had worked on in training, something which required no conscious thought from me. Something which worked out exactly as it was meant to work out.

Shanks coming over, Hooky going underneath him and away and me getting put in the space between them. That was the theory. In the moment? Jonesy gets to one, Shanks sits down two and then Hooky takes three away from them, and because I come so late, they don't see me and I just piss through the middle of 12 and 13.

You don't plan your reaction, when you're suddenly clean through and the posts are coming towards you and there's not a single South African defender who's going to get between you and the try line. That's the only reason I can explain the nervous arm, the way my left hand was suddenly waving about in the air as I crossed the line. In hindsight, it was horrendous. But in that tiny fragment of a second I was just so happy. I was genuinely awash with ecstasy, and then this weird arm comes out of nowhere, even as I'm looking at it like it doesn't belong to me. 'What are you doing, you sausage? Put it down ...'

There was no sense of playing it cool, as I slid over. I was screaming like a teenage girl. I stood up and all the lads were all over me, and then Shane was holding my face like he was going to kiss me.

'Told you so. It's easy!'

I watched the review, on the big screen. Their centre Jean De Villiers was flapping his arms about like he had been blocked. He hadn't been. He just got a howling read. Then it was the deep booming voice over the PA – 'Try for Wales, number 14, George North!' – and a roar from the stands that just filled my heart with pride. It's like your pecs have pushed out and your shoulders have grown and suddenly your chest is 50 inches broad. I had no idea where the wider North clan were in the stadium. I just knew they were there somewhere. I was so excited I was waving to everyone.

Suddenly so relaxed. Suddenly at ease in this foreign environment. Before the move I hadn't had much involvement. A couple of what I called dead carries, except dead carries aren't dead, they're just into brick walls. So I'd had a couple of those and I'd thought: 'It would be good to have a proper run at something now, or have a crack,', and then Block Tune had happened and that yard of panic was gone from my stride.

It was just as well. The speed of the game, the absolute speed of it … Normally I'd had, in club rugby, a bit of time: you see something, you call it, you act on it, it's still there. I could still see it here, and you could call it, but if you didn't get it straightaway, it was gone. Three or four times in that first 20 minutes I remember thinking, 'Shit! We've got to go now … ah, it's too late …'

The senior boys had kept saying to me in training. 'When you get up from a ruck, just scan, and if you see it's on, just go. Don't hang around – just go.' And I'd thought: 'That's a bit weird. That's not really a thing. You can't just go.' But already, in these opening exchanges, I'd missed a couple of jumps on open-play stuff. It wasn't set piece, so I wasn't going to get bawled out at half-time, but I'd noticed it. 'I could have had an extra touch there.' 'I might have got a carry here.'

I'd missed them because I couldn't comprehend the speed of it all. Doors didn't just shut. They slammed. Gaps were there and then suddenly they weren't. As you wondered where they had gone, the next thing came at you and blew past. The hits were bigger, the brick walls harder. You weren't just tackled. You were deconstructed.

It was baffling and beautiful at the same time. Even with your lungs in your arse you wanted to get to the next carry or the next slamming door. Even when you were adjacent to the carnage you were viscerally aware of it. The sound of muscle hitting bone, the fat hard slap of shoulder smacking into bare thighs.

I had another rumble down the right. Tracking across to cover a kick deep into our 22, giddy to be involved, like a puppy chasing a crisp packet on the wind. I probably should have worked harder earlier to give Lee Byrne more of a hand, but he was so good he gathered the loose ball and beat the first chaser anyway, and I could get striding away down the wing.

'Right, George, you've beaten the first guy, carry ...'

Getting over halfway, getting brick-walled. Rolling on the damp grass to present the ball back. All the time thinking: oh my God, this is class. I'm out of breath, I'm fucked. But this is class. This is exactly where I want to be.

We went wide from there. Numbers on our left, Shane and Hooky combining to send Hooky away for our second try. We were 17–9 up at half-time. I had no idea what the plan was for me. Sixty minutes and then give the kid a rest? I was never going to ask. I had fought so hard to be here, and I might never get the chance again. If this was my only cap, I wanted to squeeze every last second out of it. Why would you not? I was in a happy place I never wanted to leave. It was also a fucked place, but I was okay with that. I liked the hard work and the hard impacts. I liked the shock and awe of it all. I was the kid who'd always loved fireworks and was now suddenly being allowed inside the ropes to run the Bonfire Night display with all the adults. I could feel the heat on my face and my ears were nearly deafened by the noise of it all, but it made you feel more alive than you'd ever felt before. I saw the lights and the explosions and I wanted to run towards them. Give me another touch. Give me another carry. Let me run into that clear empty space.

South Africa came back into it. Of course they did. That physicality, all done at speed. We were behind again and I was gone in the lungs when I saw the Springbok defence was narrow, and I was in wide open acres on the right wing, and Stephen Jones had the ball in his hands.

I called it. Didn't matter I was 18; you'll never meet a winger who doesn't think he's on. I could see Bryan Habana looking on his inside, trying to cover the threat further in. I called it once and nothing happened. I saw Martyn Williams inside me, up against Victor Matfield, and Martyn Williams is always going to beat Victor Matfield in a running race, so

I thought, worse case Nugget will have it, and I've just got to be off Nugget, so I put my hand up and called it again. And I saw Jonesy spot me, and the picture in front of him.

Oh my God, he's kicking it. Fuck.

I watched this egg coming towards me, Habana turning on his heel and beginning to panic-cover, Frans Steyn spotting me further out and beginning to sprint across.

Don't let it bounce. Don't let it bounce. Don't let it bounce. Through all those years learning the game at Llangefni and Llandovery, on windy pitches and muddy touchlines, telling myself there was no way in hell you should ever let a ball bounce, because it could go anywhere. Take it out of the air, take out the role of random chance. And then, on the biggest stage I'd ever been on, the biggest day of my life, I let it bounce.

It sat up like an absolute dream. The one and only time of my career it would ever do it – a bounce so perfect in its trajectory and timing it's almost like I'd picked it from a carousel of 50 options. 'I'll have this one, please, the one that takes out Habana, and makes Frans Steyn just check for a second, and then comes straight into my arms so I don't even have to break stride, and can just fall over the line at my toes.'

I don't know whether I had a subconscious sense that I wasn't going to quite make it on the full. Maybe I was thinking of how fast Bryan Habana is. There are things that go through your mind at that point that you don't really hold onto afterwards. Tiny calculations and adjustments that happen at some level far below consciousness and memory.

Only after I'd celebrated again like a teenage girl screaming at a One Direction concert did I have a serious word with myself. 'What the hell are you doing, boy? Get your head out of your arse. Why are you letting that bounce?'

It would get brought up in the team review early the next week. 'That's really good, George. Well done. Good communication. Yada yada yada. But don't let it bounce again.' And I remember thinking, was that like a slap on the wrist, or a well done, and then, don't question this one, just be happy with it.

We never got our lead back. We went close, at the end, and I kept looking for the ball. Went into midfield for two or three more carries, blowing out of my backside but swept along by the high of it all, but the defence just soaking it all up and us working phase after phase yet unable to get more than 10 metres into their 22, which meant I ended up running about 100 metres to get those carries and then going backwards for most of them, which was not ideal.

Still totally focused on what might be possible, even as the South African defence were trying to demonstrate what wasn't.

'Come on, George, we need to get on the front foot here. Maybe I can be that guy. Maybe I can carry it.' Instead I got absolutely mullered by their winger Gio Aplon. 'Oh George, that's a terrible idea from you ...'

We came up a try short. Final score 25–29. And afterwards my head was in the chips and rice space, which is to say it was half and half. I was gutted about the result, but as I settled into a realisation of my part in it, I couldn't ignore a quiet surge of pride at what I'd managed to contribute.

I also thought again about what Shane had told me just before kick-off. Easy? It had never been easy. What sort of bastard says something like that when they know you're going to be beaten up for 80 minutes? But then Victor Matfield said some nice words at the after-match function, something about it being one of the best debuts he'd seen from a player of my age, and that if I kept doing it, I'd be around for a while, and I got called up to be presented with my cap by the WRU president Dennis Gethin, a lovely man, God rest his soul, and although the boys kept tapping me at the wrong moment so I stood up three times before he actually called my name, it was all good that giddy night.

You have to sing a song to the rest of the team, when you hit these sorts of landmark. One on your debut, one for your 50th cap, one for your 100th. I had no inkling I would get to those other two, so I went double-top with 'Mr Brightside', forgot the words halfway through and ended up singing 'Baa Baa Black Sheep'. Both solid singalong numbers, although at that exact moment, only one of them was simultaneously blasting out in 18 different bars across the central Cardiff drinking zone.

The great thing about life as an 18-year-old is that there's always something to bring you down after a high, always another basic growing-up error to make. I'd driven to the team hotel in Eric the purple Fiat Stilo, so I could hang around a bit on the Sunday and catch up with the vast numbers of family members before they began the long trek back north to Anglesey. Being naïve in this new world, I'd also not taken with me any of my own clothes. I assumed everything you wore until you went back through the front door of your own house had to be WRU branded. As a result, as Eric and I nosed back onto the westbound carriageway of the M4 from the Vale hotel, I was heavily repping the Full Kit Wanker look.

I might have got away with it if Eric hadn't been in a cantankerous mood, or maybe I should have taken more heed of the multiple warning lights on the dashboard that time I'd given Jonesy and the other boys a lift in from Llanelli. Either way the disco lights were on again as we accelerated at pace from 40 mph to 43 mph. I consoled myself with the sort of deluded optimism found in many first-time owners of substandard first cars: 'Ah, it'll be fine, it's just a sensor.'

We were just past the bright lights of Port Talbot when I heard an almighty bang. It was like something deep inside Eric's vitals had exploded. He was swerving all over the dance; fortunately, because of our great speed, we were still in the inside lane, so I was able to wrestle him onto the hard shoulder. A panicked inspection revealed that the exhaust, already badly rusted, had finally given up the ghost and snapped off before puncturing one of the rear tyres with its jagged edge.

This proper sort of *Wacky Races* action always goes down well with your fellow motorists. Soon a large number of westbound travellers were slowing down to appreciate the sight of a Wales rugby Full Kit Wanker standing forlornly by the side of the road, trying to pull his official WRU bright blue Under Armour hoodie further over his face to hide his deep shame.

The man from the AA was similarly wowed when he arrived.
'Alright, bud?'
'Yeah, fine.'
'Oh, it's proper broken that!'
'Yeah, it's proper broken.'
'You'd better jump in with me boy. We'll tow you home.'
He went quiet for a bit, once we were in the cab of his
lorry. I kept catching him staring at my blue Under Armour
gear. We were somewhere near Birchgrove when he chirped
up next.
'You don't play for Wales, do you?'
'Yeah, yeah, I do.' Could probably have used the past tense
until I'd got through Shaun Edwards' debriefing the follow-
ing week, but still.
Another glance at the badge on the hoodie.
'Did you watch the game yesterday, by chance?'
'Yeah, yeah, I watched the game yesterday.'
Another pause.
'You didn't play, did you?'
'Yeah, I did.'
'You're not that fellow, are you?'
'I don't know. There's 15 of them.'
'No, no. The young one.'
By now my embarrassment levels were moving through the
gears from painful to intense. No-one wants to be the one to
say their own name, but I was also leaving him in his own
world of discomfort.
'Oh, come on now.' Clicking his fingers, furrowing his
brow. 'What's your name now?'

The time had come to rescue us both.

'Ah, George North.'

'Aye-aye, you're not him, are you?'

'Yeah.'

'Oh! Well, what are the chances?'

He dropped me at the garage down the road from my flat. It was shut, because it was Sunday afternoon. I left the rusting shell of Eric on the forecourt, took my giant bag of kit out of the boot and trudged up the deserted street to my cold empty flat. Truly a hero's return.

I texted Stephen Jones later that evening. 'Jonesy, you won't believe this. My car broke down. Can I get a lift on Monday?' He's a good man, Stephen Jones. He took us both in. And when we got there, Paul James came over with a puzzled look on his face.

'Hey kid, did you break down on the M4 on Sunday on the way home?'

'Yeah, yeah, that was me.'

'Oh, I thought so. I passed you.'

But you didn't bother to stop, did you, I thought. I didn't say it. I was 18 years old. I was back in the Wales camp for another Test week. I might get picked to play Fiji next week, and then the All Blacks the following Saturday. What did I have to complain about?

FIVE

PORTHMADOG TO DOLGELLAU: SETTLING IN

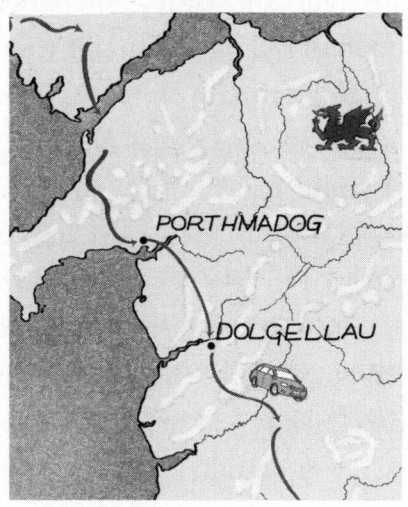

IN WHICH WE TALK ABOUT:

*Good news and bad news/post-op protocols/dirty plates in the
sink/a summer in Spala/Big Bad Wolf/World Cup countdowns/
Rob Howley gets angry/I can't feel my arms/Christmas
happening every day/a rugby form of PTSD/Magnums at dawn/
stitched up by an Argentine legend/'Here we go now, George …'*

I did get picked to play Fiji. And while the game wasn't a classic, from the strange blue kit we wore to the 16–16 score-line and the equally divided reception that followed, I began to feel I might belong. Not just in the adjustments and improvements I was making to fit in at this level, but the way the other players were treating me. After training sessions I was still being invited for milkshakes, but I was starting to push my caffeine aversion aside, and I didn't feel like a youngster in a squad of old boys. Often I wouldn't say much. I was happy being the ultimate cling-on, taking it all in. But the others were happy too, so it was all good.

On the pitch I could feel the same invisible bonds being established. No-one took a backward step in international rugby. People preferred to take several forward steps, usually straight over you, and if it got heated and you were on your own, you knew about it. But when it did, all these stars I'd looked up to for so long would magically appear shoulder to shoulder with me. You couldn't always control these scenarios. Sometimes you'd find yourself in the wrong place in the wrong ruck and shit happened. But if your team-mates could get to you, they would. And when you saw that, as an 18-year-old, it was quite the thing. You don't back up some-one you don't believe in, or who hasn't been putting the work in. You can arrive later or slower and no-one even notices, except the one on the deck with the shit happening to them.

Something else became apparent in the aftermath. My shoulder hurt. It really hurt. I put it down initially to the meta-physical – 'Ah, we've not played well, the crowd weren't happy, I'm going to feel the impacts more.' Then we went back into training ahead of the New Zealand game, and it stayed sore. Weirdly it was still functional. I could do all the things I wanted to do – tackle, pass, lift weights – as long as I could soak up the pain while doing so. Since it was the All Blacks at home and I was 18 years old, I was happy to do this.

I had it strapped before kick-off. I warmed up. I made my first tackle, and the pain reached a level where it was no longer politely knocking on the door but trying to kick it down. I hit someone else, and it felt like my shoulder almost popped out, but then reversed back in as it bounced back off their body. 'Holy shit-balls, George, this isn't normal ...'

Adrenaline got me through the game. Adrenaline didn't get me through the aftermath. The next day I was down in Cardiff Bay, getting it scanned with our team doctor, John Williams. 'Prof' had been around the game longer than I'd been alive at this point, which might be why he slightly misjudged his approach when he showed me the results of the scan.

'George, do you want the good news or the bad news?'

Me thinking, I'd rather have two bits of good news please. Me saying, 'Give me the bad news, then.'

'You see this black hole here? That shouldn't be there. Your labrum should be there covering it in white.'

'Oh, Where is it?'

'It's down by your pec.'

'Ah ...'

'You're going to have to have surgery on this to fix it, George, because it's not going to be good for your long-term health and career.'

'Okay, so what's the good news then?'

'Well, you'll get Christmas off this year.'

Perhaps this would have been good news to a grizzled 32-year-old with children. I was only six months on from legally being a child myself. I had never played a classic Welsh rugby Boxing Day game. I'd been rather looking forward to one.

It would be 11 weeks, from operation to playing again. In a period of just over two weeks I'd completed half my list from the back of my bedroom door in Llandovery. I was exactly where I wanted to be. On consecutive weekends I had played against the reigning world champions, the most exciting team in world rugby and the current number ones. It was all rather perfect. And now it felt like I was on some cruel gameshow where I'd got a key question wrong and not even understood what I was being asked. Look what you could have won, George. Instead you're going home empty-handed. For Christmas.

Christmas was actually okay. I went back to Anglesey, and my mum picked me up and drove over the speedbumps a little too quickly for Prof Williams' post-op protocols, and apologised when I swore, once I'd apologised for swearing in the first place. I tried to do a good job of pretending the news hadn't destroyed me. And then, when I realised the futility of being over-dramatic, I took a few deep breaths and tried to work out how to get through it as well as possible.

Prof Williams had promised to send me a plan. He also said I could do it from home, but I wasn't the shy kid who hadn't wanted to leave for Llandovery anymore. I didn't want to be where Gats and the other Wales coaches couldn't see me. I wanted to be in the mixer, even if that meant Rhodri as my domestic assistant rather than my mum and me rehabbing while the other Scarlets players were hitting it hard.

I began picking out small goals and objectives along the journey. First time I can take off the sling, first time I can use a light weight. First running session, first contact session. I played games in my head. 'Well, you played when you didn't think you could. Now you're injured, maybe let's see if you can get back quicker than they think.' Trying to reframe the disappointment as something else. 'Well, yeah, it is shit. But I got injured playing for Wales, which is the biggest honour.'

Little challenges, daily competitions. If the physio asked me to do 12 decline push-ups, I'd wait until he wasn't looking and then try to do 15. Pushing the physio too – '15's a good number, but 20's a magic one …' Learning to appreciate pain and, in a strange way, learning to cohabit with it. It's something most professional athletes have to absorb: becoming comfortable with being uncomfortable. In my darker moments, heavier thoughts: this is the life I've chosen for myself, so maybe I'm destined to be in a world where I have to carry some level of pain.

Sooner or later, as a rugby player in our era, you became used to hurting. Tight hamstrings, a back that aches when you're warming up and makes it hard to sit on the sofa afterwards. A knee that needs strapping up, a finger that won't bend, a neck so stiff you have to turn your whole upper body to look past your own shoulder.

And you crack on, while you can. We all wanted to be there. None of us wanted someone else to be there instead of us. And you learn from it, as much as it sounds like a terrible way to live a young life. I began listening to the feedback my body was giving me in a way I hadn't done before. I gave the physios the information they needed, but also kept it positive.

'How are you feeling this morning, George?'

Thinking, I'm fatigued here. Got a bit of DOMS, bit sore round the edges, but everything's still attached. Saying instead, 'I'm good. Actually, I'm pretty fucking good. I feel a million dollars.'

You spoke to other players and you saw all of us doing the same thing, the same talking on two levels. You'd ask a teammate how their body was. They'd say, good. They'd make a funny face, you'd nod at them, and you both knew. It happens now when I speak to an old mate who has finished playing.

'You know that weird ache that you have in your shoulders or your knees?'

'Oh yeah.'

'You don't get that anymore.'

'What do you mean?'

'It just sort of doesn't really happen anymore.'

'Whoa …'

Meanwhile, as I healed, I leaned on Rhodri for lifts and for doing the two-handed tasks around the house, like washing-up and hoovering. One element of this strategy worked better than the other. Cow, as we called him, was okay with timekeeping. He'd get us to Parc y Scarlets and back. He'd just do it with a car like a mobile skip. The passenger footwell was like an exhibition of his best snack game: food packets, bottles, wrappers. The house was worse. The sink was full of dishes. The hoover seldom got an outing. He called me a cleanliness freak, I pointed out he was a son of farmers.

My head would go sometimes. I thought he'd done the hard stuff: the dirty plates were in the sink. He just needed to wash them. But he couldn't, and I couldn't deal with the sight of them. Every now and then, when I was really annoyed, I'd pick them up one by one with my good arm and leave them in his room. Part OCD, part desire to make everything work. I liked the feeling of doing things properly: rehab, training, housework. I hated the idea of untidiness or lack of punctuality affecting my performance, and thus my ability to play rugby for Wales. I'd worked too hard and had too many people sacrifice too much to let anything preventable get in the way. I had begun taking this to a deep level. Let's say my laces snapped in a game because I hadn't checked them beforehand. Or I missed 10 minutes of training because I hadn't packed a spare pair. If it was in my control, I could find a solution. If I could nullify any shit, I would. Never give someone a reason not to pick you.

That's why the dirty dishes bothered me so much. If there were no clean plates then I couldn't make the food I needed to recover. If I had to clean someone else's plates it would slow down how quickly I could get that fuel on board. If I needed something for rehab and I put it down in a specific place then it wasn't where I left it or it was hidden under a pile of something else – well, that would stop me doing the number of reps I should do, and take away the extra time to do the bonus reps I wanted to do. Limit the shit to focus on the good stuff. That was my way of thinking. It might have sounded harsh on Cow sometimes, but anything that stopped me from doing my job would frustrate me, and I'd have to highlight it.

I made my comeback for Scarlets on 21 February. The Six Nations was already approaching its third weekend. Morgan Stoddart and Shane Williams were the starting wingers. My chances of making it back for any part of the tournament looked slim, even if all went as well as possible against Edinburgh in our Magners League match.

But Gats brought me back in. I was by no means certain I was ready. I'd never played in the Six Nations, but I'd seen enough now to understand what a step up it was from regional rugby to the international game. I thought I might need more gametime with Scarlets or Wales Under-20s under my belt. I thought I might need more intensity.

It was also France, away. A French team less than a year on from winning the Grand Slam. A side that included a back row of Harinordoquy, Bonnaire and Dusatoir. This was less a soft landing than a crash course.

And yet Gats seemed to have faith in me. Before the game, he said as many words in a row to me as he'd ever said.

'Look, I picked you because I believe in you. I know you're not 100 per cent. But I'd rather have you at 95 per cent than anyone else.'

This was big to me. Not just the length of the conversation, which was unprecedented, but what it meant from a coach

like that, when I was still two months short of my 19th birthday, when a World Cup was coming around that autumn. In
the space of that short compliment I went from doubt to
confidence. I suddenly wanted to play. 'Do you know what?
Maybe he does trust me now and maybe he wants to see
more of me ...'

What you gradually learned with Gats was that he never
said these things lightly. I only found out later what he'd said
to the media. Maybe that was a good thing. I would have
thought the reporters were making it up.

'We just think he is a real quality player of the future –
somebody who's going to be special. And he's still learning
his trade. But in a year or two I think he's going to be an
absolute star of the game.'

So I started, on 19 March, opposite Vincent Clerc at the
Stade de France. And because of everything Gats had said,
and the long weeks of rehab, and the way I was naturally, I
gave it everything I had. I went full-fat milk into it. And
within about five minutes I was absolutely on my arse.

It was like my lungs were in my mouth. You know when
they talk about getting a second wind? I'm still waiting for it
to arrive today. It wasn't that I was rusty. I could do all the
things I wanted to do. It was just I was a yard behind where
I should have been doing them all.

We lost 28–9. We didn't score a try. Vincent Clerc did. But
we had something. A lot of young players, several of us less
than a year in, others who weren't much further ahead. A few
survivors of the 2008 Grand Slam, like Lee Byrne and Ryan
Jones, but a new generation coming through as well: Leigh

Halfpenny, Jamie Roberts and Jonathan Davies; Sam Warburton and Dan Lydiate.

We had the core of something good. We just needed to be tested. We just needed to be toughened up.

It was maybe a good thing we had no idea what awaited us when we set off for our pre-World Cup training camp in Spala that summer.

I had done pretty much a full pre-season with Scarlets the year before, give or take a Monday afternoon for A-Level exams. I understood the goal of the training camp: to get you fit for the challenges ahead. What I had no idea about was the intensity that awaited us. The volume. And the almost complete lack of home comforts, rest and familiar food.

Warren Gatland and Shaun Edwards had been out to Poland before when they had coached Wasps. They had carefully planned two 12-day camps for us, with four days off in between. They explained that the first camp was designed to get us big, dynamic and strong. There was no pretence that it would be pleasant. There was no guarantee you would even make the cut for the final World Cup squad. Men would get through Spala and never get close to New Zealand in the autumn.

All of it was a massive shock. We were up just after dawn. We would begin with weights or conditioning around 8 a.m. Then there would be rugby sessions, more conditioning, more weights. More hours of work, stretching through the morning, stretching on through the afternoon. The last session was always around hypertrophy – getting big, basically. That was around 8 at night.

One thought, as the first day came to an end: 'What the fuck?' Second block of thoughts, three days in: 'Oh my God, I can't feel my arms. I can't feel my legs. I'm 18 and my back is screaming. Why the hell am I in the gym at 8.30 p.m. after I've done five sessions before?' All the time, looking around me at everyone else going through the same thing: 'Oh my God, if I can hang onto this like I'm hanging onto these guys, I might have half a chance …'

You used whatever you could to keep going. There was a song one of the boys used to stick on the stereo first thing. A horrendous tune by Duck Sauce called 'Big Bad Wolf'. Please don't watch the video for it unless you are of a strong disposition; it's not a pleasant thing. The track itself is fundamentally no more than a big baseline, the title on repeat and some wolf-like howling. The song would come on in the gym and all the boys would be howling like wolves. Madness, in many ways, but it was our way of turning a bad evening session, 8 p.m. to 10 p.m., into a better one, of distracting ourselves from the heaviness in our arms and legs and chests and backs.

We had really good people around us. That helped. A great Canadian conditioning coach called Dan Baugh, who had played back row for Cardiff Blues. He would come in with bundles of North American energy just when you were running dry yourself.

'Yeah motherfucker! Let's get this done!'

You would briefly pretend to be Canadian yourself and answer in the same way, before realising it wasn't you and you sounded ridiculous. But he got you through your session to the point where you could stagger to your bed and fall into the deepest sleep so you could get up again at dawn and do it all over again.

Nothing about it was easy. Nothing allowed you to feel good. We were somewhere in a forest several hours' drive from Warsaw, closer to Belarus or Ukraine than Germany. It was not a forest you wanted to go for a stroll in. It was a Red Riding Hood forest. It was a Hansel and Gretel forest. You looked into the dense, dark fir trees and immediately got the creeps. You didn't think of picnics, you thought of unsolved murders.

If the boys were howling in the gym, so was the food. The salad came with caterpillars crawling about under the leaves. If you wanted something fresh, there was something we called eggy pork – a slab of pig dipped in egg and fried to a grey sogginess. If you went fast food, there were protein pot noodles which absorbed as much water as you tried to pour on them and still stayed stubbornly desiccated. None of us wanted to eat, but we were burning so many calories we had to. Necessity became the mother of terrible inventions: the protein bar with peanut butter and jam smeared on top.

Shaun Edwards let slip at one point that it had been worse when Wasps had been there. This seemed an impossibility. Were the caterpillars bigger? Was the pork eggier? So desperate were we for something edible that a group of the boys borrowed bikes from the facility one morning and went out like a patrol. When they returned with news of having found a basic pizza parlour a few miles away, there were wild celebrations. It created a new dynamic to each morning: who could secure their transport first? 'Fuck it. We're getting up early and we're getting these bastards bikes because I'm going today …'

Twelve days of this. Six gruelling sessions a day, starting as we got further in at 7.30 a.m., finishing at gone 9 p.m. Poor Wi-Fi, no films, no English TV. Not even S4C. Just pure grit and the lads around each other getting you through it.

On the 13th day we were called into a meeting. Gats stood at the front, gave it minimal small talk, and then launched into it.

'If I call your name, you can leave your bag here because you're coming back in a couple of days. Boys that I don't name, take the lot.'

Of course you wanted to hear your name. You wanted to go to the World Cup. You didn't want all this to have been for nothing. There was also a small part of you asking yourself a different question. 'Do I want to be picked to come back here? I don't know.'

They told us, the ones who were coming back, to do as little as possible in the few short days we had at home. Relax, eat, sleep. I wasn't sure I had any choice. My body was in absolute bits. Four days of recuperation was barely going to touch the sides. I ate as much as I could and slept as long as I could, and I was still back at the airport in what felt like a flash, going back to it all again.

The emphasis in camp two switched from getting bigger to getting fitter. The key word was repeatability. We had the physicality and the power now. The challenge was whether we could deploy it again and again, where other teams could not.

Maybe a tiny amount of the fatigue had gone in those four days bingeing on the couch in North Dock, but not much. At the morning session two days in, I was absolutely nowhere. It was almost less the physical side of it and more the mental. It was the first time I understood what some of the older players had been saying: 'Your body will follow your head.' We were running moves, and I couldn't catch a thing.

Rob Howley came over, as happy as you'd expect when his winger is dropping simple passes.

'Are you alright or not?'

'Do you know what? I don't think I am, no.'

'You what?'

'No, no, I'll be alright now. Give me a second.'

Through all the age grade stuff, the school rugby and even the regional challenges, you can find a way if you're good. This was no longer in that semi-comfort zone. I realised in that moment, with the ball at my feet and Rob Howley in my face, that you needed a different kind of edge here. Everyone could do it once. To get to the top you needed the mental strength to be able to get up, go again, get up, go again, get up and go again.

It would be one of the most useful lessons I ever learned. To be able to say to myself: 'Do you know what? I can't feel my arms. I can't feel my legs. Don't really know what's going on. But I've just got to keep moving.'

The senior players knew it. So too did the coaches. There would come a night, later in my rugby journey, when I would go downstairs at our team hotel sometime after 9 p.m., desperate for snacks, desperate for something to keep the weight on. There was no-one else around, at least until Shaun Edwards turned up. I was still petrified of him. What was he going to say? What was he going to do? There appeared to be no grey areas with him. I assumed he wanted nothing to do with a kid looking for contraband. I thought he would sit somewhere else so he didn't have to talk to me while we ate our respective snacks.

Instead he came over and sat down right next to me.

'How are you finding it, George? How's the body?'

We had a genuine conversation. It wasn't scary. And then, out of nowhere, after a period of complete silence, he turned to me and said, 'George, are you religious?'

Now Shaun is religious. Brought up Catholic, stayed Catholic. Goes to church every single Sunday. So in that split second, my internal monologue was complicated. 'Well, no, I'm not, but he obviously wants to talk about something religious, so do I then have to say yes to make sure he's happy? And if I say yes, I've got to have enough nous about me to then back it up.'

I panicked. This was not a conversation I could hold up. Honesty had to be the call.

'I'm not really, no, Shaun.'

He looked at me deadpan.

'Huh.'

And then he stood up, grabbed his plate and walked off without another word.

I had no idea what had just happened. If I had messed up or done the right thing. But that was the whole deal with Shaun. You never knew with Shaun. He scared the life out of me, most of the time, but he was also like Christmas happening every day, because his standards were so high. I didn't need to be kept honest. I loved the hard work. But he always kept you on your toes, precisely because you were never entirely sure what he was going to say or do next.

In a normal world, having a coach shouting at you all the time would be a bad thing. In Shaun's world it was a compliment.

I spent 10 years underneath him getting shouted at. And I kept having to remind myself, like a man with a very specific rugby form of PTSD: 'He's shouting, he thinks I'm okay. He's shouting, he thinks I'm okay. He's shouting at me, he thinks I'm okay ...'

Whenever you took a knock, all you could hear was his voice in your head.

'Boys, you're never injured in defence. Get up. Just get up. Even a broken leg, you can stand up.'

Even to this day, I still hear his voice. When we played Ireland in the Grand Slam decider at the Principality in March 2019, I broke two bones in my hand in the first ten minutes. I played on for a bit, made another tackle and completely messed it up. I could hear crunching with every movement. And all I could think was: 'Just get up, G. Just get up. If I don't get up, he's going to destroy me here ...'

We made it through to the last day of the camp. It was high fives all round as we went into the gym for our final session. The 'Big Bad Wolf' song was blasting out, howling coming from every station in the room. It was only when we were walking back to our rooms, ready to lie down and then pack

– or pack and then lie down, if you were one of the sensible ones – that the rumours started flying around.

'There's going to be another session …'

'There can't be. We're on the bus to the airport at 8.30 a.m.'

'They're going to get us up in the morning and do another session before we leave.'

'No, they can't …'

I couldn't see it happening. We were just paranoid after everything that had come before. But you know what they say in these situations: just because you're paranoid doesn't mean the bastards aren't out to get you. I was showered, in my PJs and in bed with a cup of cocoa when the message pinged on my phone.

'Be up and ready to go on the field at 5.30.'

I couldn't process it. It had to be horseshit. Whose number was this, anyway? And the messages started flying around between the boys. This is real. This is happening.

The next morning, all the lads were there on time. I thought we were going to get the mother and father of all hammerings. But it wasn't a particularly difficult session – it was really tough, don't get me wrong, but it wasn't as hard as what we'd been through. There was a confidence inside us now that we were only just starting to recognise. About 15 minutes in, I felt okay. My legs hadn't woken up yet, but I knew they would. 'Do you know what? I'm alright here. Keep going. Stay with it.'

We finished the session somewhere between half past six and quarter to seven. The sun was just coming up. It was a beautiful morning. We sat there on the dewy grass, and we were all laughing. No-one complaining, no-one talking about soreness or exhaustion. Just pulling our boots off, taking the GPS vests off over our heads, ready to get showered and pick up our bags.

That was the moment our head conditioning coach Adam Beard walked over pulling two trolleys. The first was full of Magnum ice-creams. The second was a load of ice-cold full-fat Cokes.

It was the weirdest picture. All the lads, absolutely shattered and minging, looking horrible, dripping with sweat, in various states of undress. All the coaches, mentally shattered, because it had been full-gas for them, too. Every one of us sitting there with a Magnum ice-cream in one hand and a bottle of Coke in the other, faces lit by the first rays of the sun.

Our team manager Alan Phillips was the one who broke the spell.

'Alright, boys. Stop fucking around. Get showered. On the bus!'

One of the happiest moments I would ever have as a Welsh player. The worst was done. I had survived. And I was the fittest I'd ever been in my life. It felt like I had been given a superpower.

There was something else that came out of Spala. It was a dry camp. No beers, no nothing. On the first day of the first visit, Gats had given us a speech. It was a long one, by his standards: 'This is a big year for us. We've got a great opportunity.'

Adam Beard took it on. We should all sacrifice something for each other. So we all put a tenner in a pot. The moment you had even a sip of a drink, you were out. The last man standing took the pot.

It was easy for me; I was 19, aiming for my first World Cup. I thought I had to get everything right to make it, so Cokes would do for me. For the older boys, the ones in the engine room up front, it was a different matter. Men had fallen before we played Argentina in our final warm-up game. There was a good £600 up for grabs.

We were good that afternoon in Cardiff. It was the game where the Spala dividend first began to pay off, more so than our first two warm-up games against England. In the first half I got in a line-break down the left wing, saw three defenders in front of me, stepped inside and then went out again. Two of them fell over, including the legendary Felipe Contepomi. I gassed the other one, then passed to Alun Wyn Jones on the inside to score.

My legs felt great. My lungs felt great. My second wind came so easily it may well have been a continuation of my first wind.

Gats could see it. We all could. At half-time there was barely contained excitement in all our eyes. 'Ramp it up. Let's ramp it up now and see what we've got. Intensity. Speed. Let's take a breath and just go, see what all the work was for. Let's test it now.'

We were good. We were quick and powerful and decisive. Deep in the second half we were going through the phases on the wide right-hand side, about 10 to 15 metres out. We went short a few times. Then we got a quick ball, and it went 9 to 10, 10 to Foxy and then Foxy bounced and I crashed through on an inside ball off him. Blowing my cheeks out as I jogged back and Hooky got ready for the conversion. 'I feel good. We look good. I like how this feels …'

It was a good place to be after the game, Cardiff. We went out to celebrate in sensible fashion. While we may have been in Tiger Tiger, and I was keen to enjoy myself, that kitty was mine. I wasn't a nightclub sort of person, and I wasn't going to let it slip. I didn't even fancy a beer. And when you're in Tiger Tiger and you've scored one try and set up another and you still don't fancy a beer, then truly your resolve is strong.

The boys were trying to peer-pressure me, of course. I raised my Coke towards them and felt serene. That was when we noticed the Argentina boys were in the same venue too. And Felipe Contepomi was coming towards me with two pints of lager. Actual legendary Felipe Contepomi.

He had a smile on his face.

'Hey. Don't ever do that to me ever again. Show some respect.'

'Ah, I'm sorry.'

He laughed. Then he gave me one of the pints, and of course I had to drink it, because it was Felipe Contepomi and while I really wanted to win that kitty, and I was so close to it I could almost feel it nestling in my pocket, I was not a total idiot, and a pint with him in this moment, after what had happened on the pitch, was worth more than any kitty could give me.

They announced the final World Cup squad a couple of days after that. I was still worried I wouldn't make it. It was always the same with selection: I was always scared. I don't think that ever went from me, especially with Wales and the three feathers on my chest. Somewhere buried deep inside me was the feeling I shouldn't really be there. It was like when Yves Lampaert won the first stage of the Tour de France in 2022 to go into the yellow jersey, as an established and experienced rider, and said afterwards, in astonishment: 'I'm just a farmer's son from Belgium.' I was just a kid from Anglesey. People from North Wales didn't go to World Cups at 19 years old. Generally they didn't go at any age.

Maybe that was part of what drove me on. So when I was picked, and the most enormous stash of kit turned up at the team hotel so there could be no avoiding the fact that this was actually real and happening, I thought it was the best day ever.

'Here we go now, George. Here we go ...'

SIX

DOLGELLAU TO LLANBRYNMAIR: GOING PLACES

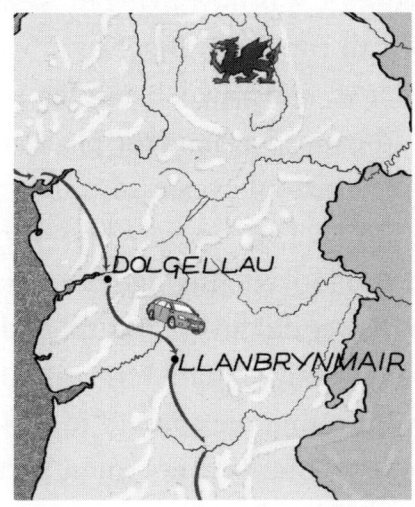

IN WHICH WE TALK ABOUT:

*World Cup fever/heavyweight Springboks/Warbs speaks out/
everything clicks/Lyds' head in the spokes/jet-boating,
go-karting, food eating/the opposite of an invisibility cloak/
a heartbreaking red card/14 men, 26 phases/a bastard I can't
switch off/drinking the elixir of youth/Sam on the toilet with his
iPad/sport is a beautiful thing/'George! Why are you crying?'*

Here's how wet behind the ears I was, heading to that World Cup in New Zealand. It was the first time in my life I'd ever flown long-haul. It was the first time I'd ever seen business class. I almost lost my mind before we'd even left the lounge. It took me a while to realise I didn't have to eat all the food, that it would keep being replenished. I didn't have to stare at all the little cans of Coke. They weren't going anywhere.

My parents were also heading out. Barry Banks, the legend of Llandovery College, was now living in New Zealand. That was one port of call for them. But New Zealand being the sociable country it is, and Kiwis being the rugby obsessives they are, they road-tripped around the place and met so many families it was like a school exchange.

Gats always told us it was family first. Rugby came after that. He wanted you looked after and he wanted your family looked after too. Never did he live this more than during that tournament in his native land. His wife Trudi set up a network of friends around the country to look after the families as they drove round. For my mum and dad, who are proper socialites, it was the stuff of dreams. My mum will talk to anyone, generally at great length. Now she couldn't quite believe the chat she was getting back.

'George, we stayed with a lovely couple. Their son plays rugby too!'

'Yeah, Mum, we're in New Zealand. Most kids play rugby.'

We had South Africa for our first game. The hardest possible start, against a team that hadn't got any less heavyweight and lumpy since my debut against them 10 months before. The Beast, Smit and Du Plessis; Danie Rossouw and

Matfield; Brussow, Burger, Pierre Spies. Du Preez and Morne Steyn, Fourie and De Villiers, Pietersen and Habana on the wings. You can see why people wrote us off before we even started.

We were 10–6 down at half-time but right in it. When Taulupe Faletau scored on 54 minutes we were 16–10 up and really fancying it. At this level you don't really have many opportunities to stand still and process what it all might mean. You're right in the moment. 'What's the time on the clock? What's the scoreboard saying? What's momentum saying? Where do I need to be?' It's only later the context comes back – 'Whoa, I'm 19 years old, at my first World Cup, and I'm playing against probably one of the best South African sides ever, and we are right in the mixer …'

We lost by a point. François Hougaard went over and Morne Steyn banged over the conversion. We had a penalty from out wide that James Hook was convinced he made and referee Wayne Barnes was convinced he did not. Maybe it all came down to conviction. In the heat of it, maybe we didn't think that we should have been there, in that position, at that time. But afterwards it sort of switched around. We had come up a point short against the reigning world champions. We hadn't won, but we could compete.

And we had Spala in our bodies and in our minds. When we spoke to each other before our second game against Samoa, that was the theme. 'We've worked too hard to crumble now and not make it through.'

It was a terrible first half. We were 10–6 down after Anthony Perenise's try and Paul Williams' conversion and penalty. Samoa were typically physical, aggressive, and well supported in a Pacific islander's home from home.

But so were we. Hamilton was Gats' hometown; he still had a house there. We were the city's second team. And Gats could be hard to know fully, in many respects, but he was never one for a panic. At half-time it was his usual concise clarity: 'Go back to the system. We've got our plan. You've got to build a game against this team. You've got to force them to go repeat sets, and then they'll break. Back all the hard work we've done.'

It went quiet for a few moments. Then Sam Warburton spoke up. He was only 22 at this point, but he already had what we all required from a skipper. He lived what we wanted to be – the commitment, the extra sacrifices. That was enough for any of us.

'We've all worked far too hard to be out in the second round of games. And I don't know about you but I'm not fucked, I'm not blowing. So let's ramp this the fuck up. Let's trust in ourselves. We've done the graft. Now we deliver.'

We didn't destroy them. It was never that sort of match. It was work-hard play-hard up the field, force them to go repeat sets. Basics rugby done well enough. Penalties won for Rhys Priestland to kick, space created for Shane Williams to score late on. That's what World Cup group games are like: you just win them the way you can. Same against Namibia, in our third game: play the way you want to play, don't get dragged into their style, keep the standards high.

So far, so … steady. It was Fiji when everything clicked and everything flowed. We didn't have a great recent history with

Fiji. Not just the draw the previous autumn where I injured my shoulder, but the defeat that had dumped Wales out of the previous World Cup in France, although my fingerprints were nowhere near that one. But we put 66 points on them, and I felt I could run all day. The Spala superpowers had been unleashed. There was a point in the second half where I went looking for a carry, didn't get one, worked to get another one, didn't get it, and could keep going. I pretty much sprinted two widths. Priestland went to the line, pumped, then I came on his shoulder. Line-break, sprint, off-load to Jamie Roberts. I remember just walking back, and I was blowing, but I wasn't goosed. And then I sprinted again, off-loaded, and we scored. It was impossible to ignore how good you felt. We were onto something. As Ronan O'Gara would later say in a different context, *l'opportunité est fucking énorme*. It was happening.

Which took us to Ireland and a quarter-final in Wellington, since Ireland had beaten Australia in their group game, and so they topped theirs as we came second in ours. I'd missed the Ireland game in the Six Nations, not that it made much difference. Even the casual rugby fan knew most of the players in their team. It was the bulk of the group that had won the Grand Slam in Cardiff in 2009: Rob Kearney at full-back, Tommy Bowe and Keith Earls on the wing. O'Driscoll and D'Arcy at centre, Conor Murray and O'Gara at half-back. Front row of Cian Healy, Rory Best, Mike Ross; Donncha O'Callaghan and Paul O'Connell behind them, and then your back row of Ferris, O'Brien and Heaslip. A strong Irish side, to be fair.

They were the favourites, at least outside our camp. But this was knockout rugby, now. It didn't matter how many points you scored, as long as it was one more than them.

You know Ireland are always going to be well-drilled and skilful, when you play them. It takes a lot to break them down. But the strange thing about watching Shane Williams score our first try, pretty early on, was that it wasn't a particularly complex move. It was just classic early Gatland rugby: physicality, speed, round the corner. Asking constant questions of the defence, working a two on one, Halfpenny fixing Earls and then Shane just flopping over.

We were so physical. Everywhere. Jamie Roberts was carrying, carrying, carrying, punching holes, sucking in defenders. Dan Lydiate was head in the spokes all day long. Luke Charteris made 16 tackles in the first half alone.

Even their try through Keith Earls owed a little to luck. A couple of bouncing passes, which is always hard to defend against. Earls sliding over from about 5 metres out, O'Gara with the conversion from out wide for 10–10.

It never bothered us. Philsy went over in the corner, down the short side, classic Philsy power and strength. It felt like everything was coming together, everywhere you looked. We didn't need spectacular plays. Our fitness, our understanding, our knowledge of each other – it was all just ticking along beautifully. The most perfect example of periodisation, like we were Olympic athletes, like we were part of the British Cycling track revolution.

And then Jonathan Davies scored, and you knew. An unreal try from Foxy off a dead move, dancing feet, palming defenders off. Spotting a prop and a second row inside him, Earls looking outside to the threat of Shane Williams, then a burst of acceleration to send him through and away.

In the first half you could hear the crowd, and there were Welsh voices, but there were many more Irish. It felt like they'd won the stadium. But when Foxy scored, it didn't feel like we were ever going to lose that match unless we made a load of basic mistakes and then backed them up with another bunch. We were in control of everything, a lot of it coming through Rhys Priestland. Not everyone's first-choice pick at 10 for us, but he came so good in that game and that tournament.

The boys all looked so fit. I know everyone looks fit in a World Cup. But even a front row like Gethin Jenkins looked in shape, and there was no room for error or imagination under our tight Under Armour shirts. We had a focus I hadn't experienced before. I hate this cliché, but it was coming to pass at this tournament: we were just focusing on one game at a time, never looking further, and it was working.

We had an instinctive respect for each other. We understood each other's work, how each player did things, why they did those things. The longer we had stayed in New Zealand the more that had grown, and the more it showed. It wasn't an arrogance, and it wasn't an over-confidence. It was trust in those around you and in the work we'd done.

And we had fun together, too. That World Cup was one of the very last of the old-school tours, that and the 2013 Lions. Professional to the gills, but room to let your hair down too. On our one day a week off, boys were spending the whole day together, jet-boating, quadbiking, go-karting, food eating. Each Monday, the squad entertainment committee would post the local lowdown: 'There's a cinema close by; these are the films, these are the times. There's go-karting available. There's golf. Put your names down by Tuesday and then pay your money and we'll sort it.'

We saw the country and we met its fabulous people. Some say New Zealand is like a supersized Wales. That's not entirely true; Wales had Wi-Fi in 2011. But the spirit of competition and rivalry, and the hospitality was always there, and we all embraced it, and it brought us together as a unit even more.

I probably didn't fully realise what it all meant, before the semi-final in Auckland against France. I didn't appreciate how well we were doing or how special the moment would seem, years later. Why? I was surrounded by players I had watched for years, and I wanted to be part of that. That was me in the week of the semi-final, and in the hours before. Looking at someone like Gethin Jenkins, who could be happily grumpy but was a constant through the success of that period, a legend of Welsh rugby. Stephen Jones, one of the best players I'd ever line up alongside. Shane Williams. It almost gave me the opposite of an invisibility cloak; it gave me the confidence to stand up and be seen and do all the things I wanted to do. Around me, all the other younger ones who were coming through and would one day be seen in the same light as those greats: Halfers, Sam, Lyds, Foxy, Taulupe, Scott.

We all know what happened in that game. It was the sort of foreign night or early morning at home that none of us ever forget. The weird thing is that I never ever thought we were going to lose it. Never felt it. Not when Morgan Parra was kicking the penalties that established their lead, not when we missed a few of our own, not when Sam was red-carded for his tackle on Vincent Clerc.

Sam is one of my best mates. There was no doubt what he brought to us. There was no hiding from the challenges that would come from being a man down for an hour in a World Cup semi-final against a French team who had been Grand Slam champions the season before. But we were still calm. We still felt in control. As soon as he went off the messages came on: 'We'll go one into contact. Don't compromise the backfield. Bring the line speed. Just go mano a mano now and empty it out.'

It didn't surprise me when Philsy scored. It didn't worry me when Stephen Jones' conversion hit the post rather than give us the lead. I never asked myself, 'Is it going to happen?' The question was a more straightforward one: 'When is it going to happen?'

France were a big team and they had experience but they were blowing, pretty much. In that game and that moment, it just didn't feel like they had anything. We had 14 men and we were nowhere near as fucked as they were. We had a unity of purpose and a shared vision of what we were going to do. 'Let's just keep the pressure on and it'll come.'

When Leigh had his penalty from the halfway line with six minutes to go, I would have happily put my house on him making it. Even with all that rain, and the soaking pitch, and the troubles all the place kickers had been having, I believed in him. 'Leigh gets this, then we've got five minutes to then get out of our half and then keep the pressure on.' That's what the training camps had given us: the sort of trust that only comes through adversity and hard work. A trust in ourselves that we would deliver. Because there are not many people, at that point in that sort of game, who would say: 'Yeah, I'll take it.'

It fell short by maybe six inches. Those are the margins you work with, in elite sport. Even after that, the same weird feeling: there's still time, there's still time.

At the end, we went through 26 phases. That's 26 phases, 60 minutes after being reduced to 14 men.

I ended up having a beer with Warren Gatland in my final Six Nations campaign with Wales, 13 years after that match ended in Auckland. He was asking me about the current group. 'What do you honestly think? Who do I need to push? Who do I need to look after?'

It was maybe the first time he spoke to me properly like a human, rather than a player. So I opened up to him. I said: 'There's something in me that I can't ever switch off.'

He asked me what I meant.

'It's not a good thing. It's not a bad thing. But there's something in me and there's something in the crew I came through with that we won't ever be able to switch off.'

He asked me the same question. 'What do you mean?'

So I told him. 'Well, the only way I can describe it is there's a bastard in me that I cannot switch off. There's a robustness, a mindset, a drive in us that you've given us. We relied on it heavily when we won games that we shouldn't have.

Even when kicking back at the local indoor soft play facility, it's important to represent.

I pretty much spent my entire childhood outside. Here I am with my brother Josh, ready to ford a mighty river. Or at least mess about on the banks for a bit.

Traditional Welsh costume from the 19th century, traditional Welsh fireplace from the late 20th.

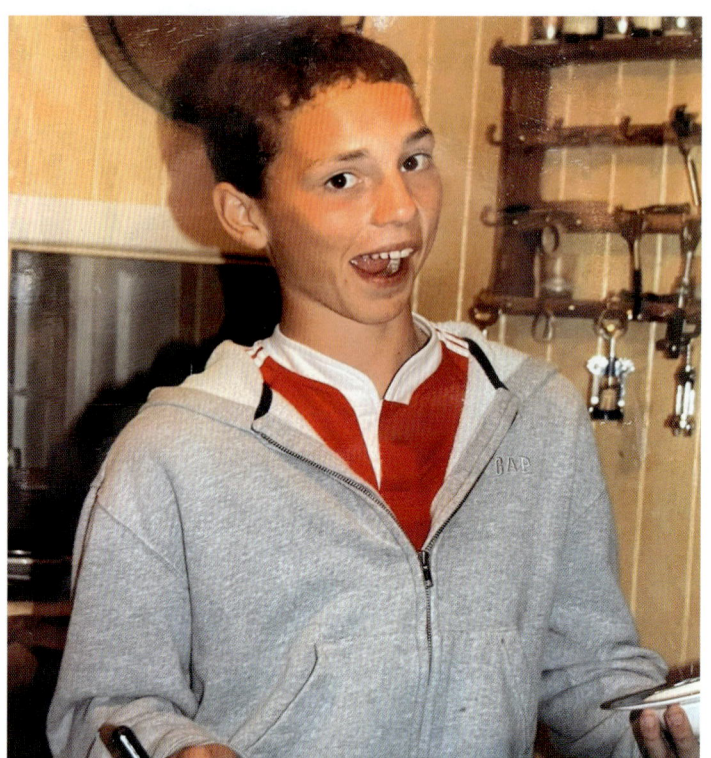

My mouth is open here because I'm smiling, but also because I'm about to eat something. Which may actually also be why I'm smiling.

You can't move for great beaches when you're brought up on Anglesey.
Of course my family and I were always on them.

I feel so lucky to have come from such a big family. Free mates, free fun. Here we see my Auntie Bessie, my mum, Josh, Beth, Georgie and Emmy.

Second from the left, back row, lining up for the Llandovery College 1st XV for the massive Brecon match.

ABOVE: I couldn't quite believe that I'd got picked to make my Wales debut at 18, against the reigning world champions. Then I scored two tries . . .

LEFT: A Grand Slam night in Cardiff is not a quiet one. And nor should it be.

BELOW: What's the only thing that feels as good as a Grand Slam? Beating England in Cardiff by a record score to deny them a Slam and win yourself the Six Nations championship.

Scoring for the Lions in the opening Test of the series against the Wallabies in 2013. I'm excited. Of course I am.

I didn't plan to carry Izzy Folau on my back. But it happened, and it's not the worst thing to look back on.

ABOVE: I loved my time at Northampton. Winning the Premiership with Saints in 2014 did incredible things for that town.

BELOW: Yes, that's my own father, invading the pitch at the Stade de France after I scored a late try against France in 2015. I'm still embarrassed by it.

Hard times with the best of friends. Walking off the pitch at Twickenham with Sam Warburton after our late World Cup quarter-final defeat to South Africa.

I was lucky to have Warren Gatland as my coach with Wales for most of my career. He didn't say much to you, but when he did, you listened.

My last game for Wales, against Italy in March 2024. It didn't end the way I had hoped. But what a journey, what a journey . . .

BELOW: Family time is good time. And, I reckon, the more the merrier. (It's expanded further since this picture was taken.)

Because the mindset was: we're always going to win it because there's time.'

Until you've been to those camps, until you've been put to the sword every day for weeks on end, every day being pushed beyond your limits – maybe that doesn't make sense. But you can see it in others when you've got it. A certain level of athlete, and you can look at the way they are and know they're happy to go to a point where very few do.

It shaped my answer to Gats' initial questions.

'Look, you've got to put these new lads in a place where they're uncomfortable and leave them there for a long time. Then you'll see very quickly who will step up and consistently deliver for you and who's going to shy away. The ones that shy away, don't bother because they're not worth your time. If they don't get up and do it again, then again, there's no point. The ones that stand up, run them into the ground again and see what they do.'

I'm aware how horrendous this must sound if this is not your life. But it's a skillset, and it's one Gats had given us at that World Cup. And it's there inside me still. They could see it when I arrived at Provence in the autumn of 2024, and I'm not sure they liked it, entirely, because they sort of got it but not to the level that it needs to be done. I could hear myself talking to Gats all over again: 'You never gave us a day off. You were always full-gas all the time. And then we earned the right to be in that position.'

That's what I said to him, and it's why we never thought we were going to lose against France, even after Pens' kick didn't make it. It wasn't just in me, it was in all of us. 'Well, we'll just keep battling until the end. It is what it is. Let's go one man in the contact. We don't have to compromise the backfield because we've got the same personnel. So we just go one-man hit and fire and then we compete when it's on.'

What I didn't know then, because I was still drinking the elixir of youth, was how seismic it would forever be. I thought I'd always have another go. Then 15 years pass and you don't get another opportunity like that, and you think: fuck, that was the one that got away.

Some players went out and got drunk afterwards. Some players went out and dodged the Auckland traffic to buy copious amounts of Dairy Milk, which isn't the same in New Zealand as back home so there's that to cope with on top of everything else, and then they went to their mate's room to eat it all and then sat on the toilet with an iPad looking at all the abusive tweets that had come in while their mate tried to persuade them not to reply, and as he did so took a picture of his broken mate on the toilet with his iPad and chocolate all over his face.

It's still my favourite photo of Sam, and it still takes me back to that moment whenever I look at it on my phone. 'Just sleep on it and then maybe reply tomorrow.' That's how I'll caption it, when it eventually goes up in the National Museum in Cardiff. I'll text Sam to wind him up again about costing us our World Cup bonuses.

But even talking about it brings back those heavyweight pangs. The one that got away.

You could throw in a load of what ifs. What happens if Alain Rolland hasn't sent off Sam? Or if Sam has tackled someone who isn't Vincent Clerc and half his size so hasn't flipped him? What if Jonesy's conversion hasn't hit the post, or Pens' long-ranger has less rain to pass through on its way to the posts?

Now don't get me wrong. This one sits with me even today. Some of the boys held onto it for weeks and weeks, for months on end. Always the same tormentors of questions: what if this, what if that. It hurt me for weeks. But I processed it because I had to. The way I had navigated my journey to that point was to keep learning, keep adapting, keep getting better from every situation. How do you do that when you've just lost a World Cup semi-final 9–8? I like to remember France being absolutely goosed. We had played three-quarters of the game with one man fewer, and we looked like we were going forever. We weren't ever going to stop. That's how I comforted myself, in the days and weeks afterwards: the image I saw, when I looked around with a minute to go, and all their players were hands on knees. If we'd had a couple more minutes, they were nowhere. We'd have absolutely steamrolled them.

But it still grinds my gears. The one-game-at-a-time strategy doesn't work after you lose a semi-final and the next match is the third-place play-off when it could have been the final. I think we would have given the All Blacks an even better game than France did, and definitely made it a more attractive spectacle. They weren't there for the taking, but they certainly wobbled. When you have to call upon your fourth-choice fly-half and he's so late onto the scene that his jersey doesn't even fit, you've deviated significantly from Plan

A. That's the only 'what if' I can entertain: what if we had played in the final, when France had used up all their emotional energy on us, and New Zealand were hanging on?

You could look at the score in three of the matches we've talked about here, and wonder who could ever have predicted them. We lost by a point to the Springboks in the group. We lost to France by a point in the semis, and they then lost by a point to the All Blacks in the final. Well, sport is a beautiful thing. It's amazing. It creates the most intense emotions, it brings people together. It creates rivalries and friendships and nights you'll never forget. But the short and curlies of it, when you're on the inside, is that no-one remembers the score. They just remember the W or the L. And if you take the hype and all that magic and the beauty away from it, it's just a field with 15 men on each side going hammer and tongs for a W or an L, really.

It's admittedly a miserable way to think about it. It's also at odds with how I feel about this sport. Rugby means so much to me. But it is all about results. And my miserable summary of it is a reflection of how brutal elite sport can be. You do all these hours, you do all this work – the public and the unseen work. You push yourself to a point where you're almost breaking everything in your body, and then it comes down to two letters.

People say of sportspeople that we're in the entertainment business. We're not, not really. It's not like going to see Coldplay or Paul McCartney and being happy they played some of your favourite songs. It's not the cinema to see a film that's won loads of awards. With sport, the content is beside the point. It's just the result. I went to four World Cups, and I never got close. That's the harsh reality of the way we lived.

Sometimes with these feelings we're told to sit with them, not to fight them; we're told to just accept it, and not pretend it's any other way. That's what I did, after Auckland. When Sam had finished his Dairy Milk and wiped his backside and closed Twitter on his iPad, when my parents had flown home from their extended school exchange trip, when a cold northern hemisphere Christmas came around. I didn't ignore it. I acknowledged it, I used it. I refocused and I got ready to go again. Now there may be a point in 25 or 30 years when I've had a little bit too much to drink and I just start crying and mumbling stuff in the corner of a room. That will be natural too. The sadness will come from realising the enormity of what we could have done.

The emotions today aren't as raw, but the feeling is the same. Maybe that's a better way of trying to explain it. I put it all in a box somewhere inside me. When I re-open the box, the emotions aren't as raw as they were. At least until that point in 25 years' time when I've had too much to drink.

'George! Why are you crying?'

'2011.'

'What about 2011?'

'The box has opened!'

'Oh no …'

'It's the one that got away! It suddenly hit me!'

SEVEN

LLANBRYNMAIR TO LLANIDLOES: WINNING TROPHIES

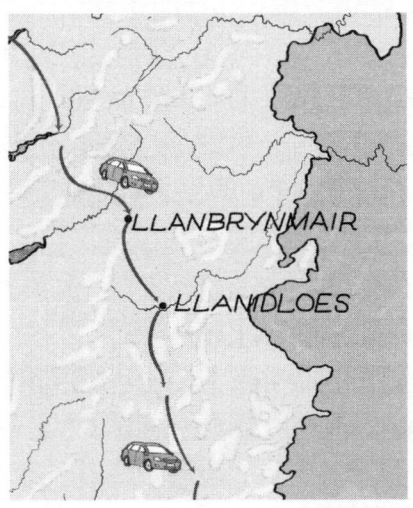

IN WHICH WE TALK ABOUT:

a pitch under snow/passing drills in eight layers/a Polish overload/Straight Tune/'The power of North!'/Leigh comes good, again/trust in delivering/a carefully planned rip/Scott's big day/not dead until it hits the floor/days that define you/Cuthy and the Chopper/Cardiff gets messy/start at the Hilton, end at Tiger Tiger/meeting a talented young cyclist called Becky

The good news, before the start of the 2012 Six Nations, was that we weren't going back to Spala for a pre-tournament training camp.

We were going to Gdansk instead. And the bad news? It was going to be worse.

We had optimism in our boots that winter. The World Cup had gone, but the Six Nations felt like the way we were going to get over it. A young team getting more experienced and better at coping with what international rugby can throw at you. A young team better at coping with what Warren Gatland and Shaun Edwards could throw at us.

The place where we stayed was more modern than Spala. It wasn't in the middle of a forest where bodies were almost certainly buried. It was under a foot of snow, and the coldest place I had ever been in my life. And I had been to Rhyl in mid-December and Anglesey in August.

It was snowing hard when we arrived, and it barely let up. When we got up each morning at 6 a.m. to weigh in, we had to trudge through the snow to get to the gym. Our head of strength and conditioning, Adam Beard, would kindly stack the morning with indoor work – off-feet fitness work, weights. He was a creative man, Adam, probably the best in his field I ever worked with. He'd get us working in the big wrestling area, which had a floor soft enough to allow contact. He'd get us doing the classic yoyo test, but starting it at certain levels so you got hit with the intensity without an unnecessary volume of running. But then we would go out to the 4G outside pitch to do our units, and the snow had buried the entire pitch. They'd get a tractor out and try to snowplough a rugby pitch out of it. By the time we completed four runs from tryline to tryline, the parts cleared on the first run were already covered in snow again.

We were wearing so many layers against the cold that it was hard to move properly. In a session working on taking the high ball, I couldn't get my hands close enough together because of the sheer volume of cloth around my shoulders and arms. Passing drills with eight layers on were similarly bizarre. As brutal as it was physically, it was also a mental test. How much did you want to be there?

That pitch turned out to be one of the nicer parts. One morning we were told we were going to do runways as a finisher. You start on the tryline on your stomach, sprint to the five-metre line, then sprint back to the tryline, do down and up, sprint to the 22, down and up, then sprint as far as you can until the whistle blows. It would be 40 seconds on, 20 seconds recovery, so the further we ran in that 40 seconds, the further we'd have to get back in the so-called resting 20. A lose-lose situation.

But we weren't going to be doing them on the snow-covered pitch; we were going to the snow-covered beach. Now the beach in Gdansk may be lovely in summer. The sand may be soft and the waves inviting. In January it was quite literally Baltic. The sand was frozen. On top of the sand was three inches of frozen snow. It wasn't like running through treacle, because treacle still has elements of liquidity. Everything about that beach was designed to stop you moving. It may have been the worst surface for running ever invented.

The sea was angry. The weather was spiteful – sleet and snow, coming in sideways. Runways are horrible anyway. Now we were face down in layers of frozen, abrasive hell. It was hard to keep the existential questions at bay. What were we doing? Why were we doing it here? None of it mattered. We were, so we had to carry on.

We trained against the Polish national team – units, so scrum into attack versus defence. It was the last day of the block before a day off and we were absolutely goosed, but without disrespecting the proud history of rugby union in Poland, or underplaying the size of their forwards, we fancied our chances. Shaun Edwards was pumped, because the weather meant we hadn't had much field time. Attack coach Rob Howley was similarly hissing. Everything would have to be perfect.

First move, they sliced straight through us. You couldn't tell exactly what Shaun was saying, because of the number of layers he had on and the fact that it was snowing into his face, but you could have a good guess. We had a word among ourselves. 'Heads on, boys, this is ridiculous. Let's sort this shit out now.'

Second one they cut us again, clean. Same on the third, same on the fourth. Absolutely sliced us and diced us. We were now losing our heads. Shaun and Howlers were raging against the darkening sky. It all seemed apocalyptic. We weren't going to win the Six Nations. We certainly weren't a team who could pretend they might have won the World Cup. We were being destroyed by Poland, who had never made a World Cup and would probably need the Six Nations to be expanded to double figures to get a look in.

It turned out there had been some miscommunication. They had eight backs on the field. Literally anywhere they went they had a two-man overload. It had taken us four scrums to notice because it was so cold nothing made sense anyway.

So we went to a relatively mild Dublin for our opening Six Nations match against Ireland in improved spirits. It was the first time we had met since knocking them out of the World Cup in Wellington, five months before; two teams who had both won Grand Slams in the past four years, the two nations that had contributed the majority of the starting Test XV on the last Lions tour.

We started okay. Jonathan Davies scored in the left-hand corner after a lovely offload round the back of the tackler from Rhys Priestland. But we weren't really firing the shots we wanted. We kept allowing them to build momentum, and when Rory Best polished off a great team try, we were 10–5 down at the break.

It was a game to hang in there and wait for your moment. It just didn't feel like the moment was coming when Foxy scored again. It might even have been the worst move we ran in that campaign – off the top of a line-out on halfway, a Straight Tune, but we rushed it and our timings were poor. Jamie Roberts didn't seem to hold anyone. But I bumped one defender and had two others coming in to cover when suddenly all I could hear was Foxy's voice outside me: 'Yeah, George, George, George!'

It wasn't a technically perfect offload, but when you're in heavy contact and you're going down, anything that works is a result. You trust in the call, and then you're rolling over on the deck and Foxy is away with that magic scuttling running motion of his, legs all go-go-go, and he's finishing it off like an absolute dreamboat.

This was the era of the tip-tackle clampdown. For Sam in the World Cup semi-final against France, read Bradley Davies in this one. A yellow card rather than a red card this time, but they still had the numbers to put Tommy Bowe past me into the right-hand corner. We were 21–15 down, into the last five minutes.

I never panicked. You look up at the scoreboard and you see the time left, and you understand where you are with this game – 'We need to do something now, otherwise this is gone. We haven't got many chances left.' But I didn't think it was out of reach. That was our team, at that point in its evolution, after we had survived snowstorms and frozen beaches. If we went with tempo and speed and physicality to the end, we were alive.

So it came left. Philsy off quick ball, Jamie to Foxy, me on the left touchline eight metres out.

It gets simple now. Instinct and training.

'I've got to do everything I can in whatever I've got left. This ball, whatever happens, has to be recycled. There's no way that this can ever, ever, ever die here now. This ball has got to come back.'

Ball into hands. Hit the floor, drive that left leg and drive as hard as you can back in.

Run at someone who's got their shoulders turned in defence. Aim for the inside shoulder. Go full-fat milk into it.

It's horrible defending from there. Maybe Gordon d'Arcy's expecting Tommy Bowe to take me low and he's going to hit me high, but they sort of end up doing the same job. And they're a centre and a wing, so they know exactly what they'd be doing if they were me: take a deep breath and hit them as hard as I can. Because, in this moment, it comes down to the crux of what rugby is about: a combat sport, where momentum is everything.

Their feet are fixed. Their shoulders are square. I've come onto this ball full steam.

Then you feel contact and you're getting battered by about four or five blokes, and you can't tell if it's the Irish team or your own players. But there's enough weight moving in the right direction that stopping you is a lot harder than you keeping going.

It's all sound, when you touch the ball down. Your teammates in your ears, the crowd just beyond. I was extra lucky: I had the great Eddie Butler delivering a line of commentary up in the stands to make my heart swell.

'George North! The power of North!'

As you're running back, there's so much excitement in you that you have to make a conscious decision to get on top of it. Philsy was screaming in my ear. You tell yourself this is exactly the scenario you want. 'We've given ourselves a huge chance. There's time to win this …'

And there was, even when Leigh Halfpenny narrowly missed with his conversion. But only just. Stephen Ferris was yellow-carded for a tip tackle of his own, and Halfers stepped up 35 metres out and sent the ball straight between the posts.

In all the time we played together, I never, ever thought Leigh wasn't going to make a kick. That was the confidence in him and the confidence in where we were – the trust in the team and the people around us to deliver, the same way they're trusting you. My try and Leigh's penalty were the parts of the iceberg sticking out above the stormy seas. If you wanted to look, that trust was being fulfilled all over the pitch – Scott Williams absolutely rattling Brian O'Driscoll in a tackle, the biggest hit Drico said he ever felt; us taking high balls out of the air not just into our chests but with our hands outstretched high above our heads. We looked at each other on the pitch in the hard times and knew we got things done.

Things don't happen by accident in elite sport. From 2011 to 2015, we were one of the most dominant teams in the world because we just didn't give in. We could dog out results that maybe we never should have. There were a couple of times when it got too close for comfort and there were times when we didn't quite do it, but that resilience was always there. 'Do you know what? Stay in the fight. Stay in the fight. We're here …'

Only when you work at a high level of elite performance do you really truly get that trust within a group. You see it in the medical world: the top surgeons with their anaesthetists and nurses by their side; you see it in the military, where teams go into places where they shouldn't be to do whatever they've got to do, and they know their guys are next to them. Going into the unknown, the hard, the scary, knowing that you've got this next to you – it settles you, where others might be falling apart.

Leigh epitomised all of that. He was exactly as you might imagine him: hard-working, quiet, liked a laugh and a joke, but when it was go-time and he was working, he would be so intense and driven. He is a great friend. As an athlete, as a professional, you'll get no-one better than him. But it was the depth he would go into with his prep that set him apart. I would do my analysis – look at the players I was up against, the players on the bench, the ones already on the pitch who could cover the opposing position. I would study how they moved, what their traits were. I'd look at how the 9 and 10 kicked – was the scrum-half a left-footer or a right-footer, and what his preferred kicking option under pressure might be. I'd do the same for the fly-half. Can he kick off both? What does his body shape look like when he kicks a cross-field kick?

Leigh would go even further, because this was the level of information he wanted. If they go to an aerial bomb, how many steps do they take before? Because they can still pass it. He would work out which area in the backfield he should occupy to negate those favoured kicks. Defensively, he would look at how players would run at full-backs, whether they would try to square him up early or go round him or draw his cover and pass. Then he would practise all of those scenarios.

'Ah, G, there's going to be a lot of heat on me. But big guys. So can you just run at me after training?. Can we just do a couple of different scenarios too where you come back inside, and then go out again?'

You'd do that, and then the next level would come out.

'Okay, but now you pick. So don't tell me what you're going to do.'

Anything he felt he needed to be the best he could be for every game, he would do. The same with his physical preparation – his rehab, activation, how he'd have to change his training week because he wanted to kick after a captain's run, how him and Jenks would be out on the field kicking on the morning of the actual game.

Most people never saw that. For those of us who did, it wasn't just about the detail. It was him doing it every week without question. And until you feel what it's like to carry that fatigue day-to-day, week-to-week, match-to-match, and then constantly deliver on it, it's hard to understand the strength of character it takes to be able to do that.

Rugby is arguably a truer team sport than any other. Football matches can be won by one fabulous player. In cricket one batter can score a double-hundred or a bowler take eight wickets. In rugby, you share your discrete skillset with maybe one other player, and none of you can win unless the majority of your 14 team-mates are also on it. You are different-shaped cogs in the same machine. We all loved Leigh for his commitment in defence, for his bravery. We respected the insane level of work he put in with our kicking coach Neil Jenkins, and that he never did anything apart from his absolute best. And our confidence came from those things, but also the more straightforward matter of seeing him make big kicks on multiple occasions. It became instinctive, when you saw him crouching down on one knee by his kicking tee: 'Well, he's got this. Halfers, he's got this …'

There's a flipside to it too, something that doesn't get spoken about as much. On the odd occasion someone doesn't deliver, it becomes about the ability of the team to get around that individual and say, 'Mate, don't worry. You've delivered every time before that.' That something, to me, is as special as the trust in delivering.

Halfers was at it again the following week, when we beat Scotland 27–13 in Cardiff. Two tries, three conversions, two penalties. Just the 22 points for him.

In the fallow week that followed, with Wales two wins from two and England two wins from two and the two teams meeting at Twickenham in the next round, all sorts of pressure was coming on us. The coaches ran us ragged, the spirit of Gdansk brought 1,000 miles east to the Vale of Glamorgan. Everyone in Wales wants to talk rugby with you all the time. When you've got England next and there's expectation in the air, something that never needs building up gets built up even more. A walk out for a coffee brings heat from the barista with your flat white – 'Oh my God, England next week. How you feeling?' In the supermarket, people make comments on your basket in the five items or less queue. 'Oh, do you need those? You've got to be focused for the England game.' And you're thinking, it's only a packet of Haribo, I had Shaun Edwards all over me for three hours this morning, what the hell is going on here?

I had never played at Twickenham before. Just the trip there as a kid, to learn how to whistle and to stare dreamy-eyed at Jonny Wilkinson. I got told plenty of times in those two weeks what it would be like and what they had done to us. The spirit of Phil Bennett in the 1970s channelled for a different era.

I respected all the antipathy, but it didn't connect with me. I hadn't been around when the English took our jobs, our water and our steel. People came on holiday to Anglesey for two weeks a year, and I'd become mates with them. There were quite a lot of English people I liked, including my dad.

I didn't need anything extra. I would be playing for my country against their biggest rivals, with players around me who I was growing to love. It was going to be a great day. A simple narrative that did everything I wanted.

I was still only 20 years old. Still in my rugby education. The first time I saw the Range Rovers with their tailgates down in the car-park, the jam sandwiches and cocktail sausages. I'm pretty sure that's what they were eating. The supporters watching your coach drive in and making the sort of gestures that suggest you enjoy solitary pleasures, as if they themselves had never considered such a thing.

All of it on fast forward. The hostility when you arrived, the noise as you came out of the tunnel. The referee's whistle, and then straight into it.

Looking back, it's little moments for me. Thinking I was clean away for a try in the second minute, and then David Strettle tap-tackling me, which is always the worst way to go down because you don't see it coming. One moment you're racing and you're clear, the next you're trying to run on your knees and the rest of the game has suddenly swept past you like a wave past a beached fish. Sam Warburton chopping

Manu Tuilagi about a metre from the line, one of the most technically perfect tackles you'll ever see; Owen Farrell chipping over our defence and running straight for me, and me timing the hit low and hard so he stopped and went backwards in the same second.

But this game was all about one moment, when Scott Williams did the Scott Williams thing. Except, since everyone remembers his steal and try so vividly, it illustrates how the story in sport is written by the winners. No-one seems to remember it was Scott who prevented a certain try by tackling Mouritz Botha when Rhys Priestland had been charged down in front of our own posts. No-one ever talks about the overlap Scott ignored when he had Foxy and Halfers outside him with 13 minutes to go, and chose to go alone instead. Then again, why should they, when he scores the try he does to win it? And in that was another truth about elite sport: things don't happen by accident.

It started with Shaun Edwards, as things usually did. As the seasons piled up, so did Shaun's aphorisms. You're never injured in defence – we had that off-pat by now. A more recent one came when he first clocked Justin Tipuric in training, having clearly not seen much of him in regional rugby, and began to understand how quick he was. That gave birth to, 'Keep up with Tips!' A drill where we went berserk line speed, and the game was just keep up with Tips. When, years down the road, Tips wasn't playing and Foxy's little brother James Davies came in, the line would get a upgrade. 'Keep up with Cubby!'

Then there was the Carousel of Defence. A series of inter-connecting drills where you started at the first station, completed that drill, and then kept moving through the subsequent ones until you were spat out on the other side. Each sequence worked a different element of your defensive skills. The first might be a two-man hit, where one guy would carry the ball, he would run into you, then your partner would get on the ball and you would hold them up. The next one might be a retreating ruck: your mate would hit a tackle shield going backwards and then it would be the contact fire around that retreating ruck. Next: about speed into position, two bags set up, a jackal and then the support to the jackler.

In there was the Rip. One man coming at you with the ball. You sprint to him, get hands on the ball, and rip – one up, one down, one extra. Up meant a different arm placement to down. Both took strength and an explosive force.

Shaun had us doing it from the start of that Six Nations campaign. We'd practised it in Gdansk. We'd worked on it at the Vale, sometimes before the team session, sometimes before the backs' units. There's a phrase you hear a lot in elite sport: 'Doing your extras.' It's usually taken to mean things like stretching or good nutrition. The stuff outside the main training sessions that everyone does.

With Shaun it was about specific extras. He would be on you from the start of the day. 'Ah, George, today you're going to do your defensive extras.' So we would do retreating ruck, we would do second-man approach and first-man approach, we'd do it coming through the gates, working. But it was always specific to your role, and it was every day. There was no point me just hitting big blokes because I wouldn't do it in a game. His thing with our defence was, they don't come through us, they have to go round us. He would get players with a crazy head-start to run away from me, so I had to turn and chase them down. That way, in the worse-case scenario of an opposition centre making a break, I would be on my winger or in the passing-lane, making it as difficult as possible for them to turn a line break into a try.

So was it a surprise that Scotty ripped that ball off Courtney Lawes, who was a great ball-carrier, and then turned on halfway and accelerated and kicked the ball ahead and gathered it to dive across the line and win us the game, with five minutes to go? Probably not, because we'd practised it so much he may have thought we were doing a session. Was it lucky? Absolutely not. Was it deserved? Yes.

And what a thing it was to watch. What a momentum swing, when a game is level at 12–12 and it's there for whoever can play the way they want to play, rather than the way the clock wants them to play. It was all going on the left-hand side and I was on the right-hand side, and you hear the noise more than anything – that electric charge, the excitement that lights up the pockets of supporters in red shirts and links them together. Chasing after Scott's heels, thinking, 'Oh my God, we're on here …'

Then England attacked at the death, and Shaun's words and drills saved us again. I made a bad read, this time, as England went right from under our posts, coming in and leaving Mike Brown free to find Strettle diving for the corner.

Halfers got across to go low. Foxy tried turning him as he crossed the line so he couldn't get the ball down. I slid in as his right hand came out, and tried to scoop the ball off the line.

We've talked about relying on your team-mates to do a job. I never wanted Halfers to be in that position, when it was my bad read that has helped put him there, but I'd bet my house on him making that tackle. Same with Foxy getting there half a second later. They both covered me, and then I did everything I could to make up for my error.

Which is where Shaun comes in again. Another of his favourite lines: 'The ball's not dead until it's hit the floor.' An attention to every moment, on every play to make sure that you're hissing and in the play. When you made the wrong decision, he didn't want you to switch off. He wanted you to compete until the ball had hit the floor, or gone out of play. You fought until it went dead. Occasionally you laughed at Shaun's one-liners, because some of them could sound a little nuts. They were also one of the reasons why he was one of the best coaches any of us ever worked with.

It was never a try. Trust me, I was closer than anyone else. As the referee sent the decision upstairs and the TMO kept looking from multiple angles and slowing the frames, you do wonder. A minute feels like an hour. When the ref called no try and blew his whistle, it was a straight wall of noise again. Like nothing else I'd heard before.

Now Shaun did give me a proper debrief after that one. It wasn't particularly nice; I just had to put it in my Shaun Edwards box and crack on. In those moments you're making split-second decisions, and I hadn't made the right one at that time. The speed of it overtakes you sometimes. But the quality of the players around me meant we were able to adapt and scramble and stop a misread becoming a try. That was where we were as a squad. You know the famous Gary Player line about the more he practised, the luckier he got? That was us as players. That was our coaches.

These are the days that define you, as a player. Scott and I were always close. Our mutual love of anything stupid with an engine, our shared love of motorbikes. He doesn't do much talking, when you first meet him, and I do. But he's happy floating along, speaking when he has to, and he likes a practical joke as much as me. Maybe we didn't realise that Saturday night, on the long coach ride back to Cardiff, spotting other happy travellers making their way back west along the M4 and across the Severn crossing. But we'd just played a game where those people would say, for the rest of their rugby days, that they were there, and Scott had just done something, as I would with Izzy Folau on the Lions tour a year later, that eclipsed the rest of his career in those same eyes.

He was my best man at my wedding. Also in attendance, as my team-mate at Northampton, was Courtney Lawes, and his wife Jess. The opening line of his speech went like this: 'Hi everybody, I'm Scott Williams. If you don't know me, speak to Courtney – he'll tell you who I am.'

Scott is so much more than that one afternoon in south-west London. But if you are going to be remembered for just one thing, it's not a bad one to have, is it?

* * *

We beat Italy at home a fortnight later, comfortably enough. That left us France at home in late March to win a third Grand Slam in eight years – 1970s sort of numbers.

I was too young to know any different. My first full Six Nations, the Triple Crown already secured, a World Cup semi-final just behind us: I knew we were doing something special, but at the same time it all felt quite normal. It was like that for most of our side. You had the players who had won Grand Slams before: Gethin Jenkins, Matthew Rees, Adam Jones, Alun Wyn, Mike Phillips. You had the younger crop I was part of: Dan Lydiate, Sam Warburton, Taulupe Faletau, Jonathan Davies, Leigh Halfpenny, Alex Cuthbert. This was the ride we were on. This was our momentum.

I'll never forget the energy around the country that week. The buzz as we drove into Cardiff that Saturday afternoon. But I never felt stressed. We had our mantra now, honed out in New Zealand the previous autumn, proven in the seven weeks of competition that had taken us here. One more game, one more game. Don't over-think it, don't over-do it. Focus on each play and every moment.

And it worked. It was a tight game, where France had the lead early, and we fought back to be ahead 10–3 at half-time thanks to a brilliant Cuthy finish from an Alun Wyn turnover. When France brought it back to 13–9 with seven minutes to go, I was never stressed. We had Dan Lydiate felling everything in sight, man of the match, player of the tourna-ment, spending his entire afternoon chewing grass and French laces, earning his new nickname, the Chopper. We had the partnership between him and Warbs, a dynamic in its early stages that would do so much for us for so many years. Everywhere you looked, that trust in the system and in each other.

I felt lucky. And while you should always try to stay in every play, in every moment until the final whistle goes, there was no point where I ever felt we were going to lose. When Rhys Priestland put a good kick downfield in the last 10 minutes, and Cuthy and Jamie Roberts caught their defender and threw him into touch – I knew it was done. You shouldn't do that when you still have Shaun Edwards barking the plays. It's only over when the ball is dead works both ways. But this was different. You felt you could actually enjoy the last few minutes, even if at 16–9 a converted try for France would have levelled it up – take in the crowd's singing, take in the atmosphere, savour all the toil and sacrifice that had taken us here.

Our old crop wasn't old. They had just been there a while. They were still delivering. Those of us in the young crew – pretty quickly a lot of us had accumulated 15 or 25 caps, a lot of them in big pressure games. It's only with the passing years you look back and realise how rarely the sporting stars align like that. Talent in the obvious ways, ability in some dimensions that were changing how we thought of certain positions: Gethin Jenkins, a loosehead who tackled like a blind-side, jackalled like an open-side and got around the pitch like a number eight, one of the fittest men I've ever come across; Alun Wyn, a second row who could pretty much do it all; players across the pitch who were multi-faceted enough to cover multiple positions and do it well.

Of course it was messy afterwards. Cardiff is alive early and kicks on late on every matchday. When a Grand Slam Saturday comes along, it goes off the rails. That night we had to go in black tie to the post-match function at the Hilton in the middle of town, and the numbers waiting outside to see us come in were staggering. We walked through a tunnel of cheering people, all of our happiness reflected back from them and bouncing around between us all. Being slapped on the back, lassoed for photos, programmes shoved at you for signing.

In the moment it was too much to appreciate. It almost seemed over the top. I was young and naïve, and the harder times were far away. But it solidified something I'd been feeling on the long drives from North to South Wales, through Caernarfon and Eryri, Dolgellau and Llanidloes, through Builth Wells and Brecon and Pontypridd. I wasn't just representing me, or my family. When you played for Wales, the journey was for all these people. You were doing it for the nation you saw around you.

When we lost on a Saturday, the whole country spent Sunday and Monday and Tuesday depressed and upset. When we won like this, it lifted us all for long happy months. In these magical, heady years when we were able to live it not once or twice but repeatedly, it changed the nation. Each title or landmark win would bring greater pressure and expectation next time around. But it was all worth it. Every single part of it was worth it.

I started on the beers that night. Got a little burpy, switched to the vodka lemonades and the vodka Red Bulls. At some point a drop of WKD in there, because I always needed a little bit of sugar after a game. The classic parabola of a Welsh rugby night out: start at the Hilton, end a short crossfield kick away at Tiger Tiger. Some of the boys took in Revs, but it was always going to come together in the space upstairs at Tiger Tiger. The whole place heaving, so many in red jerseys, so many shots going down and pints being offered and the dance-floor a mess of jumping bodies and wild singalongs. Gethin Jenkins was grumpy; Gethin was always grumpy. Philsy lead-ing from the front; Philsy always led from the front. Everyone pretty loose. Everyone wanted to live in that moment.

It doesn't happen anywhere else. Next time England win a Grand Slam in London, whenever that rare event might be – the players aren't all out in Soho, surrounded by all the fans who roared them on at Twickenham earlier. The French aren't out around Gare du Nord with the thousands piling down on the RER from Saint Denis. Unless you've been out in Cardiff after a Wales victory, it's very hard to explain. But we are unique. Some of that meant hacking your way through the detritus of a big night on St Mary's Street and Chip Alley. That was fine. This was Cardiff. We were Wales, every single one of us.

Life was changing, in more ways than one. The year before, I had been nominated for a SportingWales Rising Star Award. A tweet was put out, listing the nominees. One was a cyclist called Becky James.

Naturally, being a young, inquisitive man, I looked her up online. Naturally, being a young man who hadn't won much, I went to the awards ceremony with my mum and dad. Becky didn't turn up. Then the award was given to taekwondo player Jade Jones, leaving me to give it my best celebrity-at-a-film-awards frozen grin/happy clap. 'Well done Jade, fellow North Walian, delighted for you ...'

In the muted aftermath, I decided to follow Becky on Twitter. Neither of us had many followers, so I noticed when she decided to follow me back. A DM was attempted. A DM came back. I sent a friend request on Facebook and tried my hand at some light flirting – 'So, what sort of cycling do you do?' I should probably have looked up the answer to that one before starting the conversation. It turned out it was track, primarily the sprint. But I was young and naïve. I was also unable to differentiate between a personal page and a fan page, which meant I sent a poke and a message to a total stranger who just happened to like track cycling and Becky James in particular.

I went to the World Cup in New Zealand. Becky went on training camps and to competitions with British cycling. Our time zones were off but our text conversations found a way through. It all felt rather natural; chatting to her helped take my mind off rugby things. When rugby things intervened, and our World Cup came to an end, and the team embarked on a three-day bender, I came back to Wales determined to actually speak to her with my voice, rather than just text. Which would have been fine, had the three-day bender and long-haul flight back from New Zealand not left me with a voice that came out teenage-boy squeaky.

The first time I ever clapped eyes on her was in the St David's car-park in Cardiff. It wasn't Pont Neuf in Paris or under the clock at Grand Central Station, but was close-ish to the tenpin bowling, and it was handy for those driving from elsewhere in Wales, so all was good. She was coming off the back of some good results in competition, so I opened out with another devastating line: 'I've been looking forward to meeting you, and giving you a congratulations hug.' Remarkably she continued the date, rather than getting in her car and driving home again, and she turned out to be quite good at tenpin bowling, although naturally I won, because both of us were professional sportspeople and we understood that neither liked to lose.

I knew from that first date that I really liked her. She was an amazing person. She was beautiful. We just got on, very easily. We lived miles apart – me in the flat in North Dock, Llanelli, her in one of the British Cycling flats in Fallowfield, Manchester, close to her training base at the national velo- drome – so we saw each other only sporadically, for a while. She was always away training and racing. I was always away training and playing. But I was forever smitten. I'd drive from Llanelli to Manchester, and it would take forever and I wouldn't mind a bit. She'd come to watch my bigger matches, when she could, and I loved the idea of her being up there in the stands.

Wales were playing Australia in the autumn of 2011 when I decided to formalise things. We hadn't talked about being boyfriend and girlfriend, even though, to all intents and purposes we were. After the game I had a hell of a dead leg. I was icing it at the hotel as the two of us were chatting, getting ready to pop out for a few beers.

And I said, nice and quick, because my patter was improving ever so slightly at this point, 'Well, would you like to be my girlfriend?'

So it was sort of official, from that moment on 3 December 2011. We were going out. We were together.

A year later, Becky became double world champion. I missed her sprint final because I was on the pitch at the Stadio Olympico in Rome, playing Italy in the Six Nations. As we landed back in Cardiff the next day I caught the last few laps of her keirin final on my phone. I was familiar with wanting my mates to succeed because they'd been shoulder-to-shoulder with me. Well, it turned out to be nuts how intense it felt when your partner is that person, and you love and admire them and know exactly what they've sacrificed for this and how much it means to them.

It worked the other way too. When Becky missed selection for the 2012 Olympics, I could feel all of it. When she watched me in action, she worried about injuries and pain and all that stuff. But we both understood each other. We knew performance was everything. We could empathise, and we were always there for each other.

And neither of us forgot 3 December. The date we officially began, together; the date, a few years later, when I would ask her to marry me.

EIGHT

LLANIDLOES TO RHAYADER: CREATING MAGIC

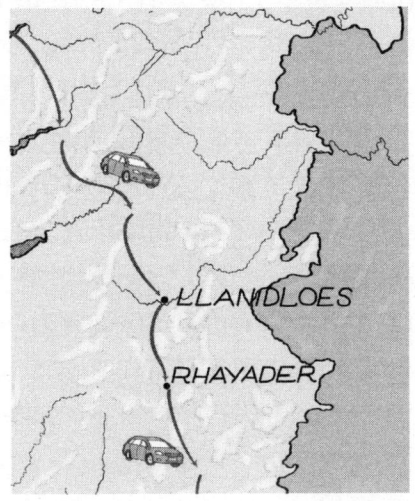

IN WHICH WE TALK ABOUT:

Wallabies woe/late tries against Ireland/a freezing night in Paris/a paternal run-in with the gendarmes/'Mon fils! Numero onze!'/flogged by Gats/18 penalty kicks/Warbs comes good/ Foxy destroys himself/England come to Cardiff chasing a Grand Slam/Howlers plans a riot/Mayhem at midday, carnage at 3 p.m./Cuthy's finest hour/holding it close to my heart/ Titanium/a piece of our lives

It's a very Welsh rugby thing, the way the national team swings from great heights to horrible lows and back again in the same time period as most national sides might just blood a couple of new players and stay marginally just above or below where they were before.

So it was in the aftermath of that Grand Slam win in March 2012. Gats sent us on a summer tour of Australia, Rob Howley in charge, because he always liked to check out the place and opponents of the next Lions tour, a year before it would take place. See also Wales in New Zealand in 2016. We hadn't won Down Under in more than 40 years, and we didn't this time, although we should have done. It finished 27–19 in the first Test; then 25–23 in Melbourne in the second, where I stepped past Wycliff Palu and Rob Simmons for a try in the third minute, and Foxy added another, and we were still ahead going into the 80th minute until we got penalised at a maul and Mike Harris banged over the three points to steal it away; and 20–19 in Sydney in the last, Berrick Barnes waiting until five minutes from time for the match-winning penalty this time.

It kept going in the autumn. Beaten 26–12 by Argentina, 26–15 by Samoa, 33–10 by the All Blacks. Then the Wallabies did us late again, 14–12, when Kurtley Beale went over in the corner with about 30 seconds left.

It meant we started the 2013 Six Nations on a run of seven consecutive Test defeats, which isn't a great place to be as the reigning champions. It was our year to be playing the blue teams away: France in Paris, Italy in Rome, Scotland in Edinburgh; Ireland at home in our opening match, England coming to Cardiff for our last. Traditionally this was seen as the tougher of the two seasons. So when we found ourselves 30–3 down to Ireland with half an hour still to go, it felt sub-optimal for all of us, to say the least.

Ireland were good in that first half. Converted tries for Simon Zebo and Cian Healy, Brian O'Driscoll crossing for another just after half-time. It was the match where Zebo flicked a loose pass up with the outside of his heel, caught it and nearly went over in the corner before they recycled and Healy powered over.

We came back, when the game was gone. Tries for Cuthbert and Halfpenny, Cuthy's the same Block Tune move that had given me my debut try against South Africa, another score too late from Craig Mitchell. The final score-line didn't appear disastrous: 30–22. We were also yet to realise how important those three tries of ours would turn out to be, seven weeks later. It was a very good Ireland team, and they had a strong record against us in that period, particularly in Cardiff. This was their 11th win in 14 visits. Players in that Irish team they're going to talk about for years: Healy and Rory Best; Donnacha Ryan, Jamie Heaslip, Sean O'Brien, Peter O'Mahony, Rob Kearney, Gordon D'Arcy. Conor Murray. But it didn't feel okay. We had been outclassed.

Then there was Sexton and O'Driscoll. The two of them in harmony, pulling the strings, operating at their own tempo and in their own space. Pure class, the sort of thing that has you admiring their patterns and precision even as you're chasing around in their slipstream. It was both impossible to play against and incredible to watch, which is an awkward place to be for a professional rugby player.

We always ran out onto the pitch believing that day was ours. An attitude that came from the bonds between us and all we had been through together. That afternoon against Ireland, I began to doubt it a little. Not just Zebo's flick and catch, but the Best charge-down that led to it. It was all going a bit like Jim Carrey's sign-off in *Bruce Almighty*: 'That's the way the cookie crumbles ...' Sure, we showed resilience and doggedness to get back in. I also felt I'd learned an unfamiliar lesson: sometimes, even if you train hard and have all the best intentions, it's not always going to go your way.

I didn't like that feeling. None of us liked the idea of eight defeats on the spin. That same old negative whirlpool that can drag everyone in Wales down: we're going to Paris next, we got beaten at home by Argentina and Samoa, what hope have we got against the French?

So we were honest with ourselves that week. Boys, we didn't fire a shot against Ireland until it no longer mattered. We start that slowly on Saturday and it's nine without a win. We don't double down on this, okay?

It was freezing on that Saturday night in Paris. The Stade de France often seems to be, in a way that a stadium so much further south than Edinburgh and Dublin and Cardiff shouldn't. There was sleet and there was rain so cold it should have been sleet. My parents were in the crowd, and although the tickets you get as players' family are usually in the main stand and under cover, there was almost nothing in the first half to get anyone on their feet and jumping around. A Freddie Michalak penalty for France, a Halfers pen for us, 3–3 at the break, as gripping as the scoreline suggests. The weather didn't allow us to get going, but nothing allowed us to get going. It was rugby as a battle of wills. It was rugby as effort and stubbornness; don't give them time and space when they won't give it to us.

Into the dressing-room at half-time, and nothing to reflect back on except the absence of a defining blow. Voices from all corners, looking for answers.

'Bloody hell boys, what have we done for 40 minutes?'

'We've done nothing. They've done nothing.'

'Like I'm not even shattered.'

'No-one's hurting. No-one's in the locker.'

'So we may as well go out and have a go in the second half now.'

'Yeah. Let's go out second half and really open the taps …'

We stepped it up. Not breaking the game wide open and running in try after try, but going more direct, bringing the physicality. Gradually getting the sense of a momentum shift, of the home crowd getting frustrated with their team's lack of progress. When the crowd turns against you in Paris, it can get ugly quite quick.

And then the moment arrived when my father became a world-famous criminal. Eight minutes left on the clock, 6–6. Four penalties to show for 72 minutes of frozen toil. What a game for the spectators, hey?

A line-out for us just inside the French half, left-hand side. A word between us as we walked into position: let's go direct here, boys. Let's see how much they've got left in the tank. Keep the ball in their 22, squeeze the pressure on. Let's smash them up the middle at pace, and see how much energy they've got left to cover wide.

I got a good carry in. Off my wing to give us some go-forward. Warrenball tactics, quick ball and physical. Forwards round the corner. Speed beats D, as we used to say. Defenders can't cope when it keeps coming at them fast.

Us up deep into their 22, central. France overcommitting at the ruck because of that speed. Quick ball, Philsy having a look both ways and then going back left to Dan Biggar. Biggs taking the pass off his toes, spotting the space in the corner, floating a little kick through.

Suddenly it's like my first cap all over again.

'Don't let it bounce, George. Don't let it bounce, don't let it bounce …'

And, once again, it bounced straight into my hands. Straight into my personal list of the top two luckiest bounces I've ever received.

Next thought: 'Oh my God, I'm not close enough.' But that bounce was perfect. Now it was about staying in the field of play. It was about riding the tackle.

François Trinh-Duc ahead of me. Shouldn't be at full-back, so someone's gone off. If you could choose one man to have ahead of you as the last defender, a replacement fly-half would be right up there.

Him understanding the same sums and going low. Me dipping my hip into him. The classic case of big man against slightly smaller man. Over Trinh-Duc and in at the corner.

I was bouncing. All the boys were – absolutely hissing, knowing how big a score this was for us at such a late stage in such a tight game. Knowing that all we had to do now was close the game out, jogging back from that corner flag giving the thumbs-ups and fist-pumps to all around.

That was when strange things started happening. Foxy running over to me with a look on his face.

'G, was that your old man?'

'What?'

'Was that your old man behind you?'

'You what mate?'

I couldn't understand this question he was asking. We were on the pitch at the Stade de France. I'd just scored a try that could transform our season. I felt quite annoyed.

'Foxy, focus on what we've got to do here, like. We've got maybe seven or eight minutes to finish this game out, and you're asking about my old man? Come on, mate ...'

I ran back towards my position for the re-start. And that's when Cuthy ran all the way over from his wing and really put the fear of God into me by asking me exactly the same question.

'G, was that your old man? I'm 100 per cent sure that was your old man that jumped on you ...'

I did remember someone jumping on my back after I scored. But our subs had been warming up in the in-goal area, and then came steaming over to join in the celebrations. But now this idea was in my head. It couldn't have been my dad. He was probably high up in the main stand. And anyway, there was no way any spectators could get onto the pitch.

There was a barrier and a load of advertising hoardings in the way, plus a load of well-built and better armed gendarmes.

We closed the game out, Halfers doing the business from the kicking tee. All of us buzzing – an away win in Paris, our Six Nations hopes alive, a long tough slog of bad results finally at an end. We walked off the field and up the tunnel towards the dressing-rooms, all back-slaps and big grins. Which was when I spotted our analyst Rhys Long coming the other way with his laptop, aiming straight for me. Now Rhys was always very good. He used to call it 'role patrol' – going around the boys and asking them what their job was in different scenarios on the pitch. Whenever you saw him coming your way during the week, you readied yourself for the deep dive on your detail, or a ticking-off delivered to make you improve next time around. But you never saw him approaching someone after a match had actually finished, which put the fear of God into me for a second time. What sort of howler had I made for him to be making a beeline for me now? The closer he got and the more obvious it became that it was me he was coming for, the faster my heart was pounding.

'Okay, Rhys, spit it out. I've clearly absolutely dropped the *ballon* here. Just get it out of the way and tell me where.'

That's when he turned his laptop around so it was facing me, pressed the space bar, started laughing hysterically, and showed me a replay of my try from the perfect angle to see a man in a black beanie hat and black coat vaulting over the barriers, running onto the pitch, jumping on my back and then running for cover.

My dad.

I sat there in the changing-room, the coaches saying their piece, and all I could hear was the phone in my blazer pocket vibrating as multiple text messages came in. Of course I couldn't touch it. I had to wait for Rob Howley to say what he wanted, then Sam Warburton, then Shaun Edwards. All the while my phone buzzing and jumping.

It was my Uncle Eddie Who Isn't An Actual Uncle whose message I read first. Uncle Eddie is known in the extended family as a wind-up merchant cut from the same cloth as me, and he had dived in with a mass-sent text to the entire extended family.

'Sorry to hear about your father. Don't worry, we're having a whip-round in the family. If you all put some Euros in, we'll get Dave out of prison.'

My dad out of prison? To get him out, he had to be inside prison in the first place. What the hell was I reading here?

To the rest of the boys it all seemed like the best possible joke. There was talk of me having to post bail; there was discussion of extradition treaties. There was certainly talk of what might happen to innocent men from distant lands in French prisons where no-one spoke Anglesey.

It took about 20 minutes for my dad to answer his phone, a period of time in which every possible negative scenario went through my head.

'Dad, what the … what the hell are you doing?'

Me astonished he could actually answer his phone under arrest, let alone get a signal to take a call in an underground cell.

'Oh, what's wrong? I'm just down the road having a pizza with your mother.'

'You what?'

'You know I like pizza.'

'I don't care what you're doing now. What I mean is, what the hell were you running on the field for?'

'Ah, don't worry about it, it's all fine. I polished it out with the French police.'

That was when I got his version of events, which seemed at odds with the replays I'd seen in several significant ways. The explanation went on for a bit, but basically featured the following key themes: no good seats given to players' families, stuck instead in the rubbish ones right in the bottom corner; some liquid courage taken on board after the boring and freezing first half, and a growing sense of annoyance at how stodgy we were playing.

Come the second half, realising we were now playing towards his end, and that my wing was now the part of the pitch directly in front of him, he uttered these ominous words to my mum: 'Oh, we're here for a reason, Jan.'

Now when he re-tells it, there's a laughable number of references to getting the hot chocolates in. I'm not saying he didn't purchase a *chocolat chaud*, but these were not the beverages that led to his later actions. He claims he told my mum that I was going to score in the corner in front of them, and that she replied, 'Don't be stupid,' which is the first note of realism in the re-telling. Then, when I do score, he claims he hurdled a three-foot hoarding, showed one steward the outside, stepped another and left the other 10 in his wake.

There's more, if you give him time. Claiming he used his O-Level French from 1974 to persuade the Stade de France security staff to let him go – 'Mon fils! Mon fils! Numero onze!'. Insisting that when he got back to his feet all the other players' fathers were congratulating him, but that my mum wouldn't talk to him for an hour.

Her side of the story? It's freezing cold and miserable. I score in front of them. She hugs my big sister Natalie, who's on one side of her, and then my brother-in-law, Ed. She turns to hug my dad, except he's not there. She looks down, assuming he must have fallen over. One too many hot chocolates. When she looks up again, all the other parents around her are looking shocked and pointing at the field.

My dad's only regret, in the aftermath, was that he had lost his favourite beanie hat in the carnage. What he didn't realise, until it was returned to him the following Christmas, was that my siblings had found it, and that my sisters had got it framed, so it could be presented to him as his first Wales cap in front of the rest of the family.

There had been so many opportunities, when I was coming through the ranks, for my dad to stroll onto a pitch. At Llangefni, at Llandovery, at age-group matches: no stewards, no hoardings, no ropes. He never moved a muscle. Didn't flinch. I would hear his voice bellowing, of course, but his decibels were the only thing that crossed the touchline. He had to wait until the hardest place of all, where no-one knew him, where he couldn't speak the language, where the rules are strictest.

I've softened, with age. Now I've got two boys of my own, I see the world in a different light. I still wouldn't do to them what my dad decided to do that night. Sure, I can see the romance behind it. Had it been Foxy's old man or Biggs' uncle, I'd probably have found it charming. But it wasn't. It was my dad, and therefore it was so embarrassing I still don't quite know where to look.

The only consolation is that I wasn't the most upset person in the Stade de France at the end of that match. That honour went to France coach Philippe Saint-André, who at the final whistle looked ready to punch his way back to Gare du Nord. I never lost against a team of his in my professional career, which made it slightly awkward when I arrived in Provence to begin my spell there; he was the club's head of performance.

I chose not to mention Paris 2013. So did he.

Everything felt different after that night in Paris. Gats looked after us at the start of the bye week and then flogged us at the end of it to keep us on our toes, which was par for the course. We had momentum again. The fixture list had looked horrible at the start of the tournament: Ireland and their record in Cardiff, us travelling to Paris. The kicker now was how the remaining three matches were falling. Italy away, Scotland away, England at home.

We beat Italy the way you usually had to beat Italy at this stage in their Six Nations development: dog it out for the full 80 minutes, trust that your physicality and fitness and skillset would be too much for them in the end. I went in there full of my usual optimism – 'I'm going to have a decent game today. Have a go. Play some rugby' – and then the weather was terrible, and we had to scrap instead, but we did a job, even if it wasn't a particularly sexy one.

Suddenly we had two big games to come and a huge opportunity. Ireland had lost to England in an Owen Farrell v Ronan O'Gara kickfest after we had beaten France, and then Scotland did a job on them too. The title was still there for someone to claim. Only England were unbeaten, and they had to come to us on the last weekend.

So we flipped it round, when we travelled to Edinburgh. Our record against Scotland was great, so we called this our stumbling block. Push the complacency away, forget about being comfortable. Did it turn out to be a classic? Only if you had also enjoyed the Faz/Rog face-off in Dublin. Once Richard Hibbard scored an early try for us, it turned into tee-time: eighteen penalties attempted in the match, a record for an international. Halfers knocked over seven from ten attempts. Greig Laidlaw landed six from eight. An ugly game, but a nice sum at the end of it.

It didn't ever really feel like they were going to break us, Scotland. That's the difference with international rugby; sometimes you've just got to stay in the fight, build the pressure, take your points, keep the scoreboard ticking over. When you do, bad streaks turn good. The stats start looking pretty again. At the start of the tournament it was all about the losing streak. By beating Scotland, we had clocked up our fifth consecutive away victory in the Six Nations, which was both a national and a tournament record.

Five away wins in the Six Nations doesn't happen by fluke. It comes from dedication. It comes from the sort of horrible work we did on those repeated camps in parts of Poland no-one wants to see. We were happy fighting tooth and nail – or rather, we were programmed to. Happy wasn't the slog that got you there. It was where it left you at the end.

Sam Warburton had been taking flak going into the Scotland game. Not from anyone inside the camp, who could see how he set standards every day in training and did all that stuff in a match you want from a modern open-side and so much more. It was from the Twitter warriors who were starting to bang their flimsy swords on their hollow shields around this era.

Warbs was immense at Murrayfield, delivering just when we needed him, and rightly made man of the match. We were tight as mates. I looked after him when times were hard and he looked after me. We'd shout at each other to get ourselves going, both of us in on the same joke. So at the end, before we walked off the pitch, I embraced him. Proper man-love.

For Sam, as a young captain with a great weight on his shoulders, representing us, representing the nation – that's a heavy burden to carry at times. But you ride it together, and that's the beauty of the squad we had for so long. When you needed big players to step up, they stepped up. When someone couldn't, another player would sense the gap and deliver instead.

Rugby union is maybe the most collective of all team sports. No-one succeeds without everyone else. Our team under Gats, right the way through to the 2015 World Cup, embodied that in a way you could never forget if you were part of it. You always felt anxiety; you always had a fear of losing, because it was something you never wanted to do. But you believed in everyone around you – each of us either cut from the same cloth, or reshaped by what we were going through.

I've talked about Sam's dedication to training, even when he was long finished with playing. It was there in all of us who went through these days together. When Jonathan Davies and his family came out to see me in Aix in my first few months with Provence, we decided it would be fun to do a workout in my garage gym. That quickly became two extra sessions. Then it went mano a mano. It started getting weird. When you've hit a Wattbike hard, you learn to understand the difference between a man who's pushing and a man intent on destroying himself. It's the sound the bike makes. It's the noises the pedaller makes. And when Foxy jumped on that bike, from the first rep in the first set, it was clear he was still the same as we were back then. If you're going to work, you go and work.

These results in the early part of 2013, as we turned it all around – they weren't glamorous, and they weren't sexy rugby. None of them will go down in the great playbooks of international rugby lore. But it was the brutal truth of elite sport spelled out once again. You take the emotion out of it. It didn't matter if we won by a single point or 50. All we were judged on was the W or the L. And, because of that, you find yourself in a world that only others who survived it can understand. When you hear Foxy destroying himself on a Wattbike in retirement, when you hear Warbs calling himself a little bitch for pulling up a rep short in a hotel gym he doesn't even need to be in – those moments can only truly be shared with those blokes. You tell these stories to someone not in the circle, and they can listen, and they can be polite. They can say they can imagine what it's like, and understand it. But you can't, unless you lived it. And that's why, even thinking about it again, I have the biggest smile on my face. It was brutally hard, rocking up to every day and every session knowing you were going to be pushed past your physical and your mental and your emotional limits. But you chose it, and you got an unfathomable pleasure out of it. You know you've done everything you can; there's nothing left for you to do but go out and share it with these friends alongside you.

We were all weirdos, after surviving that life. The French boys at Provence used to look at me like I was nuts, when I went to do an extra Wattbike session after training, or when I went back to the gym to do my hamstring and calf rehab for my Achilles afterwards. They were in the canteen having food while I was loading up the weight plates again. But while they couldn't comprehend it, it was second nature to me. It gave me confidence. It made me feel safe. I could go into tomorrow happy, rather than worrying. Rather than being just another winger who liked scoring tries.

This is the way a championship can fall. Wales, three wins from four. Ireland and France, one. England, four. England coming to Cardiff for a 5 p.m. kick-off on the final Saturday. England needing a win to clinch a first Grand Slam in a decade.

Wales needing a win by more than seven points to beat them to the title.

There are certain facts that grow bigger as a decisive match approaches. This was one of them. Every person in Wales wanted to talk about those seven points. Every dog-walker I bumped into that week reminded me about them. Sometimes I even thought the dogs were mentioning it.

After all that had happened in the past seven weeks, the second-half rearguard against Ireland had come to matter in ways we might never had guessed. Had 30–2 just after half-time ended up being 36–12, no-one would have been talking about seven points now. Our hard work in defeat, our three tries when we could have let it slip away – that's what had kept the title just about within reach.

In any case, what all the street sages seemed to forget was that you can't set out to win a game by seven points. International rugby is not a precision missile strike. None of our coaches were talking about the magnificent seven. The message was a simple one: win, and win well. Don't watch the scoreboard any more than normal. There was no pressure on us. Everyone had written us off after week one. We can come all the way back from the edge of the abyss. What the hell did we have to lose now?

Because how could it be complicated for a Welshman, when beating England would deny them a Grand Slam? None of us wanted to imagine the uproar on the streets of Cardiff if they came to our backyard and started launching champagne corks and drinking out of trophies. Forget those seven points. The story was perfect as it was.

We all knew Gats would be loving it, wherever he was watching on his sabbatical ahead of being the Lions' head coach that summer. But this was Rob Howley's tournament, and this was his week. We all liked Howlers. We liked the way he worked. We were also slightly scared by how tough he was on us. He would strip you down in a debrief, show you all the things you did wrong, show you all the tiny details you could do better. At the end of it all he would look you in the eye and say, 'Fair?'

We knew it was a rhetorical question. No-one was going to argue with one of Wales' greatest ever scrum-halves, not least our own scrum-halves, who got a particularly tough line from him. So you'd take that feedback on and you'd carry it with you inside and you'd use it because it was brutal every day.

'George, what are you doing?'

'Ah, we're doing this …'

'No, no. You missed the call. Why did you miss the call?'

You wanted to debate it. 'Well, hang on …' But you couldn't, partly because it wouldn't get you anywhere, and partly because he generally had a point.

'George – fair?'

'Yeah, it's fair. I'm an absolute idiot, don't worry.'

It was the detail that got you. He expected the highest standards all the time. Our kicking coach Neil Jenkins would tell us stories about sharing a room with him when Jenks was banging over the penalties and Howlers was sniping through sleepy defences. Jenks was the relaxed one – clothes all over the floor, telly on, cheeky chocolate bar as a reward for a good day off the tee. Howlers had plays and moves written on the walls.

Detail, then detail, then more detail.

'Right, we're going to run this play. As a non-jumping line-out man, you're on the second ruck. Then we're going to play a 31-pattern. Then you're going to be at the short ball coming back off 15 on the open side.'

If we ran it and you weren't there, it was not a nice world to be in. I found it really hard at times. There were very few soft edges. Every day, I was being torn apart.

But it set the tone. If you didn't do your job, you'd be found out. What a focus that gave you, on both sides of the ball. Going backwards, Shaun Edwards was going to come at you like a banshee. Going forwards, Howlers would be barking his impossible rhetorical question. Rhys Long stalking the sidelines with his laptop and his role patrol.

Howlers would also praise you when it was needed. Never huge amounts, but when it did come, it was like being given an ice-cream on a scorching day. And the combination worked, and we could all see it and feel it working. A mutual understanding: everything we do each day will be watched intently, but everything we do each day is to get better. A slow but satisfying realisation: if we can absorb all this in training, if they can stress-test like this and we don't break, then when the pressure comes on in a match, and England have won four from four and fancy themselves for the Grand Slam, then we can deliver.

We heard afterwards that England's players were shocked by the reception they got when their coach arrived in the middle of town that Saturday afternoon. Ten of their starting XV had never played at the Millennium Stadium before. Their coach Stuart Lancaster had never been to a game there. Even if he had, and more of the team knew what was coming, it wouldn't have prepared them for that day.

I'd never seen Cardiff like it. Mayhem at midday, carnage at 3 p.m. It's hard to explain to you what it feels like to be riding that kind of support as a player. The flipside comes when you visit Twickenham and they're all flicking digits at you and calling you that thing that most men are, after the age of 13 or 14. You get it. It still doesn't make up for what you get as your own team coach comes through the western suburbs, and every single person you see looks overjoyed to see you coming, and every single one gives you a look that says: 'I'm with you, we're doing this'. Also often, 'I'm already hammered,' but that's fine. The 5.30 p.m. kick-offs are not designed for abstention and decorum. Not on Super Saturday of the Six Nations. Not when it's them and us.

We didn't say much in the dressing-room beforehand. No mentions of Everest or heads sent banging into walls. There was enough hype out there in the media and on the streets. 'Boys, we're here now. We've got a great opportunity. We've prepared super well. Let's just go out and enjoy the day and enjoy the performance.'

I was still a young kid, really, 21 years old. I had to keep my head on my processes to stay somewhere close to calm. Go through my checklist, take comfort in the familiar rituals at habitual times. As a fan, there's nothing that fills you with more pride than your team on a day like this. As a player, this is exactly why you put the hard yards in. You want the people you care about and the people you see on the streets to feel like this. You want to give them this excitement. You feel it reflecting back to you.

For a game that fills me with so much pride and happiness, it wasn't a particularly good first half. Us 9–3 up, me a Mike Brown tap-tackle away from going the length of the pitch for the opening try. I saw Biggs pick off a Ben Youngs pass, and then the ball came to me and I was cantering away, until the longest fingers in the world from the angriest man in rugby hit my right ankle.

You know when you see someone slipping on a muddy bank, and their legs are going all Scooby Doo and there's nothing they can do about it? That's the feeling I had in that moment. Falling, falling, falling, and all of it inevitable. I could hear Tips screaming, either on my inside or my outside, but I couldn't work out how I could fall on my face and pass the ball all in one go. All my dreams ripped away by Mike Brown's fingertips, a scenario no-one wants to consider.

But we were calm amid the bedlam, at half-time. Not counting the six-point difference and trying to work out how to edge it past seven.

'Keep going, boys. Keep going. Stay in it. We're exactly where we need to be. Just keep churning away at them and they're going to break.'

And we did, and they did. It was one of those games when it was really tight until it suddenly wasn't tight. Justin Tipuric was on fire. You could have played him at centre and he would have been the best player on the pitch. Warbs was on fire. Every one of us was at least smouldering.

Was it Alex Cuthbert's finest hour? It's hard to think how it could have been better. In about six months he had gone from being at uni and playing Sevens to winning a Grand Slam and then scoring two tries in the all-time record-breaking win over the nation Wales want to beat more than any other. The social media warriors would have their way with him, too, over the following years. Him and Rhys Priestland, all of us, at times. Wild swings of opinion, horrendous personal abuse sent straight to your phone for you to wake up to the morning before or after a match. None of them could have done what he did that night. None of them.

His first try was absolute gas. A hand-off to the chest of Mike Brown, an acceleration into the corner. His second was about Taulupe Faletau's feet, Warbs' break and Tips' centre skills – a pump, a delayed pass, a perfectly timed offload.

There were very few games in my career where I ever felt I could relax with time on the clock and know we had won it. This one should have been too big an occasion. There was too much riding on it. But after Cuthy's second, on 66 minutes, I had a rather lovely stream of thoughts.

'Holy Jesus, we could … I don't think … we're not going to lose this. Even if we have a catastrophic meltdown, there's no way we're not winning this …'

I don't remember the chants of, 'Easy! Easy!' that went round the stadium. But I'll never forget the pure pleasure of that last 10 minutes. The certainty of our victory, how it felt to those of us on the pitch, what it was doing to our supporters all around. It was as if I could tune in to the frequencies all around in a way that when you're fighting for every second you cannot. What had been a wall of noise was now 73,000 people. It was the nation beyond. I could pick out the chants and I could hear the change of songs. I could take it all in and I could hold it close to my heart.

So there you go. Seven points don't matter when you win by 27. Howlers said afterwards it was a bigger achievement than the Grand Slam the year before, winning the title from where we'd been. To me it just felt different. Is a Grand Slam better than a championship? Probably. But for where we had come from, and all the things we had to overcome, Cardiff on 16 March 2013 was an incredible place to be and an amazing time to be there.

There's a song that brings it all back, for all of us: 'Titanium', by David Guetta. Blasting out when we were handed our medals on the pitch at the Millennium, in our heads and on our lips at the black-tie dinner at the Hilton, as we marched through the crowds six-deep, all of them trying to whack us on the back and tell us how we had made them feel, when it was them making us feel like this too. Absolutely in Tiger Tiger, and in the streets of Cardiff where there didn't seem to be an empty square metre of space anywhere.

It was Becky's song, too, when she won two golds at the World Championships later that year. On her playlist before she raced, when she celebrated afterwards. We put in on now and it sucks us both straight back to that time and those feelings. We really did feel bulletproof. We had nothing to lose.

A city full to the brim. Full of people so happy that they all just wanted to hold onto you. Maybe only now, looking back down the years, do I truly appreciate what it all meant – how we were collectively creating a moment in time, a piece of our lives none of us would ever forget. A very Welsh rugby thing, a very Welsh rugby swing.

NINE

RHAYADER TO BUILTH WELLS: MAKING HISTORY

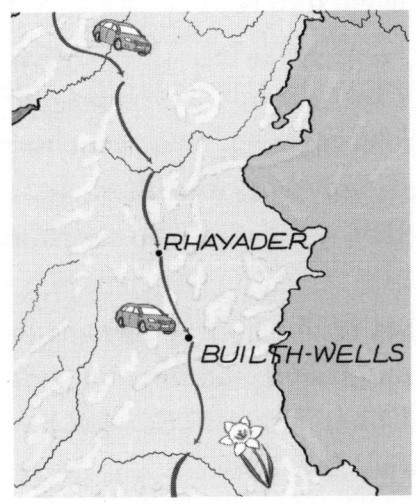

IN WHICH WE TALK ABOUT:

*Jim Carrey lines/Pauly sings Shakira/Philsy's back-seat blast/
Hong Kong ding-dongs/learning from the best/serious Jason
Bourne shit/'This is where I want to be'/the sea of red/Berrick
Barnes goes to the air/'Oh my God, I'm clean here ...'/white try
line, space/a proper old caveman fight/Block Tune, the reprise/
Kurtley slips/taking Izzy for a ride/Mike Tyson memes/Drico the
legend/one of the best games I would ever be involved in/
JAMES FUCKING BOND/a Saint, at last*

There's an easy narrative around the British and Irish Lions, when you're a kid. You dream of one day playing for them, because they're the pinnacle.

But I didn't dream of playing for them. Not because they weren't the pinnacle. It was just the pinnacle seemed too far away. I never thought playing for Wales was an option. I dreamed of winning one cap; that would have been enough, exactly where I wanted to be. The Lions were way out of my grasp.

The maths swings your way, as you get older, just as it does with each incremental level. You want to play for North Wales Under-16s; you work out there are five or so other wingers you've come up against who are handy, so you've got a one-in-six chance. Same thing when hoping to make my full Scarlets debut; we've got four wingers in the senior squad, and that one's out injured, and now one of the others has a knock too. Same thing when the Scarlets boys were winding me up ahead of my first international cap – 'George, you're one of eight wingers playing for a Welsh region this weekend, and one of them's Irish, and another is too old, so …'

Wales, Ireland, Scotland, England. Four nations, eight wingers. A different Jim Carrey line for this occasion: so you're saying there's a chance? I naturally found my focus on playing well for Wales. It had been such a long road and so much hard work to get here, and once you have a hold of it you never want to let go. But 2012 had brought us the Grand Slam, and 2013 had been a good Six Nations, in the end, for all of us, and Gats was the Lions' head coach. I moved on from *Dumb And Dumber* to *Hunger Games*: may the odds always be in your favour …

They announced the Lions squad for the tour to Australia on 30 April. Four wingers: Tommy Bowe, Alex Cuthbert, Sean Maitland … and me. Stuart Hogg in there as someone who could cover anywhere in the back three. Now the game had changed again. I had to stay fit and in-form. I also had to avoid injury. And I didn't want any of those other wingers making a melt of me, which is why Tommy's display when Scarlets played Ulster at Ravenhill in the Pro12 semi-final 10 days later was somewhat sub-optimal. Ulster were different level. Tommy took me on one-on-one out wide and beat me all ends up for their first try.

That was my last game for Scarlets. My move to Northampton was on. But I couldn't spend too long lost in reveries of the jersey and my compadres, because we were into the initial Lions camp at the Vale pretty much straight off the back, and then, as other teams' seasons came to their own end, another camp in Dublin with the full set of lads. And this is when the big build-up begins.

First day in Ireland, and a scan of the rooming list to see who I was in with first. I knew it wasn't going to be one of the other 14 Welshmen; that's not how the Lions works. That it turned out to be Paul O'Connell was both thrilling and intimidating. I'd only met him very briefly after the Ireland game earlier in the year. I struggled to think of him as a man, because he was quite clearly a legend, and so I came to some quick decisions in the lift on the way to our rooms: I'll take the smaller bed; I'll offer up whichever side of the room he wants, closest to the toilet or furthest away; if he wants right side, I'll take left; if he wants all the hangers in the wardrobe, he can have them. Actually, forget what I should offer him. What should I even say to him?

I opened the door. I could hear the shower going. I looked at the beds, and saw Pauly had already picked his spot. Perfect – he liked the right side, so I would take the left. I began putting my stuff on the bed, making sure to leave the bedside table in between untouched. Now the nerves were really kicking in. What exact words should I choose to greet Ireland and Lions legend Paul O'Connell?

'Hi, I'm a big fan.' Too kiss-arse.

'Hi Paul, I see you like sleeping on the right.' Too creepy.

Then I hear him singing, in the shower. He's doing Shakira. He's doing Shakira, but not as Shakira, as a big strong man from Limerick. 'Oh baby, when you talk like dat …'

There's nothing to settle you down like a legend in a towel skirt singing South American pop hits in a west of Ireland accent.

'Ah, hey Paul, I'm George.'

'Yeah, I know. I know.'

What a lovely man he turned out to be. He couldn't have done any more for me except ask me to duet with him as Beyonce.

'George, I'm going down to the team room. Shall I take your washing?'

External voice: 'You're fine, thank you, I have no dirties yet.'

Internal monologue: 'Fucking hell. No, do not touch my washing. What are you even thinking? Let me take yours. I'll wash it with my own hands.'

It's amazing what spending time together can do for you all. We all learned from each other, and we all loved doing so – how these other lads worked in training, what their mindset was, how they ran moves and thought about the game. Hard work bonds you too, which was a good thing the way Gats was tucking in to everybody. The heat was coming on from the coaches very early, and it came as a shock to some of the lads who'd only seen him on the opposition bench. 'Jesus Christ, I knew he pushed you, but this is a bit nuts, isn't it, especially after a long season?'

Inevitably there were a couple of piss-ups. Hard work bonds, but so does hard drinking. In Dublin we went out to eat at one of Jamie Heaslip's restaurants, and then on to a traditional old bar called Keogh's. It started raucous and ended up with a lock-in. Naturally we all got a little giddy – boys climbing on the bar, boys singing songs, boys urging each other to climb on the bar and sing songs.

There are certain rules you instinctively stick by on tours like this, one of the most important being, if you leave somewhere, make sure you're either leaving with your roomie or your roomie's okay and in someone else's vision. Come the end of the night in Keogh's, I couldn't see Pauly anywhere, which when someone is six-six and nearing 18 stone, is something of a worry. I looked round the back of the bar. Nothing. I looked for Mike Phillips, usually a good place to start for the well refreshed. Nothing again. Charging around like a paranoid mother – 'Where's Pauly? Was Pauly here?'

I found him in the corridor. On his back, sprawled out in the perfect shape for a chalk outline on *CSI*.

'Oh my God, Pauly, are you alright?'

Turns out he was only briefly resting. A stumble coming down the stairs, a moment taken to gather his thoughts. That was another lesson for me: if I was still able to walk about at the end of a team bonding session, so too would Pauly.

The end of the lock-in was not the end of the night. It just meant the action switched to the team bus. Now was the time for Philsy to get to work. He was on the back seats, all on his own, beginning his own chant.

'If you're a rugby legend, come and sit at the back.'

Spotting the re-animated Pauly coming up the coach steps, upping the volume.

'Pauly, you're a legend pal. You come to the back with me ...'

So now it's him and Pauly at the back and Pauly doesn't know if it's all a brilliant joke or the start of an irrevocable split in the ranks, he's got that much Keogh's in him, and Philsy is bored of the first game, so decides to take it up a level.

Stuart Hogg, the next man on, one of the few even younger than me.

'Hoggy! The only Scotsman here!' Which seemed harsh on Sean Maitland and Richie Gray, but this was only the start of it.

'Hoggy, I don't even know who you play for, Edinburgh or Scotland.' Meaning Edinburgh or Glasgow, although this was not an evening for factual accuracy.

Owen Farrell coming up the steps. 'Faz! You're only here because your dad is the coach ...'

It is all about getting to know your new team-mates in those weeks. Getting rid of the preconceptions, getting to know their foibles and the things you'll eventually love about them, which might be the same thing sooner than you think. Philsy was a case in point. If you didn't understand him, you'd think he was the most arrogant man in the world. When you did, you realised he was one of the loveliest fellows you'll ever meet in your life. You're just going to have to get used to the idea that his idea of humour is winding everyone up. And assuming you'll enjoy it as much as he is.

He never took the mick when it was time to go to work. When he trained, he trained hard. We all did. For all the good times off the pitch – the drinking games, the bad rounds of golf on beautiful courses – the thing that bound us all together was the desire to do everything better than we ever had before. When you're a player coming through, you want to train at the best facilities with the best coaches. You want to be surrounded by the best players. And when you look around and you're surrounded by all that, and everyone's on exactly the same wavelength, it makes you happy in your secret obsessional place deep inside.

All of it was bigger – the sponsorship days, the formal dinners before we left, our reception en route to Australia in Hong Kong. It comes thick and fast on a Lions tour – games against Western Force, the Reds, Combined Country, Waratahs and Brumbies, before the Tests in Brisbane, Melbourne and Sydney – so your recovery becomes even more critical. If we weren't training, we were travelling. Long distances, long days. If you weren't training and you weren't travelling, you were playing.

Sometimes you went start-bench. Sometimes you went start-start. You never complained, even with the fatigue of a full season still in your legs, because you understood it was all about the bigger picture of building to the Tests. You finished a session and the ice-baths were full to the brim, ready to go. You were ready to ask, 'Could we …' and someone had already thought about it and would finish your sentence with, 'we have already.'

I loved the quality of the training, and I loved sensing us becoming a single team rather than four discrete nations. I enjoy talking to people; I'll make an effort, and I like bringing a positive energy each morning. I could see new groups forming, not around national groups but shared interests. I could see lads finding a common ground they might not have believed existed.

I was tight with Hoggy from the start. Two youngsters, two boys who grew up with a love of going fast. I liked hanging out with Richie Gray, and the Leicester boys were great. Three weeks in, I'm not sure there was a single bloke I wouldn't have a full pint with.

It wasn't an optional extra, this togetherness. The weight of expectation, the pressure from outside and inside – if we weren't on the same page very early, we would be found out. You have the build-up games to find the combinations and work on the performance and the confidence to underpin both. But if you weren't on the money, those teams would be hissing. Every Aussie player wanted to say they had beaten the British and Irish Lions.

There was an obvious blueprint for how we might play. Gats as head coach, those 15 of us used to the way he ran things and the way Rob Howley liked to groove the attack. But everywhere boys were bringing added value. Howlers enjoyed picking their brains; there was the influence of Johnny Sexton and how he liked to run things compared to Owen Farrell, the way the dynamic worked between those two 10s and what they preferred to run with the backline they had. There was Brian O'Driscoll, and all he brought in attack, and what he could bring out of Jamie Roberts when Jamie didn't want to do anything but run.

Conversations popping up on buses and in airport lounges and hotel breakfast rooms.

'Oh, that's really good. But why don't we go the winger one out?'

'Yeah, or get him on the outside shoulder of 10 on the return ball?'

You find a groove. I was used to Shaun Edwards' version of defence. In Andy Farrell we had another strong northerner with a very detailed understanding of exactly what he wanted. He wasn't forgiving. You were there to do a job, and he would drive you hard. He could be scary at times, just like Shaun. But it was all because he knew you could be better, and he wanted to make sure there were no mistakes at any key moment.

Every day I was learning – from the coaches, from these other players. It was a dreamy sort of brains trust with the hardest possible edge. You think you have the game half worked out, and then you go on a Lions tour, and you realise you haven't really scratched the surface, not yet. You see boys doing different skills and different activation and different recovery, and you soak it all up, and you start questioning yourself – 'Am I doing enough?' 'Am I doing too much?' It's like when you go on Instagram and see these hacks people put together, and you suddenly realise you've been peeling bananas wrong all your life.

It was serious Jason Bourne shit at times. It was also full-on. When you were picked for the tour games, you were looking at the team you were playing, you were training hard, you were working on stuff – not just for that game but for the next game, and then stuff you could drop into the Test series. You played, you reviewed it, you wanted to rest, and then a coach would come up to you with the realpolitik – 'Right, G, we've got a couple of niggles. So you're on the bench, and we need at least half-an-hour from you.'

Maybe that's why those tour games race by, and the Test series is suddenly upon you. How was the odds game looking now? Well, they'd had to bring Shane Williams in for one game, and Christian Wade and Simon Zebo came out from back home as cover, and Tommy Bowe had an injured hand. So it was going to be two from me, Cuthy and Maitland, and with the season we'd had with Wales, and the way my form in the warm-up games had gone, I thought the best chance of me starting a Test was this first one.

They announced the team to us 1 to 23. Not alphabetically. As a result, by the time they got to number 11 I'd forgotten the entire starting pack. You play it cool, until you eventually hear your name called, but your heart still pounds hard in your chest, and your hands still go clammy. Someone asked me, months later: what's better, playing for Wales at a World Cup, winning a Grand Slam, or playing for the Lions? And it's very hard to compare, because there's nothing like any of them. It felt nuts to me that I was on a Lions tour. Training. Playing. I felt I was contributing, not just being here, and I was loving every second. To be about to play for the Lions in a Test match? That gave me an overpowering sense of belonging. 'This is it. If I have to be anywhere in the entire world right now, this is where I want to be.'

You feel where you are in your season, at this point on a summer tour. I worked out I had probably played 30-odd games already. Just when you want to be at your freshest, like you're a million dollars, like you're absolutely pristine, it's arguably the worst of all moments, physically. There are multiple aches and pains and a few bits hanging off. But this is rugby, and it's the Lions, so what are you going to do – complain about it, and ask to be stood down? You focus on the good things you can do. You fall back on your pre-match system, on your processes. You get yourself towards a place where you can perform and deliver.

I've always felt like I've had to graft above and beyond to get certain things, to be in certain places. In the last few days before that first Test, which just flew by – I slept, I ate, I sneezed, it was game day – it was one of the very few times in my career where I felt everything clicking for me. I would be okay, physically, because my commitment was total. And as you looked around the camp, you could see that in the other boys, too, and as you walked out from the team hotel into the streets of Brisbane, you could see it again in the thousands of Welshmen and Irish and Englishmen and Scots.

They were using that tagline for the first time, around this series: 'The sea of red'. Well, the tide had come in. I had a little game I liked to play, in the last few days before the game on the Saturday. As a group of Lions fans walked into the coffee shop we were in, or towards us down a street, I'd try to work out from the way they looked or walked or held themselves which nationality they were, before they even spoke or you heard their accents. It was a good game, but after a while, I realised I'd got it wrong. It didn't matter where they were from, any more than it mattered that our back row was made up of an Englishman in Tom Croft, a Welshman in Sam Warburton and an Irishman in Jamie Heaslip. They were all Lions. We were all Lions.

It was the sea of red that I saw first as we walked out of the tunnel at the Suncorp Stadium on Saturday evening. Opposite us, across the stadium, I could see only one colour. I don't think I saw one dot of yellow. It's quite a narrow field of vision, when you first begin walking out, but as we got closer to the pitch, and more of the stands opened up to us, that sea of red grew and grew.

It was the start of one of the great romantic three-part series of sport. You don't know it yet, of course, in that unique moment, but you could feel the atmosphere in your ears and your chest and through your legs. It was incredible. You both wanted it to last forever and to tear into the game like a lunatic hound.

The Wallabies scored first. That epic try where Will Genia breaks from deep and cuts through us, and then kicks through for Israel Folau to gather and go under the sticks. Quite some debut from Folau, although that was something else I couldn't know at that point, how our fates in that series would be so wound around each other. I did get hounded in the post-match debrief, because I hesitated for a split second and stupidly didn't trust Halfers to get last man and ended up jumping out of the line.

But I didn't panic in the moment. In these games you know there's always a threat there. It's coming, even if you can't see it yet. You can get so caught up in everything else – energy pouring down from the stands, noise in your ears, red blood in your veins – that an early score against you is quite a handy reset. It's a boxing match where, rather than circling round each other, firing and missing with jabs, your opponent catches you with a clean shot to the nose. Not the chin, and you're never going down, but you're awake now and you're alive. 'We're going to have to fight tooth and nail for every second of this …'

Blow by blow for the first 10 minutes. Looking for an opening, for a chance to get my hands on the ball and make a positive impact. About 10 metres inside our half, doing the winger thing of covering our back left field with the Aussies ball in hand and coming towards their own 10-metre line.

Berrick Barnes decided to go to the air. I positioned myself in the sweet spot, where if it went long I knew I could get back, but if it went short I could give myself enough of a run-up to clatter on.

The ball went high, but not long enough. It was mine to field. Blow by blow, so a simple enough initial thought: catch the thing. Do your job.

Next thought, working out where I was going to be – 'Well, I'll have to run this back now, won't I?'

Pat McCabe the first man in front of me, charging up. A little shimmy onto my left, space opening up. James O'Connor diving in with an ankle tap. Wobbling over it, and suddenly I felt clean free.

Running as hard as I could, as fast as I could. Crowd in my ears.

Barnes coming across at pace from my right, the left-hand corner up there ahead of me.

'I've just got to go. Just go ...'

Not thinking about what sort of step it should be, what he might do.

'Just got to get on the outside of him ...'

Running. Running as hard as I can. Putting the ball in my opposite hand in case I have to fend.

'Oh my God, I'm clean here. I'm free ...'

Then I looked over and absolutely panicked, because Genia was tracking across, and Genia is quick.

'Just run, run, run as hard as you can. Just get there ...'

I'm halfway through celebrating, my right arm going up, when Genia is almost on me. I stick my arm out at him, for the fend, but it looks instead as if I'm taunting him. It looks as if I'm pointing into his soul.

Corner flag ahead. No Genia. No tackle.

White try line. Space.

I slid over, legs first. And I didn't go wild, to start with. I just lay there in the grass with the ball under my chest and my heart hammering against it. Squashing it into the turf with the pressure of my pounding blood.

Disbelief, pure excitement, pure enjoyment, pure … I don't know how you describe that feeling. A solid wave of noise in my ears. Almost frozen by all the emotions.

Foxy was there first, two hands slapping my back. Climbing to my feet and feeling Brian O'Driscoll's palm on the back of my neck, pulling me into his shoulder.

'Oh my God, that is probably one of the best things I've ever done in my life …'

Only when I started slowly walking back did I begin to appreciate that the sea of red was now like a storm. Up and down and bouncing. I thought about my mum and dad in there somewhere. I thought about what would be happening back home in Anglesey, in Llandovery, in Llanelli. I almost couldn't comprehend what had just happened. Only when I was back in position to receive the kick-off did all the pent-up energy release out of me. Screaming in the middle of that busy field.

There would be times ahead when I would be injured or chasing form. Times would get hard in ways I couldn't imagine. When they did, I would take myself back to this moment. This would be one of the fuels that kept me going – this energy, the warmth it gave me.

But it wouldn't happen yet. There are very few Test matches I've actually enjoyed as I'm playing them. The enjoyment comes post-game when you've got the time to process, when you're having those conversations – 'Do you remember that move?' 'We did that …' 'Oh, we had him turned on that attacking strategy.' 'Oh, that was exactly the picture we've seen all week …'

I was ecstatic. Don't get me wrong. I was hissing to the gills. But I couldn't give myself to all that emotion, because it was so early on in the match. It was so early on in the three-part series. We hadn't just won it. We were ahead on the scoreboard for the first time, and only just. So much rugby to be played, starting with exiting from this re-start.

That's why I took a water bottle from our doctor James Robson when he came on. I didn't need fluids. But it's the default action. It's normality. 'Okay, doc's there. I'll take a drink. I'll give it back to him.' It's the way you reset, it's the way you refocus.

Into the usual sort of chinwags in the middle of the park. The moving debriefs, the tweaks to the plan in the heat of battle.

'What are you seeing? What are we seeing in attack? What are we seeing in the defence?'

'Let's tighten it up.'

'Let's put a bit more width on that first phase so we get in round the corner.'

'Right, what else needs to be done?'

It's not romantic. But elite sport isn't about misty eyes, not until it's all done. You're in a process. You're in an 80-minute battle. You're not a spectator who can launch their pint in the air and climb on their mate's back and enjoy every second of it. Imagine if you went all cock-a-hoop midway through the first half and then lost the match. Enjoy? Not yet. Not for a long time.

It was always going to go back to blow for blow. A proper old caveman fight. I thought I'd gone over in the same corner again, when I smashed into Genia and Folau and the referee went upstairs and the TMO decided my left elbow was in touch as I grounded the ball. What did I think? It was a try. I still do.

We went back for a penalty. Leigh Halfpenny kicked it. We went ahead. All living out the truth we instinctively knew: in the heat of battle you haven't got time to think, you just do. How quickly it all shifts and changes in a Test match: the early waves of pressure, their score, them all over us; a loose kick, we score, we stay down there, then I almost score again. Elite sport may not be romantic when you're in it, but it can be beautiful.

Folau then scored another ridiculous try. Not that I was seeing an individual battle between the two of us. I was just feeling those blows coming one way then the other. I was living my caveman life.

It was one of those games where you don't really say much at half-time. The score's 13–12, and everyone is so tuned in there's no need for an *Any Given Sunday* speech. A collective understanding of where we were, how far we'd come and the opportunity ahead of us.

From 13–12, and then 18–12 after Alex Cuthbert sliced through, to 20–12 after Halfers converted. The move Cuthy scored off? Block Tune. Foxy did a great job on it, and this was peak Cuthy, unstoppable from that distance out, with his gas and strength, but it was our good old trusty classic. The one that gets me my first ever Test try, the one we score with against Ireland in the World Cup. Rob Howley's favourite ever play, and why not?

Still a lot of time left. That was when the Wallabies started winning penalties and kicking them. O'Connor with three points, Kurtley Beale with three more. Three from Halfers, Beale going on a crazy mazy run and nearly getting all the way through, but them winning a penalty and Beale banging it over to go 23–21 with 12 minutes to go.

That's the sign of a good Test team, when you can keep that scoreboard going. The best sort of battle to find yourself in, going blow for blow, hit for hit, point for point. Doing everything you can to stay in it, doing everything you can to edge in front.

Beale had a very kickable one to put the Wallabies in front. He sliced it wide. Then, clock almost in the red, they won a scrum penalty near halfway.

It's the same as when you score yourself. You don't lose yourself in the emotion of it all. You process it. Okay, anything can happen here. He could kick it, so do we have time for a re-start, and if we do, what's our best option for contesting it? He could miss it – who's making the catch, who's kicking the ball dead? He could hit the post or the crossbar – and if that happens, it could be chaos, and they could gather it and score, so where should I be to gather it instead?

Beale missed. His standing foot slipped on the churned-up turf. The ball scudded long but low. Bod and Halfers watched it bounce and roll over the dead-ball line. We had made it.

They left 14 points out there, the Wallabies. O'Connor had missed a conversion and two penalty shots too. A big number, when you think about a night like that, when you think about a Test series. I got heat, afterwards, from some of their fans, in some of the media, about the moment with Genia. They thought I had been taunting him. I hadn't. It had been the celebration that turned into half a hand-off that turned into an accidental wave. I spoke to Will after the game, because he's such a good bloke. I explained and I apologised. He told me not to worry about it.

I didn't lose sleep over it, even when questions kept coming in the press conferences that next week. One of my favourite ever Test matches, one of my favourite ever tries, the second Test closing in fast. Eat, sleep, recover, train, get ready to go again.

Cavemen do as cavemen will. The second Test was nothing like the first, in some ways, but exactly like it too. One try rather than four, a kickfest, a drawn-out slog; a penalty missed at the end to win it, an even narrower victory margin, another moment to stick around with me for the rest of my days.

Oh, and the intensity went up a notch, too. That's what happens when the touring team win the first match of a Lions series. Revenge is in the air. It might not have been pure running rugby, and Halfers and Christian Leali'ifano may have taken it in turns trading penalties, but it never let up, when you were in the guts of it. Seeing the best of these 30 players, and the ones coming off the bench: their physicality, their determination, the little bursts of excellence.

A flash of something from one side, shut down by the other. A moment of something outrageous, then a reaction and scramble to recover. Defence trying to squeeze the space and cut the time; a furious level of concentration, an absence of air in the lungs.

We were 12–9 up and an hour was on the clock when it got messy in the middle of the pitch and Drico grabbed the loose ball and passed it back to me between his legs.

'Oh my God, that's a nuts pass!'

The last thought I had before I looked up and saw Folau right in front of me, coming in hard and fast. Now Folau is many things, but he's also a big old lump. I had the ball in my hands but I was isolated. One mistake or moment of invention could win this match. I had to get some go-forward before he took me down. Without momentum we might not secure the ball. If we didn't secure the ball, they would be coming at us with turnover space ahead of them. And those Wallabies loved a broken backfield and disjointed defence.

Folau all over me. Me trying to get under his grappling arms, to get my legs going. Dropping my shoulders and driving.

Just like that, he was on my shoulder. No time to do anything much but keep driving with the legs.

One step, two steps, three steps.

George, what the fuck is going on here?

Four steps, five steps, six.

George, what are you doing?

George, this is not going to end well …

It felt like an eternity, when it was happening. And then one moment I was driving him backwards and his feet were in my face, and the next he was falling backwards and my head was going straight down with him and I hit the ground and pain was blasting up my neck.

I know a little bit about pro wrestling, and I believe that move is known as a DDT, when you have someone in a front headlock and you make them fall on their own head like that. It was not a pleasant sensation. You may be familiar with the Mike Tyson meme where he says, matter-of-fact: 'I broke my back. It's spinal.' That's what I thought, as I lay there with the game moving on a few yards away. My neck was in tatters. The doc came on and I tried to get back control of my breath, and I was able to carry on. It probably should have been a penalty, really, but to be fair to Craig Joubert you maybe don't expect to see a DDT after one player has worn another like a human backpack. And in some ways Izzy had defended it really well, because if I had got on the outside of him and got round him, I was one-on-one with their replacement second row, Rob Simmons.

The neck settled down. It was sore for a few days, when I moved my head a little too quick and it just caught for a second or two. What was weird to me, after that moment, was how big the Folau carry seemed to become, and how long afterwards people have wanted to talk to me about it. It's cool to do something that a lot of Lions supporters told me gave them much joy. It's amazing to be recognised for anything, more than a decade after it happens. But it didn't actually mean much in the context of the game. We didn't get a penalty, and we didn't recycle the ball and smash our way down the pitch. The move just sort of spluttered to a messy halt by the left touchline. It didn't change the scoreline, and it happened in a game we went on to lose. In short, it did nothing for us. It just got a huge amount of hype and I got a bad neck which eventually cleared up.

I'm still glad it happened. I'd rather be remembered for carrying Izzy Folau through Melbourne than not be remembered at all. In the words of the romantic poet Tennyson: 'Better to have loved and lost than never to have loved at all.'

It wasn't a particularly good try to concede, the one they scored late on from Adam Ashley-Cooper. Drico was covering O'Connor, Foxy's got two and Tommy Bowe had last man. But Foxy went slightly to O'Connor too, and then there was a momentary gap, and that's all you need, at a level like this. Neither does it really matter, whether you rate it as a piece of attacking play or a fractional defensive misread. They all count, and what it meant in the series was huge. We were one Test-apiece with one to play. Now the romantics could sleep happily in their beds again.

Gats took us up to Noosa before that epic decider down in Sydney. Back up north of Brisbane for some sunshine and good food, jump in the water for some bodyboarding and surfing and just take a clean break from all that tension before we dived back down into the haunches of it all. A classic Wales move, from that time: stay away from the pressure pot until the Thursday, then hit the captain's run on the Friday and get into the game. No messing about, no letting it get to you.

It did all boot off that week, around selection. Maybe it was always going to. You win the first Test, lose the second, there are always going to be changes. I didn't see the big one coming, but I knew Gats too. When he dropped Drico, it was because he had a plan. Sentiment didn't come into it. And if it were possible to have any more admiration for a man than I did already for Ireland's greatest ever centre, I experienced it after the way Drico reacted to being left out that week. He made no pretence about being happy; there were big conversations between him and Gats, and if some of them were private, some of them were hard to miss. Sometimes you weren't quite sure where to look. But when you got to the actual training days, the last few critical hours before we went back into battle to see which of the two teams would prevail – then Drico was the one driving the standards, and Drico was the one building the energy. The hurt he was feeling was obviously huge, and yet he could stick all that in a box for later and throw everything he had into doing what was best for the team. I still felt like a callow kid, compared to him. And that week I realised you couldn't ask for a better role model. The quality of the man was impossible to miss.

Gats loved those sorts of occasion. A chance to show what he was made of, to flourish under that pressure. He loved firing off a few rockets in his press conferences, just as Eddie Jones did too with different teams. I tried to ignore them, in the main. It already felt like the biggest game of my life. We were the ones who would have to go out there and perform. You wanted to keep it as simple as possible. Train hard.

Know your roles. Trust in each other. That's how it works, when it works well.

And then it ended up as one of the best games I would ever be involved in. As a team, but from the selfish point of view of individual performance too. Genia knocked on from the kick-off, a minute later Alex Corbisiero was burrowing over for our first try. We got dominance at the set-piece, they had a man in the bin, Halfers kept kicking pens.

We were 19–3 up quite quickly, and we probably should have been out of sight. I got a good whack in on Izzy. One more score and we probably would have broken them. We had enough dominance to be at least another score up.

Instead, almost as fast, we were back at 19–16. O'Connor danced and wriggled his way through. Leali'ifano picked off a couple of penalties. The exuberance we saw from them in the first two Tests, that rapid offloading game, those little half line-breaks – they were suddenly coming at us again, and we had to do something about it.

And we did, and it was beautiful to be part of. Cutting through them down the left, Halfers in space and me in support on his outside, and him choosing to go inside and put Sexton away instead. He's never asked my forgiveness for not making that pass; okay, Genia was maybe covering me, but I'd have fancied beating him again at that point. Then Halfers made up for it with another break, and this time he did find me accelerating up on his outside, and that left-hand corner was free and empty for me to slide into once again.

I think we knew, then. I think they did too. The momentum and match had gone. The mountain they had to climb, the timeframe they had to do it in. When Jamie Roberts ran onto Conor Murray's short pass for our third try in 12 minutes, all doubt disappeared into the fresh Sydney air.

So you could relish and cherish every second of the last 10 minutes or so, because you knew that even if every one of us had a howler, they were never going to make up a 25-point deficit. I had the single Welsh cap I'd dreamed of; now the Lions had come calling, and we had a record-breaking victory, and a series win. Even thinking about it all over again takes me straight back to cloud nine.

Actually, it takes me past that. The memories make me so happy I can barely talk about it anymore. I just smile. Afterwards, when we were back in the changing-room, bouncing around the place, screaming, joking, it started to get silly: James Bond turned up.

Now I'm a big, big James Bond fan, by the way. I'm 21 years old. And one moment I'm pouring beer over Jon Davies, and the next I look up and it's FUCKING JAMES BOND.

I don't get starstruck by many people. I was so starstruck by James Bond that I could only call him James Bond. Not Daniel, not Mr Craig, not mate. Just holy fuck, it's James Bond.

Maybe it's good I didn't know, in that beautiful moment, that I was in the peak of the Lions for me. I didn't know what would happen on the 2017 tour and I didn't know what would happen just before the 2021 one. I was still working out that sport can be cruel as well as wonderful. It was all still moving in straight lines for me: up, up, and away.

So let's leave me there, for now. Surrounded by all my mates, old and new. Grabbing souvenirs when I could find them. Wondering how my mum and dad would be feeling out there, what I might tell Becky when we spoke later. A British and Irish Lion, whatever else might come to pass. Sitting next to James Bond. JAMES FUCKING BOND.

Life was already changing, before that Lions tour. The time had come for me to leave Welsh regional rugby and begin a new chapter in the English Premiership.

Scarlets were keen to sell me to a French club. Maybe the money for them would have been better. For me, it was about silverware. I wanted to win trophies; I'd got a taste for it, now, with Wales. I wasn't ready for a move to France at that point. I could barely speak English and Welsh, let alone French, and it was a sight easier driving from the east Midlands to Manchester to see Becky than from south-west France. My sister Hayley also lived in Northampton. For the first time since leaving Rhoscolyn for Llandovery at the age of 16, I could have family around me. Hayley had three kids. They were three miles down the road, rather than 180. I could babysit, do the school drop-off, do pick-up. It was a prospect I absolutely loved.

It worked out a treat. I lived with Hayley for the first month. When I found my own house, I could pop round for a cup of tea anytime I liked. Northampton reminded me of Holyhead. It didn't fancy itself, but it was friendly. I could have felt under pressure when I first signed. I was a relatively big transfer, and then the Lions tour had happened. Instead any initial apprehension soon turned to excitement. It was a rugby town, and I was a rugby person. Fans would come to watch training every day. If you went out for food, people wanted to talk about how it was going.

And so the first year was incredible. We did win silverware, taking the European Challenge Cup at the Arms Park in Cardiff. Then my good mate Alex Waller scoring a try in the 100th minute to beat Saracens in the Premiership final after the longest TMO decision in history. To do it at Twickenham was special. To see what it meant to the town when we got back the next day underlined it all – the open-top bus through the town, the crowds, all of the boys in sunglasses because we were absolutely ratters. It all confirmed to me that I'd made the right decision.

We were tight as a team, and it showed on the pitch. We played for each other, and we enjoyed every minute, in those first few years. In any rugby squad there are players at different stages of their lives – married boys, engaged one, ones with young kids, single lads. I was lucky that at Saints there was a good group of younger guys. We would train hard and then enjoy each other's company, go to a café for lunch and recharge and play a few games of Monopoly Deal before I lost too many and got angry with myself and left. On the team WhatsApp group a message would go out – 'I've booked this place for food. The biggest table they've got is eight or ten. First people to reply will all go and meet there at 7 p.m.'

Other times it would be about helping each other out without thinking about it.

'I'm moving house, I need a hand moving stuff.'

'Oh, I've got a van.'

'Yeah, I'll come and give you a couple of hours.'

The thing I loved most about Northampton was that rugby was the heartbeat of the town. Everyone looked out for one another. Players, fans and owners all had a common goal, and an understanding of what we wanted to do and where we wanted to be. It made it an amazing club to be at, at the time, and if that changed towards the end, and the dream soured a little, with some of the personnel who came in – I'll always have a place in my heart for Saints, and I'll always have a place in my heart for the supporters, and for the Barwell family who owned the club. The Barwells were absolutely incredible with me. They were the heart and soul of that club, and I hope the love and respect were mutual. I could have happily finished my club career there, had things been different. That's how I feel about the place.

TEN

BUILTH WELLS TO BRECON: HOLDING ON

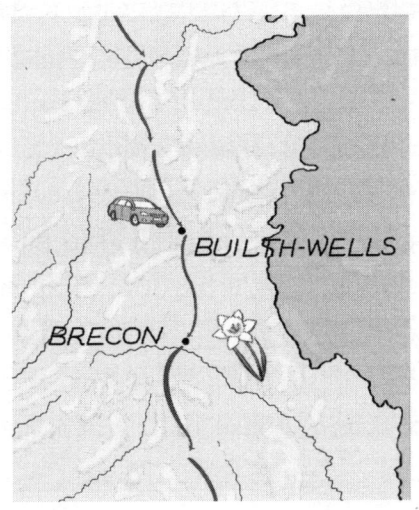

IN WHICH WE TALK ABOUT:

the C-word

I'm going to tell you quite a lot about concussion. Some of it will make sense. Some of it won't, unless you've been there. A big part of me doesn't even want to write this chapter, and not only because, as a rugby player, you don't want concussion to be part of your life story.

When you're knocked out in front of nine million people watching on television, and then it happens again in the same match, your personal health becomes a national debate. People you've never been in the same room with discuss in depth on TV and in newspapers something they have no specific knowledge about. I have a slight fear that by talking about it here, I'm going to trigger that all over again. But I've got to be honest about what happened to me, and what I did about it, and why the single hardest thing I've had to deal with in my career might actually be one of the best things I've done too.

What does concussion feel like? Each one happens in a different way, and each one feels different when it does.

My first came in the autumn international against New Zealand in 2014. Alun Wyn Jones and me in the defensive line together, coming in to tackle the same man and cracking heads and going down. Alun Wyn got up. I did not, for a while – at least not until the All Blacks had exploited the space left out wide to put Jerome Kaino over in the far corner for their second try.

I was aware something had happened. Like something had just stunned me. I wasn't out cold but I wasn't good either. You know the thing where a dog gets tapped on the nose, and it looks confused and stops in its tracks? That's what it felt like. A glitch in time, a jump cut that doesn't quite make sense.

I didn't feel worried. Certainly not panicked. I wasn't trying to stagger to my feet and get moving again. Sensible thoughts in my head.

'Oh, I've had a good whack here …'

A pause, a moment of self-appraisal.

'Something's … I don't feel quite right.'

It made the next part quite simple. Even before the medical team did the Head Injury Assessment and made the right decision, I had done my own evaluation.

'Well, if I'm not right, how can I put the team at risk and go back out when I can't do the job I'm supposed to be doing?'

And you have complete trust in the experts, in these moments. I was 22 years old, still a young man in a big world, still stacking up the new experiences. The medical team had got me through every knock and injury I'd had. In the same way as I believed in the boys I was shoulder to shoulder with in every session and every game, I believed in our backroom team. I followed the protocols and we all did everything right. I was a bit rough, but I didn't play for a few weeks, and I came through all the tests and I was fine.

There was something one of my own auntie-not-aunties used to say when I was a kid: you've only got one noggin, so look after it. I agreed with her. Why wouldn't you? But sometimes things happen to you that are outside your control. What I had no way of knowing was that this was only the start of a horrible spell for me.

Against England in the opening match of the new year's Six Nations, I took a boot to the chin from their lock Dave Atwood. I went off. I had an HIA. I passed, and came back on. Twenty minutes into the second half, trying to stop Mike Brown going over in the corner, I smacked heads with Richard Hibbard, and went down again.

This time I didn't go off. I played on.

Neither of the two were deliberate actions. There was also nothing I could have done about them. When you're rehabbing, you look after that particular part of your body. You build up other areas – do your knee work, do your quad and hamstring strengthening, bring in a lot of balance stuff. All of it to prepare you for the forces that will hit you and turn you and test you in a game.

You can't ask someone to kick you in the head. You can't practise dealing with head collisions. This is international rugby. The speed of it takes some things out of your control. You've got a split-second going into contact, and you always try to get your body and your head in the right place. But you're not the only input. There's the man you're tackling, and there's where he's going, and where his team-mates might be trying to shove him, and where your own team-mates are coming in from and the split-second decisions they're making.

So it happened twice in the same game. And whereas with the concussion against the All Blacks I knew straightaway, with the kick to the head I didn't. I had ultimate trust in the medical team. They do the right thing at the time, you follow it, and you pass it, and you go back on.

The Hibbard one? Of all the heads I could have met, I hit one which is about four days' thick. This time, I was out cold. I was gone.

Why did I stay on? There was an investigation from World Rugby in the aftermath. It found a systematic error rather than a human one. Our medical team had missed the second head injury. They had no access to video replays. Our coaches had our analysts and their laptops next to them, but they were used to turning round instant reviews of passages of play, rather than medical issues.

That was the turning point, that Friday night in Cardiff. They would change the system after that. The medics would have access to replays. For now, around me, there seemed to be an uproar. Why wasn't I taken off? Why didn't I go off myself? Why was I deliberately making it worse?

This was new to me. There was the recovering from the physical injury, and there was trying to cope with the wave of hostile opinions. You play rugby for Wales, you expect to get told, by strangers, where you're going wrong on the pitch, just as much as you'll be loved when it goes right. This was something else. It wasn't about the rugby or the results. It wasn't really Welsh supporters, very often. It was people I'd never met, with no medical experience, who had never examined me. Advice from the wild west of uninformed opinion.

You can't do this. You shouldn't do that. This is what's wrong. This is what you should be doing.

It all seemed to miss a fundamental truth: who, out of all these random strangers, was more concerned about my brain than me? Not all elite sportspeople are academically gifted.

But none of us are stupid enough to put the long-term health of our most important organ at anywhere less than an absolute priority.

That was 6 February. Seven weeks later, it happened again. Different game, different part of the pitch, different players.

Different impact. Same result.

I was playing for Northampton against Wasps at Franklin's Gardens. I was playing well. I'd scored one try and had just gone over in the left-hand corner when Nathan Hughes jumped in late and caught me with a knee to the back of the head.

He was sent off. I was properly out cold, again. Treated on the pitch for several minutes, and then carried off on a stretcher.

Do those four incidents seem linked to you? A clash of heads with a second row on our 10-metre line. An opposition boot to the face. A clash of heads with a hooker by the corner flag. An opposition knee to the head after scoring a try.

I wasn't making mistakes. I certainly wasn't repeatedly doing something stupid. I made tackles in every game. I attempted to score tries whenever I could.

But something had to change. Four concussions in five months is bad news. No-one cared about my brain as much as I did.

I sat down with the Northampton medical staff, and I sat down with the WRU. I told them I wanted to explore it all more – what had happened, how my head was, what we should do beyond the existing protocols. What we might be able to do to stop it happening all over again.

Both organisations were very proactive. I was recommended a specialist. I felt optimistic; he had been suggested to both the WRU and Saints. The first hint that I might be seeing the wrong man came when he talked about the patients he worked with. He was a specialist in the most traumatic things that can happen to a brain: cancers, vast surgeries, incurable diseases. Not concussions. Then, when I told him how I felt, there were no tests. No looking at my brain, no scans. He just asked me about the impacts and how I experienced them. He told me to take a month off from proper rugby and come back to him. Basically, do an extended return to play protocol, spread out across four weeks.

I was not in a good place at this point. I felt a constant pressure in my head. I was sensitive to lights, and I was struggling with my balance. If I closed my eyes, I'd fall over. At times Becky thought I must be taking the mickey. I was incapable of doing the washing-up, because I couldn't stand long enough and I couldn't cope with the noises and stimulation.

'Just take a month ...'

What was that based on? How was I supposed to recover? What happened when the month ended?

None of it felt right. Sometimes I'd try to say a sentence, and I'd get my words back to front. Not on a tongue-twister, but in an ordinary sentence. I'd try to say, I'll meet you at three, and what would come out was, I'll three meet you. I wouldn't even notice. Someone else would have to point it out to me.

It was late April now. The domestic season might have been coming to an end, but the Rugby World Cup was coming closer every week. Wales' opening game against Uruguay was on 20 September. The final tournament squad was going to be announced on 31 August; the training squad was coming out 1 June.

All the time, the clock in my head ticking. The clock in my head with the minute and second hands going in opposite directions.

I wanted to be right for the World Cup. I wasn't going to put myself at any risk. These two positions didn't need to be opposing, but they had equal potency to me. So I went back to see the specialist, and I got the same troubling feeling that we were not in the right hands.

'How are you feeling?'

'Well, I've done the return to play stuff. I haven't done any skills, because that's what we agreed, and I haven't done any contact.'

Still no tests. He sort of looked at me, made some notes and then said, 'Take another month, and extend it again.'

I don't want to speak ill of him, because he was clearly very good in his area. His area may just not have been elite sportspeople with concussion. And now my frustrations began to grow, because I could no longer figure out a safe way forward. I was trying to do the right things, at the exact point where outsiders seemed to be assuming I was doing the wrong things. I was in Northampton, my mum and dad were in Anglesey. Becky was training hard at the velodrome in Manchester. I had a sister and her family in Northampton, and they were brilliant, but their lives were busy. For a lot of the time I was alone.

People made comparisons that made no sense. A few ex-players talked of their own experiences as if they were mine. I had every sympathy with how they felt and how they had been treated, but their game was not my game. There was an era when players did contact every day, not just skill-set contact, but level three – the hardcore stuff. Lads would get knocked out in a game, get up and play on. They could be out cold, get a slap in the face and smelling salts under the nose, and be pushed back on. Afterwards they'd go out on the drink; they'd eat bad food, they'd do all those unpleasant bonding games that old rugby players liked to do. Me? I was an academy kid. Even as schoolboys we had been told that a knock to the head meant we came off the field.

'Don't put yourself at risk.'

'Make sure you're okay before playing.'

Of course I will. It's my brain. Who in their right mind would not?

I lay there for hours one night, and I let the anger and frustrations lead me naturally to a point. Something had to change. I would have to be the one who changed it.

'Right, George, of course you're going to do something about it. You're not going to sit here and ignore this, because this is much bigger than anything you've ever had to deal with before.'

I went back to the WRU, and I went back to Northampton. I asked for a second opinion. And that was when I met Professor Tony Belli for the first time.

Professor Belli is director of the Surgical Reconstruction and Microbiology Research Centre at the University of

Birmingham. He is a world-leading expert in concussion. And he was brilliant.

The first time I went to see him, I was there for five hours. We did a long series of different checks: cognitive tests, balance tests, maths, problem-solving. We did two MRI scans. I had blood tests. We looked at my saliva, since he was leading some research in the markers concussion can leave. When we had done all of that, we sat down and talked frankly about where I was and what my most pressing concerns were. At the end, we had a plan.

It felt revolutionary. It felt like hope. Straight away I had a confidence that had been entirely absent before.

'George, I've seen this before. I've seen it worse. I've seen it better. And this is how we go about it.'

There are certain experts you speak to, and their knowledge is so obvious and their credentials so good you can't help but trust them. He had a confidence in himself. He had the track record and the research to back it up. So when he said to me, you will have six months with no contact in training whatsoever, I didn't worry about what it meant for my World Cup chances. It was my World Cup chances. It was my career, if I still wanted one.

I met him every month after that. A check-up every time, an assessment. Building the information they had about me, finding the patterns and the long-term implications. All the while, the experts who had never met me were giving their thoughts to the media, and the media were amplifying them. Dr Barry O'Driscoll, a former World Rugby medical advisor and uncle to my Lions team-mate Bod, was being quoted everywhere. I'm sure he was coming from a place of concern, and trying to make the game safer. But he had never spoken to me, never seen my medical notes. And when someone reads an article quoting a doctor, they tend to assume they're absolutely right in what they're saying. Well-meaning though these medical experts may have been, they were actually making my life a lot harder, because every person I saw, everyone who spotted me in the street, would be giving the same erroneous advice to me.

Social media was changing the world. So were news aggregators. An article would come out and then get spun by another news agency and be rehashed a hundred times. Algorithms would pick up the spikes of interest and outrage and fling them out some more.

Everyone had an opinion. I'd go to Tesco for my shopping and four people would tell me where I was going wrong. I'd switch to Morrisons and five more would drop their thought-bombs on me. In a house by myself, with no proper training to throw myself into, it became hard not to start questioning myself at times. I went back to Anglesey to stay with Mum and Dad for a week, not to search my soul on long walks along the beach but just to escape my own head for a bit. They did all the mum and dad things that parents should do. They also communicated their own concerns and fears, because naturally they were reading the same stories as everyone else. Each morning there would be something new. Mum would come down for breakfast looking worried sick.

'Ah, I've just read this article from another doctor. What do you think?'

And I would say, 'Mum, why are you reading it?' even when I knew she couldn't help but read it because she was being protective and it was about her son and it was about my health.

There were moments when I honestly thought about just jacking it all in. About going abroad and finding somewhere to hide away. This was not what I was playing rugby for. I wanted to play rugby to represent my country. I wanted to be the best that I could be every day. I wanted to push myself and be pushed and then, when it was all over, know that I had given it everything I possibly could.

That week I realised I had a choice. I could either bottle it up and become really angry and bitter about it all, or process it and deal with all that came with it. Because if I didn't, it was going to melt me to the core.

One morning, I told my parents something else I'd said to Professor Belli at our first meeting, around the time he was filling me with confidence about his approach and expertise.

'Look, if you turn round to me today and say: "George, it's not worth it. I can see a huge impact on your brain. There's a massive decrease in your cognitive function, your memory," then I'll get up, shake your hand and I'll walk out and that's me done.'

Then I told them his response.

'George, I completely get it and I'd be the first person to tell you that. But at the moment, I know you've had four concussions in a short amount of time. But your brain health and your functions aren't showing deterioration. You can be okay.'

So I stuck with him, when I drove back from Rhoscolyn, across the Menai Strait and along the coastal road past Conwy and Colwyn Bay, back into northern England and the M6 and the M1. I didn't go near contact in training. I did his tests, monitored all the things we should. Then we started the rehabbing: looking at ways to strengthen my neck muscles, and then the tendons and nerves that control the balance in your neck, so next time a knee or boot came calling or someone blindsided me there would be a limit to the whiplash movement of my head. I had to be realistic. If I did return to rugby, I would be hit. It's a contact sport. There would be no 5-metre exclusion zone around me.

At the same time, I tried to work out how to deal with the well-meaning people who were making it all so much harder. Losing my shit with them was not me and it wasn't helping. I would have to process it in a different way, compartmentalise it so it didn't affect me as it had been.

I made the World Cup. I felt good. I felt better than before. When our race was done, I went back to see the Prof. I told him how amazing it had been to work with him. I told him I'd like to carry on, even now there was no medical reason to – keep doing regular tests, keep monitoring.

He told me we didn't need to. But, if I was comfortable with it, he'd facilitate it all. So that's what we did. At the start and end of each season, I would go back to Birmingham to see him. The MRI scans, the cognitive and balance tests, the problem-solving. More work for the Prof, better for me. He was there for a phone call if I was ever worried about something; I could drop him an email if I wanted any testing.

I felt protected. Why wouldn't you, when you had the attention of someone in whom you had the utmost trust? The people who doubted me – somehow, they seemed to turn it back on me. I'd get the familiar line about doing damage to myself. I'd tell them that I was taking significant precautions, that I was seeing a specialist twice a year of my own choice and doing my own stuff well beyond the usual recommendations. And they would nod their heads as if I'd just inadvertently made a secret admission.

'Ah-ha, why are you doing that? There's a problem, isn't there …'

Sometimes it felt like they just wanted to get stuff off their chests, and I was the public face of their chosen topic. The poster boy for the poster no-one wants to be on. David Beckham and Freddie Ljungberg got Calvin Klein underwear. I got concussion.

I could be on a beach in the off-season, sipping a mojito. Someone else would get concussed, in some other sport, and the headlines and articles would all be about me again. I could get through season after season without a problem, all my tests clear, and the clash of heads with Richard Hibbard in 2015 would come round again, like some monstrous Ferris wheel I just couldn't climb off.

So I had to take a deep breath, and put it all in the concussion box. George, remember that what's happened to you has at least highlighted what a massive issue it is to the sport you love, and what a danger it can be. It's forced rugby to get a lot better at dealing with it – forced it to learn more and understand more, to do more and protect its players. I would think about the fantastic care I was receiving, about how that made me feel and how it made my family feel. By the end of that, I was ready to pick the mojito back up and push away the doubters for another day.

So here we are, 10 years on. I do my catch-ups with the Prof. He picks up my WhatsApps. He tells me that a cognitively-challenged brain will always be healthier than a non-cognitively challenged brain, so I have a list of different games and brain-teasers that I do every day, just to keep my head ticking over. I'm trying to learn French, with mixed results. I've gone deep into the world of supplements that help with cognitive function and brain health. I have businesses outside rugby, and I'm trying to learn from them all the time. Because it's my brain, and it's my life. Do you honestly think I would sit there and do nothing about my own health?'

Even if I explain all of this to some people, they won't hear it. They have their own experiences and preconceptions. I'm the poster boy. I'm the lightning rod. There's not much else I can do about that now.

I've always understood what an emotive topic concussion is in rugby. I know how important it is for the game at all levels, not just for us internationals but at grassroots. As a father myself now with a wife and a young family, I know inside that I'm doing everything I can to look after myself. I just never wanted to be Concussion George. So it was the hardest time in my life, and something I probably shouldn't have gone through, but I did, and I hope it's made the game a better place.

Because I don't want my career to be remembered for one 2013 summer tour and the C-word. When I sit there in my house in my dotage, slightly drunk because I've been at the rugby club, and I've got curry down the front of my shirt and my tie, I don't want someone to turn round to me and say: 'Ah, you're the fellow who lifted that guy on your shoulder and had concussions.' I'd rather my name came up when people talk about some of the best players that Wales has produced. That was always the dream, and it hasn't gone away.

ELEVEN

BRECON TO MERTHYR TYDFIL: COMING CLOSE

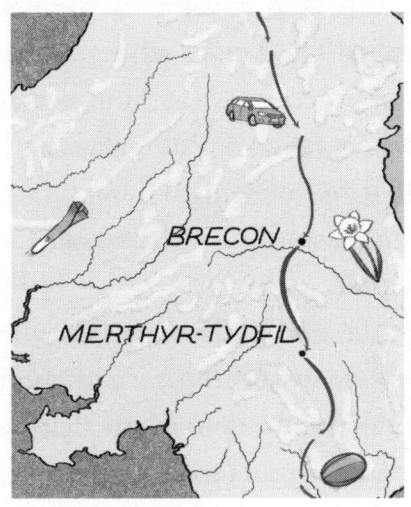

IN WHICH WE TALK ABOUT:

cable car PTSD/getting hammered in Doha/50 caps in/World Cup injury crises/Tom Jones knows Scott Williams/'They're not like England. They're tough fuckers'/a Welsh rugby miracle/ the noise, the noise/Mike Brown gets angry, again/great expectations/13 Wallabies hold out/Vermeulen goes genius/ a moment with Sam/the sword you live and die by/'Yep, I know how it feels …'

Here's a silver lining to six months as a rugby player with no contact, after four concussions in four months: when I was picked for Wales' squad for the 2015 Rugby World Cup, I actually felt quite refreshed.

The emphasis here is on silver lining. I would have liked to have been playing. I would love to have been riding tackles and diving over trylines. I would have been perfectly happy making tackles and then rolling away so Sam Warburton could get over the ball and go to work. At times it was a little weird, this loop of practising, watching, practising, watching.

But you know me, by now. I'm a glass half-full guy, and if that glass was half full of semi-skimmed rather than full-fat milk for now, the reasons all made sense, and my body was showing its gratitude.

Refreshed was a good place to be, when we went to Switzerland for our first pre-tournament training camp. You'd expect widespread celebrations that we weren't going back to Poland and its cruel forests and bang-average canteen food, and there was certainly a delusion about what might await in the sunny Alps – elite-level chocolate, a level of comfort befitting a land of bankers and easy wealth.

This would turn out to be a heinous misreading of the Gatland way. There was a minging few weeks in Cardiff to pre-heat the oven, so to speak, but when we got to Switzerland we found our gooses being well and truly cooked. Have you ever suffered PTSD at the sight of a cable car? I still do, as a result of what they put us through in those weeks.

We slept high and trained low, the classic methodology for getting fit fast. Training at 1,500 metres, because sports science tells you that's the highest you can go and still put in the same intensity you can at sea-level; sleeping at 2,500 metres, because that's the best place for adapting and making more efficient use of oxygen. We got from our high sleeping place to our low training ground via the cable cars. It was summer, and the snow and its skiers were long gone, so the frequency of the service reflected the reduced demand. This led to two unpleasant issues: if you missed the cable car you had intended to catch, you were guaranteed to be late to the session, which is not an option under any regime featuring Shaun Edwards. Even when you did catch the scheduled cable car, you knew exactly where it was taking you and which levels of pain were coming your way. It's probably an exaggeration to describe those vertical morning commutes as like descending to hell, but only just.

It became something of a love-hate relationship, Switzerland and me. I'm an outdoor person. I found Anglesey awesome, so when I found myself in a place where the mountains were much higher and the meadows greener and the opportunities to do outdoor things all the more enticing, I was all in. I loved being outside, I loved the hiking trails and I loved how far and how fast you could theoretically go on a mountain bike.

At the same time, we were being flogged. Is an alpine meadow still beautiful when you're lying on your back in it, trying not to be sick? Is a mountain still awe-inspiring when you've also got Shaun Edwards towering over you? The enjoyment was a retrospective thing, if it happened at all – when you felt that Gats/Edwards fitness coming, when you saw the weights you were lifting and the times you were running. When you went to the next camp in Doha and suddenly realised quite how unpleasant the desert is in summer compared to a mountain and its dinky cable cars.

The thinking was this: do the altitude training stimulus first, then do the heat stimulus. You might well point out that we were preparing for a World Cup at sea-level in autumnal London. We would have done, had we not been in so much physical distress. The facilities in Doha were incredible. There's a machine we had at the Vale in South Wales called a Biodex: they're incredibly expensive, something like a quarter of a million pounds each, so our one in Wales had understandably been purchased second-hand. The rehab centre in Doha had four of them; three were still in their packaging. But if the set-up was mind-blowing, so was the heat. The evening we arrived, sun long gone below the horizon, we did a late-night session – nothing too intense, just to get us moving. At one point I looked around and saw Tom Francis spark out on the floor, covered in cold flannels and wet towels. If this was happening when we were just having a gentle move-about, what the hell was actual training going to do to us?

That fortnight it seemed increasingly ludicrous that I could claim to have PTSD from a mere cable car. As we completed our first units session and conditioning at 8.30 a.m. each morning, it would already be 40°C. Because this was only the start of the day's temperature adventures, we then had to wait until last thing at night to return to the rugby field. There had been much talk about the changes they were making to Twickenham for our World Cup group matches against England and Australia. Quite how they were going to add 30 °C to a mid-September evening I was looking forward to finding out.

I won my 50th cap in one of the warm-up games against Ireland. I felt the contact and enjoyed its unfamiliarity. I didn't linger on the personal landmark because the game itself meant little, and 50 had come round so fast I was used to the concept of just keeping going and keeping going. The thing we were preparing for outweighed that particular day.

I was fit, but too many of my favourite team-mates were not. Jon Davies had ruptured his anterior cruciate ligament in May, scoring a try for Clermont against Montpellier. Rhys Webb suffered a bad knee injury in our final warm-up game, against Italy; in the second half of that game, Leigh Halfpenny did his anterior cruciate too. Gats called up Eli Walker, who did his hamstring within a week of joining up with us. Centre Cory Allen came in for our opening group match against Uruguay and pulled his hamstring too. Liam Williams hadn't played since June, after a foot injury. He went off after half an hour. We had three props – Samson Lee, Aaron Jarvis and Paul James – all in some sort of serious bother.

Forget the lingering nightmares about Switzerland and Doha. This felt like the real stuff of tortured dreams. Wales' first choice XV since I had made my debut five autumns before had always been good enough to take on anyone in the world. Where we struggled a little was in the depth of the squad around that. When you're drawing your talent from only four regional sides, it narrows the odds on your inclusion as a player, but it also means the shelves in the cupboard are seldom groaning. When you're into a World Cup that fires games at you fast – England coming the next Saturday, then Fiji in Cardiff on the Thursday, then Australia back at Twickenham the following Saturday, and a week's turnaround before any possible quarter-final – it could have scuppered us before we'd really begun.

If you were the type to enjoy a flutter, you'd have been backing the horse in white colours rather than the one in red, that Saturday night against England. This was England's home World Cup. They'd had a great Six Nations. They had pretty much all of their best players to choose from; they also had the mystery gift in the shape of Sam Burgess from rugby league, converting from flanker to centre, converting from never having started a match for England to starting in this huge one.

In all these things we saw, in all we had been through, we found motivation. I actually quite liked being written off before we had even gone toe to toe. As the injuries piled up, we trained and we focused. We drew strength from the bonds between us. When Burgess answered a question about facing Scott Williams by saying, 'Who's that?', and no-one was quite sure if he was joking, being honest or being offensive, we all logged it somewhere safe for personal interpretation. We had Tom Jones award our jerseys to us, and he definitely recognised our centre. I found a photo of Tom shaking Scott's hand and turned it into a meme to send round our group. The headline: 'At least Sir Tom Jones knows Scott Williams.'

*　*　*

So it was England against Wales, in a World Cup match at Twickenham. My thoughts were simple as we ran out onto the pitch: 'What better place to be, what better game to play?'

The atmosphere was unreal. They had transformed Twickenham, just in a way that had nothing to do with the temperature. It was like a rock concert or main stage festival vibe beforehand, and if you don't usually then progress to national anthems at a stadium gig, they successfully lifted things another few notches again. England came at us hard, as they were always going to do. We rolled with the punches, we stayed in touch. Swapping penalties, struggling at the set-piece, shipping a try to Jonny May when Ben Youngs went down the short side but never letting them get away on the scoreboard.

We were 22–12 behind at one point. We were down, but we also felt like we hadn't fired our shots yet. We weren't out of the equation, we just needed to balance the two sides of it up. And I felt okay about the hard work we would have to do, in that last 20 minutes. We had done the yards in Switzerland and been tenderised in Doha. We were quite happy being the underdogs, and we knew we could keep going and keep going.

Even with those injuries. Scott Williams went off. Liam Williams was gone, so too Hallam Amos. Dan Biggar went to full-back, I went to centre. Our replacement Lloyd Williams went out to take my slot on the left wing.

We should have been finished. Who can win a critical World Cup game against the tournament hosts at their home stadium with a scrum that's going backwards and a backline that looks like it's been thrown in the air and reassembled by how it lands?

This was us. This was Wales. There's the line that South Africa coach Rassie Erasmus comes out with in the *Chasing The Sun* documentary, before his Springboks side played us in the semis of the following World Cup: 'Wales are not softies. They're not like Ireland. They're not like England, who go away. They are tough fuckers.'

Chapeau, as the old cycling boys say. And so, on 70 minutes, we went wide. General phase play, nothing special or pre-planned. Biggs hitting the line from full-back, finding Lloyd Williams on the wing. Lloyd looking up at the covering white shirts, and putting his left foot through the ball and sending it crossfield, past the defenders, into the space in front of the posts. Into the space in front of Gareth Davies.

Here's what you need to know about Lloyd. He's one of the most skilful players I've ever seen. He can kick off both feet, he can pass off both hands. The kind of guy who starts playing golf and six months in is playing off single figures. The sort of team-mate you take on at table-tennis in the team hotel and get nilled by. He then switches the bat to his wrong hand and beats you again. That's the ability Lloyd Williams has. Nothing he did in that move was lucky. Nothing was flukey about the weight of that kick nor the bounce of the ball. That ball went where Lloyd wanted, exactly when he wanted it to.

Here's what you need to know about Gareth Davies getting to that ball. His supporting run was about seeing things happen before they were happening. His pick-up, off his toes and with his fingertips, would have been sensational in training. Such a hard skill when you're going full hiss. This was Twickenham. This was the World Cup. This was the game.

Except it wasn't, not quite yet. The conversion took us level at 25–25. But I could feel, in that moment, the momentum shift. Us under intense pressure, pressure, pressure, never breaking down. Us taking half a chance and holding onto it with both hands. It was like we'd been turbo-charged. Forget the no contact for six months. I could have run through walls all night long. I could have run through every wall from Twickenham to Rhoscolyn.

The noise, the noise! There were so many pockets of red in that stadium. Welsh fans are probably the best in the world. When it's Twickenham, they seem to find another voice. The songs were in my ears and the noise was in my chest and all of it was in my heart.

Three minutes later, Biggs putting a high kick up. Mike Brown claiming it, me the first one there to tackle him. Warbs and Gethin Jenkins straight on him to jackal, the usual suspects. And when referee Jerome Garces put his arm up to signal a penalty to us for holding on, Gethin getting a big pat on the back from Taulupe Faletau, and as he's doing that, me deciding to follow suit and give Mike Brown a good slap on the back too.

Unfortunately, this was the sort of thing I instinctively wanted to do in moments like that. And Mike Brown instinctively wanted to jump up and fight me, except I was walking away by now, and Jerome Garces was putting his hand on his chest as if to say, 'Mike, the moment's gone.'

Biggs nailed it, from all of 45 metres. Of course he did; he'd been ridiculous all night long. Now we were ahead, and when the final whistle went, six minutes later, and we were jumping on top of each other celebrating – if you could bottle it up and sell it, that feeling right there, you'd be a billionaire. If I could take a sip of it right now, it would taste like the elixir of life.

We went straight back to Cardiff that night. All the way along a dark M4 to the Vale, arriving sometime after 1 a.m. The Fiji game four days away, so not to bed, not straight-away, but into the cryotherapy chamber, a cold every bit as intense as the heat of Doha, but this time bouncing around, laughing and singing – not full of disbelief, at what we had done and how we'd done it, but joy, pure joy.

Us in a freezing wooden box in a nice hotel in Glamorgan, hundreds of thousands of Welsh men and women floating along in their own magic places up and down the country and in foreign lands. Us thinking of them, them thinking of us. All of us together, even when we were far apart.

Maybe I should have felt older at this point. My second World Cup, the quarter-finals beckoning after we beat Fiji, as comfortably as any Welsh team could beat Fiji in a World Cup. Fifty caps in and counting. But I was still only 23 years old, and if I had become one of the senior players in our group, it was through game experience, not the role I played within it. We had so many natural leaders in our squad – Sam, Alun Wyn, Biggs – that they were quite capable of carrying us onwards without needing an extra pair of hairy legs.

I drove my own standards, and I was pushing boys in training and within the camp. That felt natural and instinctive to me, and left me in a nice in-betweeny role; the boys weren't looking at me and asking what we should be doing, but when I chose to speak up, they would listen, and they would take it on board. I still had some of the minging jobs to do that you give to the youngsters, even if the pre-match dash for contraband chocolate had now moved to someone else. But I was also comfortable within the system. I'd learned a lot about myself, since our last World Cup quarter-final against Ireland in Wellington. I knew when I needed to push, and I knew when I needed to pull.

It wasn't a senior player pressure I felt, as we got ready to play Australia in our final group game. It was about expectations, and constantly delivering on them. That seemed to be the other side of having squeezed so many caps into such an early part of life, of having had a few great moments like the debut tries, and the ones in Dublin and Paris, and all those Lions adventures two summers before.

Once the question had been a basic one. 'Can this kid do it?'

Then it became slightly longer. 'Can he do it and survive?'

Now came the next level again. 'Okay, he can do it. He can survive. But can he do it week in, week out – every day, every game?'

This was new to me, and it wasn't always the easiest place to be. You know the old classic in school rugby – 'Oh, just give it to him, he'll do something ...' Possibly it was all in my head, but I felt it all, sometimes, as our denuded squad made its way towards the knockout stages. People looking at me to do something game-changing when the game-changing thing wasn't always on. 'Oh, he's good enough, so he can make it happen.'

Were these expectations a privilege? Maybe. Were they fair? Maybe not. But I couldn't complain. They were there because we were here, at the business end of a World Cup. We had beaten England on their home turf in a manner many believed to be miraculous. And once you've seen a miracle happen in front of your own eyes, you're a believer. You think the near impossible is within reach. You're all in.

We didn't beat Australia. Maybe I should rephrase that: we couldn't beat Australia. When they were down to 13 for a prolonged period, and we basically sat a metre off their tryline and battered it with different players in the same way for what felt like forever, we couldn't get through. When we did, they held us up. Maybe that spell on its own was a sign of where our campaign might end up. It certainly changed the points on the track. Instead of facing Scotland in the quarter-finals, it would be South Africa. A South Africa who under their own pressures had reverted to a familiar South African blueprint: big men doing hard yards, and then bigger men doing harder yards, before doing it all over again. The pretty stuff could wait for other teams.

Twickenham was our playground again, that Saturday afternoon in mid-October. A playground where you really fancy a go on the slide, but there's a group of massive kids hanging around it, and they don't want to let you anywhere close.

We were ready to graft. To shut the doors on the voices telling us we weren't good enough to pass this particularly brutal exam. I had a nice canter down the left wing early on before another type of door shut suddenly in my face.

Handre Pollard was doing Handre Pollard things. Dan Biggar was doing Dan Biggar things – dropping a goal, gathering his own up-and-under and then finding Gareth Davies outside him. Ten plus nine put us 13–12 ahead at half-time.

Physicality, everywhere you looked. Men going round the corner, other men trying to stop them. Biggs and Pollard trading penalties. Us 19–18 up, five minutes to go.

You can plan for most things in rugby. You can work out what might happen, and you can come up with strategies to mess those things up. And other times someone conjures up something that you didn't see coming, and even if you did it's done so well it wouldn't help you if you did, and there's nothing you can do about it and no amount of social media warriors piling in after eight pints on the sofa is going to change anything.

So it was in our right-hand corner. Our scrum had buckled on their initial push but then held, just. Then Duane Vermeulen used his left boot to keep the ball in, dug in with his hands, and set off.

Lloyd Williams went low. Alex Cuthbert came in off his wing to go high. Vermeulen's offload round his back to send Fourie du Preez into the corner didn't make sense to start with, from where I was on the other wing. It was slightly unreal, and then annoying, and pretty quickly became heartbreaking. In games that tight you know when the decisive moment has come. It's that momentum. It's the change of energy on the field and in the stands all around.

So people outside the camp wanted to fly into Cuthy afterwards. None of us did. When you've played at that level, you understand the nuances and you understand that sometimes it comes down to one player and one per cent. While it was unreal and annoying and heartbreaking, it was also trademark. Vermeulen could do that. He could do it in the last five minutes of a World Cup quarter-final. How many other players in the world could? That was the only difference.

Could we have gone further, had we held on? I don't know. When we had lost to France in that semi-final four years before, we had 59 per cent possession with our 14 men. We made France make twice as many tackles as we did. In this one against the Springboks, they made 101. We made 189.

A hundred and eighty-nine! It's brilliant in one regard, and it's absolutely the stamp of Shaun Edwards. It's also an insanely high number. Dan Lydiate made 21 tackles, and he was only on the pitch for 67 minutes. Warbs and Taulupe made 17 each, Alun Wyn 15, Luke Charteris 14, Jamie Roberts 12. In 2011 it had felt like we could have given New Zealand a far better game than France in the final. Had we got through to face them in the semi-finals this time, with our injuries, down to the bare bones physically but emotionally too, would it instead have been a game too far?

That World Cup in 2011 ended with me trying to console Warbs with chocolate while he sat on the toilet looking at Twitter haters on his iPad. This time we were next to each other on the pitch. Each with our arm around the other's waist, both of us simultaneously looking gutted but desperately trying to cheer the other one up a bit.

Now Sam is one of my best mates. He's one of the best captains I've ever played with. He's amazing with a few carefully chosen words, and I can talk like a blizzard made up of thoughts I've just plucked from the skies as I've gone along. In that moment, arms pulling the other to us, neither of us had any idea what to say. Most people had written us off before the tournament. The rest had written us off as it progressed. And apart from five minutes to go and one of the best offloads you'll ever see in your life, we were still in there, fighting shoulder to shoulder, trusting each other, emptying out everything we had.

Two years before, when Sam had been man of the match against Scotland in the Six Nations, we'd shared a full embrace on the pitch. Him riding a wave of shit in the media for weeks, being told he wasn't good enough, that he'd lost form. We both loved *Any Given Sunday*, the classic American Football film with Al Pacino and Jamie Foxx and Dennis Quaid. We loved the bit where the defensive end comes round after getting injured making a critical tackle, looks at the medics carrying him off on a stretcher and says, 'Don't you guys drop me, I'm worth a million dollars ...'

Elite sport is brutal. You have to look after your mates. So as we embraced after the Scotland game, all smiles and laughter, I'd grabbed Sam by the chest and shouted, 'Don't you guys drop me, I'm worth a million dollars ...' There's a photo you can find of the two of us laughing. It was the best of times. We were in it together, and we were winning together.

In this moment against the Springboks? There is nothing I can say to Sam to make him feel better, because I don't know what those words are. There is nothing that Sam can say to me at that point because even he doesn't know the words. We are just there with each other. And in the same way that we were together in 2011, sometimes saying nothing, sometimes talking absolute rubbish, we were together again. It wasn't about the talking. It's just being there.

That's what supporting someone is, a lot of the time. Not just in sport but in life, which is often a version or an exaggeration of what you experience in elite sport anyway. In that moment on the pitch at Twickenham, on 17 October 2015, 23 years old, I thought about all the hard work we had done to get to that point. I thought about the injuries each of us had overcome. I thought about all the nail-biting physical moments and emotional moments that had played out through us, all the incidents and instances we had given ourselves to – our bodies, our hearts. In the time it took a fantastic player to perform one of the best offloads I'll ever see, all that had been taken away.

But that's the sword you live and die by in elite sport. Sometimes it cuts you deep, other times it saves your life. Our match-winning try against England, two Saturdays before – how many times does that ball not bounce quite right for Gareth Davies, how many times in training does someone stretch for a loose ball and their fingertips don't quite grip and hold on? These are the fine margins you work with, each day in every week. It's not always fair. It's often not logical. Sometimes it just *is*, and you have to learn to live with your world standing or falling on these tiny frozen moments.

Gats told the media afterwards that South Africa had probably deserved it on the day. He told us in the dressing-room that there's not much you can do but your absolute best in every situation, and sometimes that's just not going to be quite enough. Maybe he was right, and maybe it was also part of his own coping strategy. Making us feel better, helping himself through too.

And Jesus, those are the games that stay with you forever, years after other World Cups have come and gone and players have retired and fresh names pushed you far into the shadows. For the fans they're the ones when you tell old friends you were there. They're the days that still stand out in a year that otherwise fades and drifts away. That day was horrible for us. It was horrible for a long time after. But they're also the best games I played in my career, and I feel fortunate to have been part of them. Fairytale endings are sometimes just that. Sport is beautiful and cruel and addictive and indifferent, all at the same time. You might never know what is going to happen at any given moment, and that's the whole point. In the heat of battle you'll see the best of yourself and those around you, and if you don't, you'll at least see the truth.

That's what you sign up to, when your dream of playing for your country comes to life. Things are going to be black and white now. A big part of your life can change in 30 seconds, often less. So when it does, and you're arm in arm with your mate, you don't need to talk. Be together.

Understand. Give each other a slap on the arse and think, 'Let's stand together, let's suck it in, and let's go again.'

Give them a squeeze, keep walking, share that moment. 'Yep, I know how it feels …'

TWELVE

MERTHYR TYDFIL TO PONTYPRIDD: BATTLING DEMONS

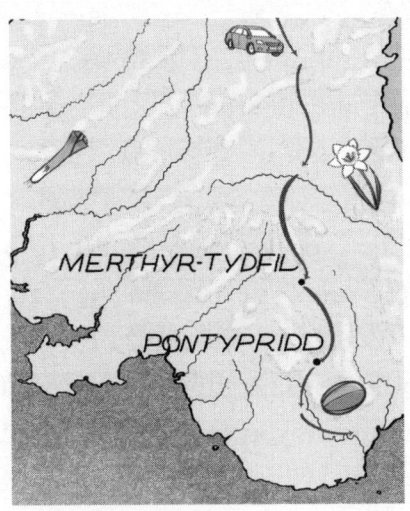

IN WHICH WE TALK ABOUT:

an alluring offer / the OG Dupont / Ten Wing Cut / going past the carefree days / shutting down my space and time / George isn't as good as he used to be / overthinking, undershaving / 'Do I want to be here?' / running reps in the rain / not talking to my mates / screaming tries v Ireland / Becky, again / moving on, moving in / Lions losses / a headstrong boy in a man's world / holes in my armour / dropped by Gats / 30 blokes standing around in tight tops / 'If you're going to be a bear, be a grizzly'

I don't have many regrets about my career, when I look back. I did the things I wanted to do, mainly. Sometimes it hurt me, and sometimes it took me a while to work my way through it all. Those late losses, the arm around Warbs' lovely strong hips. I never had a day in training when I didn't bounce in and try to bring the good energy; I never had a day when I gave it anything less than full-fat milk. That way lies satisfaction. That way lies peace, when you go home and you're lying in bed at night.

But there are two moments. The first came in the aftermath of that 2013 Lions and all it brought. I was offered the chance to play rugby league out in Australia. There were a few bids, had I wanted to set them off against each other. League is huge out there; the NRL is a great place to be, if that's your thing. Switching codes used to happen all the time, at a certain point in Welsh rugby union history.

I thought about it. The money was obviously good. It wasn't just about looking after myself. I could have made my own family comfortable, and laid down the foundations for a future family yet to come. Maybe I should have been more impulsive and given it a go. But my dreams in Rhoscolyn and Llandovery and beyond had always been about playing for Wales. When you got to the last page of the list on the back of the bedroom door, that was the bottom line. It didn't mention well-run, financially sound clubs in the Sydney suburbs. It didn't mention a bigger car or two spare bedrooms.

So I said no. I came back to the colder northern hemisphere and I cracked on, and I didn't look back that much. The second one? The aftertaste of this one stuck around a little longer. I was already invested in the 2016 Olympics in Rio; Becky was in form, months before, and looking good for a tilt at both the sprint and the keirin. Then came a surprise call: there was a chance, if I wanted to take it up, to have a crack at making the Great Britain rugby sevens squad.

When Antoine Dupont did it for the Paris Olympics, eight years later, he sat out the Six Nations in the spring before. There's a huge amount to learn when you drop down from 15-a-side to sevens. Your body shape has to change. Your engine needs significant tweaks. The way it was being put to me was slightly easier: have a go at two tournaments with Wales, see how it goes, take it from there.

It's possible that if we'd gone down that route it would have closed the conversation off on its own. I would have had to drop a load of weight. The boys in the squad were specialists, pretty much. They had been playing it for years and knew it inside out. We had Jonathan Davies' younger brother James in the set-up, who played for the national side as well, Cubby to his big bro's Fox, but he was an exception. I'm not arrogant enough to assume I could have taken the place of any of these lads.

The stumbling-block was how much time it would have meant away from Northampton. When I sat down and talked about it with the club – and it was a fair conversation – it was clear they had objections. Head coach Jim Mallinder was a good man. There wasn't much, 'No, you're not doing it.' It was more, 'Well, you haven't really mentioned this before ...', and, 'You've never done this in your previous rugby life, so why would you want to start now?'

It wasn't hard to fall into line with their thinking. There's always another game to play, another training session to turn up to bright and bouncy. You don't drag your disappointments with you, if you want to stay connected to a playing environment. Yet when those played out, and Becky won her two silver medals, and the GB boys got all the way to the final before being taken apart by a sensational Fiji side, I did look back and wonder. I could have had a silver medal to match Becky's. I could have experienced an entirely new form of elite sport and elite environment – stayed in an Olympic athletes' village, done the opening ceremony, worn a GB tracksuit. Possibly the blazer too. I could have done a Dupont before Dupont did it. I could have been the OG Dupont, without the unreal skills and French flair.

So that's the regret that sticks. And maybe it would have been what I needed, at that time, because I was slipping into a period of my career where things didn't quite come off the rails but I found myself shunted into a few tracks that I never envisioned going down.

The Six Nations that year had looked okay, from the outside. We finished second to an England side pushed on to a Grand Slam by new coach Eddie Jones. I scored a try against Scotland where I came into midfield and just kept stepping off my left foot until I got to the tryline. It was a play called Ten Wing Cut, set up off a right-hand side scrum, designed to find an over-chasing nine or ten, but perfect for a left-foot step. As it happened, I stepped so many times that if I had kept going I'd have ended up back at the same spot.

Then I scored against France, when Foxy kicked long and I chased it down, and I tried to kick the loose ball over the line to dive on it, and missed completely. Possibly the worst piece of football ever seen on a rugby field, although clear confirmation that I had chosen the right sport; when you're swinging a size 13 boot and you still manage a complete air-shot, it sends its own message. Thankfully Jules Plisson then nudged the ball over the line anyway, and I was able to touch it down. I scored against England at Twickenham when we had been 25–7 down and then came steaming back, and Taulupe scored and I nearly got away down the left at the end again to derail their Grand Slam hopes once more.

So it probably all seemed fine and dandy from a safe distance. Sunny George enjoying his rugby. Wales always a threat to every team. Gats with his blueprint, all of us understanding where we were inked on his plans. Tries coming from a winger expected to score tries.

But it was those expectations that were catching up with me again. Expectations, and the pressures that came with them.

It wasn't like I woke up one Monday morning, drove to training and someone greeted me on the touchline and said, 'Here you go, George, here's a box of responsibility for you – crack on, now.' But I felt like I'd gone past the carefree days without even noticing. There was no longer any time being allowed to find my feet, or have a few flat games. This was the delivery part of my career. I was deep into the international experience. I'd been to two World Cups. The team I was part of had won things and were expected to win more. We were expected to win more not just by playing as we had before but by coming into some new level of maturity and skill.

This was the pressure I felt. Not just to keep scoring tries, but to score more. Not just to beat a man on the way to the line, but to cut defences apart. Game after game, season after season. I had to show I wasn't just a big fast kid who played without fear, because there are plenty of them, and a fair few never kick on again. I had to show whether I'd got it or whether I hadn't.

Of course that's a very black and white way of looking at it all. But that's what happens, when you're chin-deep in elite sport. You get there by not giving yourself an easy ride. You've stayed there by being tougher on yourself still. So when you're 60 caps in and people are saying you're not scoring the same sorts of numbers and style of tries as you used to, you get harder on yourself.

So I wasn't enjoying it now, like I had done. Sometimes – quite a lot of the time – it felt like too much. In games I was getting defended differently. Opposition players and coaches knew who I was and what I liked to do. Their analysts came up with ways of shutting down my space and time, of taking away the flow of the ball every winger needs from those inside them. The cruel paradox of elite sport: the better you get, the less of a free rein you'll get to show it.

I tried meeting it head on. Trying to work out where I could go on the pitch, the runs I could make, the fresh angles I could find. But when you're my weight and my size, it's quite difficult to hide on a rugby pitch. I loved the Welsh fans then and I love them now. Because of the bumper run the team had been on, all of them wanted more. Most seemed to expect it. It was never that I wasn't doing my best to score tries. Quite the opposite. I was almost certainly trying too hard. I just had a spell where I didn't seem to score for ages, and then you notice the volume of the questions – 'Why hasn't he scored?' 'What's going wrong?' 'Is it time for someone else?'

In the same way I would always put pressure on myself and my team-mates to deliver, it was now coming from every direction. I could feel it ramping up – not twofold or threefold, but in much greater multiples. A nasty, corrosive idea – George isn't as good as he used to be – that leached into every one of my days and spread further with every match where it didn't miraculously come right.

All I wanted to do was score. What I didn't realise was that I was hanging myself out to dry by trying too hard. I was slipping in space. I was dropping the ball over the line. All I wanted to do was score, to get this immense weight off my shoulders. But I couldn't shift it. Everything I tried just added a little more weight every time.

Maybe it's not entirely a surprise that I look back at clips and photos from this time and remember that these were the beard years. I'd tried one before at the Scarlets, when there had been a charity push to 'Grow a Grav' in honour of the late Llanelli and Wales centre Ray Gravell. There had been a secondary push among some of the boys at Northampton. But I wasn't really a natural beard man. Mine tended to be wispy. I was naïve on the subjects of trim-lines and regular oiling. So there must have been a deeper psychological reason why, in 2017, I tried again. I wasn't deliberately attempting to look older and more troubled. I actually was older and more troubled.

Overthinking, overworking, overtraining. Undershaving. I wanted success so much – to perform for the fans, to deliver for my team-mates, to capture those glorious giddy feelings of only a few years ago – that I just kept trying too hard. And the harder I tried, the worse I seemed to make it for myself.

In some sports the movement is the skill. You can groove a golf swing through repeated time on the range. Rugby ... well, doubling down on the work felt like the right thing to do at the time. With the coaches we had at Wales in this era, with the circle of players I was part of, hard work trumped everything. It had always worked for me before, at Llandovery with the pre-dawn gym starts and at Scarlets and at the Vale with Shaun Edwards and Howlers watching over me. Of course I would naturally try to work harder. It's the obvious thing to do.

But it didn't work. Not at all. So I felt this ache, in my daily life. Not like a bad hamstring pull, but deep inside me.

It would come at me in waves. I would wake up first thing in the morning and it would hit me – wham!

'Oh my God, I've got to try and fix this again today. What can I do differently today to make it better?'

I would get into my training, be focused on the small details of what we were doing. I could almost forget about it for a while, because I was with the boys, and I was working hard, and I was getting stuff done. Then, at the end of training, as I was walking away from the gym or the training pitch, it would come at me again.

'Did I do enough today? What didn't I do today? Ah shit, I should have done that and this. Ah bollocks ...'

It eats into you. So you go back and do your extra bits. You're focusing again. You're chatting with the boys. It is what it is. Happy days.

Then you get in your car and you drive home and suddenly it's just you and it sits there again. It sits there and it bangs around inside you and you try to watch TV or something but you can't concentrate on what's going on because the banging is so loud.

I was lucky with one part of it. I was working at everything so hard that I was exhausted each night. Totally physically spent. And that meant I could sleep, and before I drifted off into this sort of exercise-induced coma, I would lean into the positive George and try to help myself and say, 'Well, tomorrow you've got an opportunity to fix it.'

Then I would wake up early in the morning and the whole thing would start all over again. A spiral of doubt and disappointment with myself. You do that, day after day, week after week, and it wears you down. You begin to break up inside.

I spoke to Wales' sports psychologist Andy McCann about it, a little bit. I didn't really speak to the boys because I just assumed they knew the pressure I was under. I mostly just kept it all in. That very typical male thing: just keep it all in. I don't want to call it depression. But the big questions kept coming at me, each day.

'Well, what am I doing here?'

'What am I doing wrong here?'

'Do I want to be here?'

So I talked to myself, a lot. Remember the story about Warbs in the hotel gym, long after he had retired? We all had the self-dialogue thing going on inside. If you tell me that you've never spoken to yourself, I'd think you're an absolute liar. For me, my self-dialogue was always 'you'.

'You chose to do this.'

'You wanted to do this.'

'You are here now and no-one else is here. Only you are going to see this, but if you want it, then you fucking best deliver on it.'

I know how it sounds, looking back. But these are the periods when you learn most about yourself. When I was stood there by myself, in the pissing rain, not getting picked, not scoring tries, having done a running session on my own out in a farmer's field beyond Rhoscolyn or on a messed-up old pitch somewhere near Becky's parents' house, and it's so cold and wet that not even the stupid dog walkers want to take their dogs out of the house – that's when the internal dialogue was at its noisiest.

'You chose to do this. You wanted to do this. You could have walked away ages ago but you're still here … why?'

I doubled down on training because that's what I knew. I talked to myself because it was the only thing that could keep my head in line.

'Well, you don't want to feel like this anymore. You want to be playing better for you, you want to be playing better for the boys, playing better for your country. No-one's going to do it for you. It's all on you.'

Andy helped me by going deep into that famous old line: form is temporary, class is permanent. I believed it. But in the moment, form is what drives you. Form is what energises you. If you haven't got the form, you're not showing your class, and you're not advancing your class, so you're not able to push on because you have no confidence.

When sport is new and exciting, it's easy. Your curve is always heading upwards. When you're half a career in – that's when the pressure comes on from every direction. That's when strangers are calling you every name under the sun, and all you're trying to do is exactly what they want you to do. That old classic: 'I'm trying my hardest. Fuck you …'

So it bubbled over during this time. Andy was brilliant with me. We talked about ways to – well, not fake the confidence, but to tap into it again. To take small things each day and say to myself, that went well, you did everything anyone could do, you finished your sets. And if I was in a session and that banging inside threatened to drown everything else out again, I repeated the same mantra to myself.

'You picked this. You wanted to do this. So keep doing it.'

I didn't feel I could speak to my mates back home about it. We were all still so young. Some of them were at uni, some were out and trying to get their first proper jobs. It was a fact to me that all of them would have given their left testicle to be in my position. The thought of me complaining because it was a bit tough at the moment – that just didn't sit right with me.

I did feel lonely. Even in a team sport, where there were always others around. Maybe that's the same for most sports people. There's an element of loneliness with every rep, every run. Every injury. You're on your own when you do these things, and it can be the toughest place you ever find yourself.

So I talked to myself like a nutter instead. I wish I'd felt like I could speak to someone outside. I wish I'd felt I could have spoken to one of the lads. Because I don't want to call it a coping strategy, this thing I was doing instead. It was just quite an elite sport way of being in the world. Talking about how I felt, to the people who cared about me most? It didn't feel like it was the right thing to do, at the time.

And when we played Ireland in Cardiff in March 2017 and I battered my way over for a try, all of that stuff came pouring out of me. In the expression on my face, in the noise I made. Had there been no crowd, you could probably have heard me in Anglesey, so loud did I scream. When I scored a second, off a driving maul and Rhys Webb breaking down the short side to feed me on the touchline – all the weeks and months of frustration and pain, of graft and doubt, all of it washed over me, and I lay there in the lush grass, whitewash of the tryline under my thighs, and I let the relief fill my head and carry away everything that was dark and stubborn and all too much.

Through all of these hard yards, everything stood firm with Becky. Everything got better. Each year brought us closer.

She rode a fixed-wheel bike around a wooden velodrome. I ran into people, if I couldn't run round them. She was an individual athlete, I was part of a team. But it was the same difference. I recognised in her all the things I was experiencing – when we were under the pump, and feeling the pressure; when my body was in bits, and it was hard to get out of bed in the morning.

British cycling had this motto, personified by Chris Hoy. It was all about saving your legs for when you needed them, and it went a bit like this: why stand up when you can sit down, and why sit down when you could lie? Becky and I would have days off when we sometimes didn't leave the house. If we did, it was for the shortest walk, and only then as a form of light recovery. If we went for coffee we'd drive there and park as close to the café as possible.

Some days we would sit there and talk absolute nonsense all day. Other times we'd lie there and watch nonsense on the telly and then eat food. It was all an unwritten thing. She didn't have to say she was tired, and I didn't have to say I was sore and aching. When games and races weren't going right, we both had someone to talk to who was outside the situation but close enough to be able to break it down.

They were long-distance days, a lot of them. But because we both knew we loved each other dearly, and we both wanted each other to succeed, we could both do exactly what we needed from a performance point of view. Maybe it took a tiny bit of traditional romance out of things. We were allowed to be selfish in our preparation and training, but we also had each other's backs. Becky would come to every match she could without walking there and standing up to watch. I would go to every race my schedule allowed. It was amazing for us. It all clicked.

I've talked about how communication worked with some of the boys, after a while. It was like you didn't need to speak. It was a certain nod, or the fact you were there by their side, and you were both hurting. Becky and I had the same trust and understanding.

They say when you find the one, it's easy. Part of me doesn't want to use the easy word, because it's not that we ever didn't try, or always make the biggest effort for each other. But it was all natural and all of it made sense. It was never forced. It just flowed.

Before the Olympics in 2016 I'd watched her fight back from a knee injury when some people were saying she would never cycle competitively again. When she made it through, I got to go to Rio and watch her win her two silver medals. The first time her mum Christine had ever heard me swear, when she got that first medal; the biggest wave of emotion I'd ever felt hit me.

So, at the end of that year, Becky moved in with me in Northampton. The first time we'd ever lived together. So many people do it the other way, don't they? They get together, they move in together, then they go away each day or week to go to work. We had done the opposite. We'd gone away to do our jobs for five years, we would go months and months apart, and then we went to live together. So much had happened in that time. I'd won a Grand Slam, become a Six Nations champion, gone on a Lions tour and to World Cups. Becky had become a two-time world champion, a European champion and won two medals at the greatest event of all. We crammed quite a lot into those years, but the longest we had spent together in one go was probably one week. There were times when we hadn't seen each other for four months. But the longer we had been apart, the stronger we had become.

It kept working, kept flowing. I loved her to bits. And so, on 3 December 2017, I asked her to marry me.

I thought it was romantic, choosing that particular date. Exactly six years after I asked her to be my WAG. It was romantic. It also had practical overtones; when I had the engagement ring engraved with the date, I thought, well, if I don't ask on the 3rd, I've always got the back-up of the 13th or 23rd to try again.

And, even to this day, with Becky retired and in a completely different phase of her own life, she still under-stands my world, and she is supportive of the day-to-day impacts of elite performance. She knows. She hasn't forgot-ten. And I'll forever be truly grateful, because I know that heart, body and soul she's in it with me. There's all that, and then there's the fact that she's given me two amazing boys with Jac and Tomi. An entirely new emotional wave, without doubt the greatest thing that's ever happened to me in my life.

All from a tweet about a Rising Star award eventually won by someone else. Not everything that came from the early days of social media was a bad thing.

I got picked for the British and Irish Lions again in the summer of 2017. A chance to go to New Zealand and take on the world champions. To go back to the stadium where we'd come so close to a World Cup final when the All Blacks were still in their long winless years. This time it didn't work out. I played three tour games but not the first Test. In the next midweek game against the Hurricanes, attack coach Rob Howley insisted I had to prove my form. I knew I wasn't playing as well as I wanted on a Lions tour. I'd played two extra games for Northampton at the end of the season; in the captain's run before the game against Connaught, I popped a rib out. Then, against Stade Francais, I popped the SC joint around my collarbone. You know that thing where a professional rugby player is asked how their body is, and they say, good, and they don't really mean it? That was me in New Zealand. I wanted to show I had form and fitness, even if I wasn't quite sure that I did.

Sure enough, against the Hurricanes, I tore my hamstring scoring a try. I felt so lucky to be playing for the Lions. You never know if or when it might happen again. If this was my last opportunity, I was going to make it last as long as I could. When they subbed me off, I knew it wasn't good news. My hamstring was gone from arse to knee. But I walked off. I was never going to be carried off.

It all felt rather nightmarish. All these years later, I still haven't spoken to any of my team-mates or friends about how this time affected me. I'm sure if I told them I didn't feel I could, they would put me right – tell me I should have opened up, maybe admitted they had been through similarly testing periods.

It's too late now. I dealt with it at the time, and I'm okay with it, at my age. I don't think I'd get anything out of going back into it, eight years on. Later in my career, I would be more capable of opening up about these things, about performance anxiety, if we can call it that. I could say if my body was sore, or if I was struggling with a particular block of training. But at the time, it wasn't the done thing. It wasn't that Warren Gatland didn't want boys to have help with their mental health, more that he expected us, I think, to be in control of everything ourselves because of the experience we had racked up

With hindsight, you could argue the experienced ones were the ones who needed most help. A load of us had got that deep into our careers and still hadn't worked out how to process it all. Today? Thinking about it again and writing it all down gives me that old anxiety feeling in my chest. The heebie-jeebies return fast. Maybe that means I'm not as okay as I think. I'd like to hope I'm in the fifth stage of grief. I've accepted what happened, and I can't change it, and I processed it. But it's never that far away.

Of course I spoke to Becky about it. I also appreciated that she was going through her own stuff at the time. We discussed how I was finding it tough; we didn't go into full detail, because I fell back into the observed and learned male rugby persona. Batten down the hatches, try to heal myself. A headstrong boy in a man's world.

It wasn't like no-one was offering me advice or an ear. Loads of people were trying to help me. I had just decided I was better dealing with it on my own.

Back to those statements to self, round and round and round.

'Right, here we are. This is the process. This is where I am. This is where I need to be. This is where I want to be. It's going to work.'

All those 'you' questions I asked myself – the strange thing is, I never answered them. I didn't get doubt coming back at me – 'Maybe you don't want to be here. Maybe you don't want to be doing this. Maybe you don't want to be doing shuttle runs in the rain in a field by yourself.'

The conversation never came. My head would get back into line before then. Did I want to be here? Well, I could never forget all the things I'd done to get to this point. The sacrifices, the intense physical discomfort, the games I lost and still didn't want to think about. The pain of me walking away and not doing it would be worse than the pain I was currently in. If I quit, in this lonely muddy field, then when I was retired and sitting in the fictional corner of the fictional pub I always thought about, and I started crying, it wouldn't be tears of joy. It would be tears of sadness, because I wouldn't have done myself justice and I wouldn't have done what I felt I needed to.

When I imagined looking into my children's eyes and they asked me, 'Why did you retire then, Dad?', I couldn't handle the idea that I showed them any holes in my armour. I wanted them to think: he was always ready to go.

Everything was really fucking hard in these moments. But walking away and having those regrets, 10 years on, would have been 15 times worse. That's what I thought at the time, anyway.

They scared the shit out of me, those thoughts. They also

kept me running. They wouldn't have worked for everyone, but in those hard times when no-one sees and no-one understands, it got me through.

Come the 2018 Six Nations, I was no longer a guaranteed starter for Gats and Howlers with Wales. I was on the bench when we played England at Twickenham. Josh Adams and Steff Evans were picked ahead of me. Same again away in Ireland. I came back in against Italy, but as Gats was clocking up his 100th match in charge of us, I was wondering if my time with him was coming to a premature end. I was coming up to my 26th birthday. I'd always imagined this would be my peak. Instead, I was watching younger versions of me, always the young kid, taking my place.

More questions.

'Now you haven't got it, what are you going to do about it?'

Whichever way I looked at it, the 'you' kept working.

'You got yourself here, big boy. Don't ever forget that.'

'This is exactly what you wanted. So fight for it.'

Turning my past into a positive. Finding confidence at its source.

'Well, you've come this far. You did exactly what you wanted to do – no-one else did it from Anglesey the way you did it ...'

'Well, you know, now it's not going great; you've found a bit of form, you're feeling okay but you're not getting the chance. What are you going to do about it?'

As an athlete it's too easy to forget how much you've had

to sacrifice. You always remember to thank other people, quite rightly, but if it wasn't for your hard work, you're not going to be there to be helped anyway. I would break it down and think sometimes – if you take rugby, take all the hype away, all the flapping of the lips and the nonsense we all talk about it, essentially it's just a field with 30 blokes standing around in tight tops. And when you think about what you have to sacrifice to be one of those 30 at the time, it seems a bit daft, doesn't it?

Yet the fear of not getting another opportunity to be one of those 30 blokes – fuck, that keeps you running. Gats was always very good at mind games. Maybe he saw that fear in me. Maybe he just wanted to see if it was there. Either way, the internal dialogue responded probably exactly as a wise old coach would want.

'Well, this is a test for me now.'

'I'm not going to just cave-in and show him I'm not up for the fight.'

'I know, on my day, that I deserve to be in that jersey.'

Sometimes you can't control what the bossman thinks. Particularly when it's Gats. When he decides that it's not your turn, there's no point stamping your feet, hissing and moaning at him; you may as well prove to him he's wrong, even if that means you're entering into his games.

That's what I decided to do. Ultimately, I think it worked. I got back in. We won Grand Slams, we went closer still to World Cup finals. Maybe I didn't need to be so hard on myself. Maybe I could have been more stoic: do my job as best I could, and if it didn't quite go right, then I'd played my part.

But I'm not sure you can play elite sport without giving up some part of yourself. You can't ride this train for free.

Sometimes it's a brutal place. When you're starting out in elite sport, and you make a mental list of all the attributes that you're going to need, they tend to be around your skillset in what you do. You don't know then that dealing with the inevitable tough times will be more important than your ability to step a defender or time your run onto a pass. The thing people often forget about sport is there's so much that's out of your control. Sometimes the athlete who comes out on top is the one who grasps that straightaway; the one who can process the heartbreaks and the let-downs and move on, and can learn how to use those moments as fuel for the journey ahead.

It's almost like a mad love affair, how it is between you and sport when you reach the top. It's the weirdest relationship you'll ever be in. You grow up and this thing is your obsession, it's your dream. But holy shit-balls, it's a weird, cruel relationship. You'd have epic highs – these incredible moments most people never get to experience – but also points where the object of your love treats you like an absolute bastard, where it dumps you on your arse and doesn't call you back.

The funny thing is, you keep coming back for more. And you have to embrace it, if you're going to survive. Throw yourself into this relationship, and relish all the wonders it brings you – the ecstasy, the despair, the moments feeling lost, the strength you take from finding yourself again.

Jon Davies had a nice way of looking at it. He would say, 'If you're going to be a bear, be a grizzly.'

There's no point being a teddy bear. Sometimes you just have to take a deep breath and say, well, today I'm going to be a grizzly. And then you've just got to get on with it. No-one's going to do it for you, no-one's going to fix your problems. So why the hell are you feeling sorry for yourself? Get up, put one foot in front of the other and get on with it.

Roar. Get your claws out. If you're going to be a bear, be a fucking grizzly.

THIRTEEN

PONTYPRIDD TO PONT-Y-CLUN: FIGHTING BACK

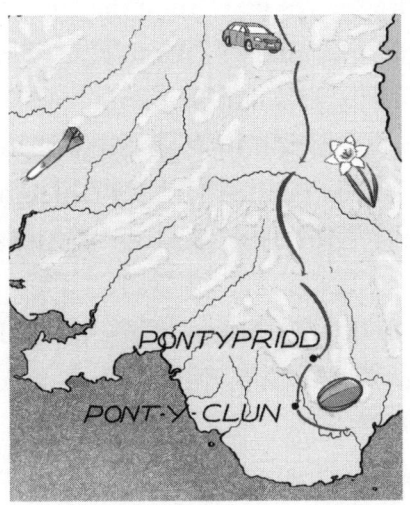

IN WHICH WE TALK ABOUT:

*loose balls/a Huget hole/the origins of Jadsy/chasing
everything/a pancake pass/ball becoming balloon/win, perform,
recover/34 phases/a lovely choo-choo line/my hand cracking like
twigs/champions again/Turkish delight/Kitakyushu kicks/
a Howlers curveball/Tuisova's calves/Vahaamahina seeing red/
we never go away/a very hamstring way/the red shagpile bar*

How did the fog lift? As fogs do – slowly, at first, so it was hard to notice, and then gradually a little more light came in, and the warmth, until one day I looked around and the sun was shining and I'd almost forgotten why it might not be.

We finished 2018 well with Wales. We beat South Africa in the summer, and we beat them again in the winter. Foolish people said they might be struggling, a year out from the World Cup in Japan. We were on a decent unbeaten run. We had a core of the old guard – Alun Wyn, Tips and Taulupe, Jon Davies, Dan Biggar, Liam Williams, me – and the settling in of a younger generation in Josh Adams, Josh Navidi, plus some boys who weren't called Josh – Hadleigh Parkes, Gareth Anscombe, Ross Moriarty, Aaron Wainwright. The big change was the change yet to come. This was due to be Warren Gatland's last Six Nations in charge. It was this tournament, then the World Cup, then he was stepping away after 11 years.

Except, with Gats being Gats, it was never going to be about him. The way he ran his ship there would be no deviation at the helm. No individual, player or coach, was bigger than the collective. He didn't always see eye to eye with all the players. He could be a hard taskmaster. But no-one was looking towards the end. We were too focused on the middle.

It was France first, away in Paris, on a Friday night. Pretty much the hardest of any possible Six Nations start, and not just for that opposition and that crowd at that stage. Shaun Edwards had also been riding us hard in training. He had never changed in all the years with Gats, in the best possible way. He was still obsessing over microscopic details in defence. His big thing in the last week had been about getting back and making sure loose balls went dead. At the end of every practice he'd been making us do repeated drills – sprinting back, touching the loose ball down, jog back, turn the right way to always see the opposition man, sprinting and putting the ball down again. He even took us deep on the specific skillset of sliding into the ball so you could gather it cleanly first time around.

When we got out to France and the weather turned wet and looked like staying wet, he went even deeper into it. Now it was about securing that ball, then turning, presenting it and the second man getting in there and over it. One of his favourite old mantras, given fresh life: the ball is never dead until it's dead. In longer form: 'Lads! Chase everything. Chase every scrap. Any ball on the floor, you dive on it, you kill it, you get it back. Anything. It's not over until the whistle goes.'

Evening games at the Stade de France kick off at 9 p.m., deep into the dark night. It's a nightmare, as a player. How many meals do you eat? When do you try to sleep? How can you wake your body up for full Gallic combat at a time when you'd usually be yawning and thinking about one final episode of your favourite show before turning in?

My technique was to break the day in half and make it two shorter days. Big meal in the middle, proper sleep, and then when I've woken up, treat it as Day Two – coffee, breakfast, get the body moving. When I opened my curtains for a second time that Friday, it was like Anglesey had come to the French capital. All of us Welshmen should have felt at home. Instead we sat back and France came at us hard. Louis Picamoles scored first, then I stepped in on Yoann Huget, when I should have trusted the defensive system and Gareth Anscombe a little more and stayed wide a touch longer, and Huget was away free down my wing and diving over the line, all screams of delight and celebrations.

Being 16–0 down at half-time should have felt worse than it did, particularly given the manner of the second French try and its scorer. I wasn't the first name on the list of Huget devotees. He enjoyed scoring tries, which was absolutely fine. He was also the sort of guy who would stand on your hand in a ruck, when the ball had already gone. He would happily leave a little something extra in there after a tackle – a loose and obviously absolutely accidental elbow or fist. The aftermath of a try would often involve his face coming too close to your face and his screaming being a little too adjacent to your ears.

But none of us in the dressing-room were turning the air *bleu*. We hadn't fired any shots. That was the main problem. The talk between us was correspondingly simple.

'Well, bloody hell boys. Just look at where we are. We haven't done anything.'

'We've been under the pump, so let's just focus on getting back into the game.'

'Second half we have to give life to the ball. We have to play. We've got to get points on the board.'

And that's what we did. A really nice break around the ruck from Jadsy, Josh Adams (J plus Ad plus sy), and then Tomos Williams on his shoulder to score. Good gas by Jadsy, great support line from Tomos.

All of a sudden it was 16–7, the weather was coming in and the momentum in the stands was shifting. I always loved playing in Stade de France for the atmosphere the home crowd create. It could be a brutal place to be, maybe more hostile than anywhere else outside South Africa's rugby heartlands. But when those fans lose a little faith, and then begin to turn – then you hear your own supporters suddenly, and it's like a wind has blown through and changed everything the other way round.

We got a scrum on the right-hand side, deep in their half. We went left. I don't think Hadleigh Parkes was meant to kick it. Maybe it was because the ball was wet. Maybe the next pass was overrun a little, or the cover was up fast, because if you're defending in a situation, you're just thinking. 'Right, ball's wet, it's pissing down, just take line speed. They can't do much.'

It was a trademark Hadleigh kick off his shin. The ball went miles ahead of us, right up towards the French line. Huget was running back into his own 22. I was 15 metres off him. It was the classic lost cause, but I was still chasing it. Even as Huget was approaching the ball and sliding to gather it, I was still seven or eight metres back.

Words in my head. 'Come on, George. Shaun's watching. Just got to chase everything. Chase everything …'

There was also something else knocking around in there somewhere. Rob Howley was always so big on this sport all being about the team, and how you have to do your job every single time.

'Boys, you may run a line 10 times selflessly. It's opened up the door for someone else, at least. You may not get the pass nine times out of 10, but on that 10th time, if you don't go, that's the one where you'll be through a hole.'

In other words, you're constantly working for the team. Not for the romantically unfulfilling promise that you might get it, but because even if you don't, you might make something happen for someone else. That Hadleigh kick was a bit of a nothing. But because you give life to it – because you work as hard as you can to give life to it – it's always got a chance. Just a chance.

Huget got there. Huget coughed it up. It bounced up into me as I slid in behind him, and over the tryline I went.

God bless you, Shaun Edwards. God bless you, Rob Howley.

I didn't scream in Huget's face. I'm not the type. If I had been, he had his face buried deep in the wet grass, trying not to see it. Also, I didn't need to. My pleasure was intense as it was. A little later in the contest, we would go wide, wide, come back in, one phase, then come back down the short side and he would get a double on me – someone hitting me first, then Huget coming in a fraction later to finish me off. As he landed on top of me, he was screaming again; the exact words didn't stay with me, because I hadn't learned conversational French at that point, but his meaning was clear enough. Soon after, we went again – two phases then coming back on the short side, and suddenly he was one-on-one, and coming in for another hit. I went straight through him. Sent him back about five metres. I didn't use French; I didn't need to, either.

It all went a bit wishy-washy for a while. Dan Biggar put us ahead for the first time with a long-range penalty. France got a penalty off our scrum in front of our posts, and Camille Lopez put them back in front. Even at international level, you sometimes get these games where it's almost like village rugby; the standard is much better, but the weather is bad and the pitch a mess, so it all becomes quite simple: do nothing fancy, play high up the field, tackle, drop back, tackle some more, wait for someone else to force it.

France tried to force it. They tried to bring the power game, to get a little momentum going in a game falling apart in the cold rain. They kicked down the short side, Gael Fickou with a great chase and re-gather, the Stade de France crowd responding again. Our defence was scrambling and it was narrow. I worked back hard down my wing, but as I turned to get into position, everyone else had squeezed in.

The defensive line suddenly seemed miles away. I glanced at the French attackers fanning out. Huget coming into my eyeline. Looking at the space inside me, the space outside me.

'Ah, bollocks ...'

Then imaginary Shaun Edwards in my head, as always.

'What the fuck are you doing lad?'

I saw Lopez with the ball in hand, looking outside him. Looking my way.

'Fuck, George, you've just got to get with Hadleigh here as quick you can ...'

Hadleigh came out of the line fast. Their big second row Sebastien Vahaamahina with his hands on the ball, maybe

Hadleigh spooking him, maybe adrenaline and excitement taking over.

His pass was an absolute pancake. Long and high and hanging in the air for an awful long time.

My first thought: I can get Huget man-and-ball here.

Second thought: I might be able to get to this before it even reaches Huget …

Third thought, barely a conscious thought at all: Oh my God, oh my God …

My speed suddenly switched up. I went from watching to going full-fat milk. An acceleration into the tiny slice of space between the arc of the ball and the path of Huget.

I had to go for it one-handed. No chance of going two hands. But it's still pissing down. I'm soaked, the ball is soaked, everybody is soaked. I've got cut grass all over my hands.

Remember what I told you about my first ever cap for Wales, and that crossfield kick coming in from Stephen Jones, and me thinking, don't let it bounce, don't let it bounce … and then letting it bounce? This felt the same. All those hours of training, all those thousands of balls you've caught – you come to understand, quite naturally, where the ball's going to be, the speed of it, the exact angle and pace you need to be cutting to pick it off. So somewhere in that acceleration, in what is probably five-hundredths of a second, I had changed my intention. From completely fixed on taking man and ball to knowing I could catch it. To understanding I couldn't go two hands, that if I went with one and spilled it the ref would almost certainly call it a deliberate knock-on and a penalty to them and a yellow card for me, leaving us a man down for the rest of the game. To working out that if I could go with one hand and scoop it to two, then I was clean free.

Right arm out high in front of me. Palm upturned, fingers reaching. Huget coming the other way at flat-out pace to do the same.

Wet ball onto wet hand. Ball popping directly into my eyeline. Both hands reaching out as Huget's right arm tried to grasp my jersey and slipped straight off.

Ball into both hands. Wet green emptiness ahead of me. I wasn't getting caught, not then.

It's not the easiest thing, dissecting these compressed, critical moments. Or rather, it is, but not to share with others. It's pretty close to my worst nightmare, for anyone thinking I fancy myself. So take these reflections as me letting you into my private places.

I'm really happy with that try. Partly because I knew I was probably going to be on the thick end of a Shaun Edwards conversation about Huget's try in the first half, and this would act as a certain amount of damage limitation, but also for what I knew it took. I knew it mattered, in the course of the match. Drop it, yellow card, they kick the penalty, they win the game. Catch it, run away, score, we win. I understood the drama of the moment. I had a pretty good idea of what it would be doing for people I cared about on that long journey of mine from Rhoscolyn to Cardiff. I knew nobody flukes these things – that it came from the aggregation of practising endlessly, and caring enough to keep practising, and having the speed to get there in the first place, and the discipline to hit the gym to build the strength and explosiveness to create the speed, and the willingness to hone that speed in a field in the rain where no-one else is making you do it. The endurance to surmount all the fatigue you're carrying in the 72nd minute of a Test match like that.

There's something strange and magical I'll never forget about that moment. When I was watching Vahaamahina's pass in the air, it looked to me like it changed from a rugby ball to a balloon. You know when you watch a balloon? You've got all the time in the world. It's easy. You just go towards it and wait for it to land gently in your arms.

That's how it felt to me. It went from a ball into a balloon and it just floated, and it just kept going and going and suddenly it became the simplest thing to meet it and catch it and go away with the afterburners on.

But as I say, I can't share any of this, because it's hidden in my secret place, and I don't want anyone thinking I fancy myself. Right?

So that was one way to win a big Six Nations game. We would have to find another, against England, after we had beaten Italy the following week.

Gats had made one of his pot-stirring predictions before Paris, something along the lines of a win over France having the potential to set us up for a tilt at a Grand Slam. Eddie Jones' team had made their own statement of intent in winning away in Ireland in their opening match, and then thumping France at Twickenham in their second. Huget had something of a nightmare at full-back in that game – not that I noticed, obviously.

They started well against us, too, on a rainy Cardiff afternoon where they wanted the roof open, and Tom Curry scored his first international try, and they led 10–3 at halftime. A proper Test match, going back and forth, always tight, the atmosphere in the steep stands of the Principality incredible.

Sometimes it seems we were always behind, in that great era. Always behind, but seldom beaten. Always believing, always finding a way. This was not the same team that had beaten England four years before in the World Cup, or the one that found something to beat them in our Grand Slam year of 2012. But it had those consistent threads, and that new generation coming through had matured into a winning side and a winning way. And when you get a group of players who only know winning and only understand winning, then it's actually Christmas, really, because they see what it takes day-to-day, and they then work on it day-to-day, and then they add their own bit to it, taking it to the next level.

That experience of win, perform, recover, win, perform, recover – that rare and sacred cycle in professional sport – it becomes a habit then. You learn to dog it out, because a comfortable win is a rare thing and a string of comfortable wins is a non-possible. We had been average at best in that first half; it was why England were ahead and looking to stretch away. We would have to problem-solve in real time, and that's the next incredible skill to have – to work out what is going wrong, first of all, then work out how to put it right, and then to actually make that happen, which is the hardest part of all, because your opposition also know what you want to do and exactly what they want to do too, so are planning specifically to stop you.

It's hard whichever way you do it – individually, collectively. Holy fuck-balls, to do it with limited time under huge pressure? It's so, so difficult.

You need near perfect communication on the field, when you can barely hear yourself shouting, let alone your teammate with their head in a ruck 40 metres away. You need total clarity in what you are trying to achieve, and exactly when you want to do it. Us? We were so well drilled at this point. We were still playing Warrenball, but we'd added different players, allowing us to bring different tactical options to the table. There was always something new now, always another option now, whereas in some previous years we had maybe been a little limited in the stylistic things we could do. We kept understanding where we were, where we were going and where we needed to be.

That's how we got back that day – all of that stuff, all of that collective erudition. We were still 13–9 down with 12 minutes to go, and we were hammering away at the England defence, and you might have thought we were getting nowhere. We were up to 34 phases and not appearing to go anywhere, which might be regarded as a defensive masterclass by your opponent. It can also be the opposite. You've gone 34 phases, and you're still going? You haven't panicked, you haven't made an error with a wet ball on a greasy pitch, you're staying patient, you're probing them and stretching them and you're still looking for openings, and you're all still communicating and believing and making the right decisions when the wrong one might be the end of the contest?

Then it came. A ruck on the left-hand side, 15 metres or so out. We'd carried strong down the right, then we went all the way far left-hand side, physicality and speed, phase after phase. Biggs sitting a little bit deeper, England now defending quite narrow, me in space on the right with Hadleigh Parkes outside me.

Biggs heard us, saw us. A mis-pass out to me. Johnny May coming across to cover, Manu Tuilagi sprinting across, Elliot Daly sort of trying to mark Hadleigh while also covering me.

You might think I should ship it on to Hadleigh. He's hugging the touchline. He might score. Why would I go myself, if I've got two, maybe three men ready to tackle me?

Here's what I thought, instead. Those three defenders were covering me, but the rest of them were still narrow. England had been under constant intense pressure. If I passed to Hadleigh, sure, he might go a little further – but, because he's so close to the touchline, he might also be put into touch, and then we lose possession and we lose all that field position we've been working so hard for. England exit off their line-out, we have to go again from 30 metres deeper against a fully set defence.

I carried, not because I thought I could score, but to be able to recycle, knowing that 11 of England's players were still on the other side of the field. So when I drew May, and Tuilagi, then Hadleigh was straight over the ball, and Biggs had sprinted over to act as scrum-half, there was Cory Hill, coming in on an absolutely lovely choo-choo line to smash over.

It looks simple in the end. Cory's a big man; he's just straight trucking. And it was. It was also everything that came before. Everything in the preceding 34 phases. Everything we had done to get there, and still believing, and able to make it happen.

It was chaos in the stadium after that. Shaun Edwards was clenching his fist, Howlers was jumping around. Even Gats stood up, which is saying something. And when we scored again, Biggs kicking crossfield for Josh Adams to leap above Daly and gather and wriggle over – we'd won another tight match, from another deficit. Twelve wins in a row, a new national record, and none of it, absolutely none of it, was a fluke.

We beat Scotland two weeks later, another try for Josh, one too for Foxy, a whole heap of defence and dogging it out. That set up another Grand Slam shootout, this time against Ireland back in Cardiff. A classically strong Ireland team at this time: Murray and Sexton at half-back, Aki and Ringrose in the centres, Rob Kearney at 15. A front row of Healy, Best, Furlong. Tadhg Beirne and James Ryan in the second row, O'Mahony, O'Brien and Stander in the back row. All eyes were on us. It was wet and it was cold again and the roof was open, Irish conditions brought to Wales. It was sure to be another tight one.

Except it wasn't, at all. Hadleigh gathered Anscombe's chip to score our first try on two minutes. Gareth knocked over penalties like it was a sunny day in June. We gave them absolutely nothing in defence. It was pretty much done by half-time. It took until 82 minutes for Ireland to score their first points.

I was long gone by then. I had tackled someone early on and heard the bones in my hand cracking like twigs. I got up because we were never injured in defence, but it was agony, and when I looked down my hand looked like it belonged to the Elephant Man. Every time I tried to catch a ball it was like someone was stabbing me. When I tried to pass it and gave the ball a slight squeeze, there was another audible clunk, and another burst of fire through it.

But I could enjoy the rest of the game, all the same. What we thought was Gats' 50th and final Six Nations game in charge, and his third Slam – the first coach in Five or Six Nations history to pull that off. Alun Wyn, our captain, in maybe his finest hour. He was amazing in that championship, voted player of the tournament. In the first 40 minutes against Ireland, he had beaten more defenders, made more metres and made more carries than any other man on the pitch. Very Alun Wyn.

He was a good friend of mine by now, and I was glad. He was good with me for the first seven years, but we didn't really speak much; Al was the last of the generation where you had to earn a senior player's respect, and then keep earning it, hard yard after hard yard, for him to let you any closer. Once he realised I wasn't a flash in the pan, and I was willing to work as hard as he was, then we were there. He had been a tremendous leader for us, always very good with his words, but never happier than when leading from the front, than when doing all his extras and more. The most consistent man in Welsh rugby, the most professional in his preparation and approach, when consistency and professionalism are sometimes mistakenly seen as less alluring attributes than some others.

So we were champions again. We weren't flashy that spring. Not once in the championship had we scored more than 26 points in a game; England scored 32 or more on four occasions. England also scored 14 more tries than us. It didn't matter, because we had conceded a mere seven, almost half as many as Eddie Jones' team. We were on a winning streak of 14 matches, and in all that time had shipped just 19 tries, and an average of 13 points per game. Scotland head coach Gregor Townsend called ours the best defence in the world. We didn't disagree with him, and not only because, if we were honest, we were still pretty scared of Shaun Edwards.

You have a solid grasp of how our World Cup preparations went under Warren Gatland, by now. The 2019 tournament in Japan would be a very different one, but our training camps in advance that summer were not. We went to Switzerland to live high and train low again, just like in 2015, and the cable car-based PTSD came back strong. We then went out to Turkey for a warm-weather camp, trying to get close to the intense heat and humidity we'd experience in a baking Japanese September, and there were no cable cars there but the same familiar levels of pain and horror.

The opportunities for relaxation were typically limited, which made the discovery of a local market specialising in knock-off fashion gear all the more amusing. You've never seen a Welsh rugby player happier than when confronted with a load of fake designer labels at insanely agreeable price-points. So many wives and girlfriends were gifted Louis Vuitton bags on our return that the market for luxury goods in the UK was temporarily thrown completely out of whack. I walked into a watch shop as something of a connoisseur, and was astonished to see a particular designer timepiece on display – astonished because I'd recently read an article about it, and knew that only 50 of this particular version had ever been made, each of them individually numbered. When I asked for a closer look, it turned out this guy had got number one. What were the chances?

Had I been a bigger fool than I am, I may have been tempted. In beating England in one of our World Cup warm-up games, we had actually gone to the top of World Rugby's international rankings. The All Blacks had been on an unbroken run lasting 10 years, but our win in Cardiff took us to number one instead. As World Cup auguries went, it seemed a decent one. As an excuse to buy a watch that would stop working the first time I wore it in the shower, it was not.

I'd heard a lot about Japan. None of it prepared me for the welcome we received when we arrived. Touring was now a very different experience to my first World Cup in New Zealand, eight years before; the rules were stricter, there was less downtime, and there was less chance of letting your hair down in that downtime, partly because rugby had changed, and partly because phones had changed, and everything you did would be filmed by someone and on social media before you were tucked up in bed. There would be less bungee-jumping and more temples. A lot more temples.

But I loved it – the country, the people, how thrilled they were to be staging a World Cup. Each touring team had been allotted a host city. We had been given Kitakyushu, partly because it was a place of ports and mining, and those threads tying Wales to a foreign land worked even for young men with lives lived purely in sport. The city had turned red – banners everywhere, big signs at the train station and in public squares saying, 'Go Go Cymru'. When we held an open training session in the City of Kitakyushu stadium, 15,000 fans turned up to watch.

Something else happened that day. During the session I trained really well. I then did my extras out on the field, and then some more passing drills. I had a little laugh and a joke with some of the boys, just to get through it. Rob Howley was on me straightaway, commenting on every aspect of everything we did, and because everyone was in such a good mood, with the weather and the fans and the pre-tournament anticipation, I said something back for a change – 'Jesus Christ, Howlers, I can't do anything right ...'

For the first time ever – for the only time, until I ruptured my Achilles in my final ever game for Wales – he said something else.

'No, George, I only do it because I have the utmost respect for you. You've always given me everything.'

I was stunned. Not just because it came from me messing about, but because it was so out of character. None of it made sense until the following day, when we were told Rob had been sent home for an alleged breach of World Rugby's laws covering betting and anti-corruption. He would later be banned for 18 months, nine of those suspended. He must have known, I think, that he was gone, when we did that training session, but it was a weird time for us players. He was a hard, hard man, Howlers, yet I always enjoyed the way he worked – the detail he brought, the energy, the pure understanding of rugby. Stephen Jones flew out to take over as backs coach, and we rolled on. Something fundamental had also changed.

We beat Georgia well in our opener. I scored, and all of us sweated like we seldom had before on a rugby pitch. At moments we even felt grateful for Turkey. We then started brilliantly against Australia, for so long our bogey team, going 10–0 up and leading 23–8 at half-time before they came back at us and we had to dig in hard until Rhys Patchell landed a penalty late on to see us home. Of course we played Fiji next, because Wales are always drawn against Fiji in World Cups, and Josua Tuisova scored early with his massive calves, and then they scored again, and Tuisova and his mates kept coming at us, and there is no-one in the world harder to defend when he's on song than Josua Tuisova.

When you let Fiji into the game early, it's going to be a long afternoon. The size of the guys running at us was ridiculous. People talk about how beautiful it is when Fiji play rugby like they can. They love the contradictory truth that you never know quite what you're going to get with Fiji. These people have never been hit by a Fijian player. There is nothing beautiful about it. It's horrible; it hurts, and it keeps hurting, and then they do it to you again. We had to stay in the fight, and then keep staying in the fight. We had to trust our fitness, and believe their casual brilliance would create chances for us as well as them. We were grateful for Josh Adams' hat-trick of tries. We were just glad when it was over.

We topped our group, a new experience for me at a World Cup. We stayed in Oita, and France came our way, and in the first 20 minutes we were wishing neither of those things had been true.

They were hissing, straight out of the bag. Running hard lines, offloading, support lines, phase after phase after phase, living off the adrenaline and the thrill of it all. The worst possible version of France to come up against.

Sebastien Vahaamahina thundered over. Charles Ollivon finished off another ludicrous team move. We struck back when Aaron Wainwright scooped a loose ball off the deck and cantered away for a try out of nothing, but then Ross Moriarty was yellow carded, and when Virimi Vakatawa smashed through again, it was 19–10 at half-time and we were lucky to have 10 and they were unfortunate not to have more.

We'd missed 18 tackles in the first half. That's the basic statty term. What the word 'missed' doesn't really incorporate is when big fast men run through your arm or your shoulder. You've missed a tackle in the same way a brick wall misses a wrecking-ball going through it.

Hanging in there, hanging in there. And then, in a little poetic return to the 2011 semi-final, a red card that changed it all around.

I didn't see Vahaamahina elbowing Aaron in the face when it first happened, but I saw the reaction from the other boys. You can tell when a red card is coming, and you're drilled to know how to play against a side reduced to 14 men. You go through the gears, you build pressure, and then you build some more. You keep the ball, and you keep going through phases, because you know that'll put them in the hurt locker. Once they're in there, you keep squeezing.

Pressure tells. A penalty from Biggs for 19–13 with 27 minutes to go. And then phases, and squeezing, and pressure.

There were six minutes to go when France were awarded a scrum, eight metres from their own line. They'd been playing for almost half an hour with a forward down, every set-piece a rearguard action, every set-piece another stick of firewood burned. So we went hard at them.

Ollivon picked the ball up from the base of the scrum. Tomos Williams ripped it off him. The ball looped in the air, Justin Tipuric caught it.

Tips dived for the line. Stopped just short.

Moriarty onto the ball.

Over the line.

That TMO decision took a thousand lifetimes. Had the rip gone forward? France thought so, although France would. Tips said it had gone straight up. Referee Jaco Peyper agreed.

The score 18–19. Biggs with the conversion, 20–19.

It had been a one-point game in the semi-final in Auckland eight years before. So it would be again, but this time in our favour.

You've always got time.

311

I'd believed that in 2011, and I believed it again. This was us, under this coaching team: an ability to hang in there, a refusal to accept defeat. It wasn't a beautiful try, to win it. It wasn't one that kids would be recreating in back gardens and parks that afternoon. Who cared? Fight it out, find a way, get it done. There's always time.

I know from friends and family sat in front of the TV in the early hours back home that it was exhausting to watch. All those emotions in the red for so long – the fears and the hopes, the wondering and dreaming, the see-sawing score. The creeping doubts and the eventual ecstasy.

You don't experience it the same way, as a player. You can't. Emotion is your enemy, until the end. The prosaic is your friend. Focus on your role and what you have to do next. Next play, next job, next play, next job. Was there a sense of revenge, later that night? Maybe. Since the semi in Auckland, we had won eight of our next nine matches against France. Only the All Blacks beat France more often in that time period. We had been 16–0 down in Paris eight months before, and come back to win; we'd now pulled off our biggest ever comeback in a World Cup match.

People look back now, in a much leaner period for Welsh rugby, and talk about how dominant we were back then. The less charitable might choose to bring luck into it. The obvious question comes up: we're a small nation, the regions don't do very well, and there's never enough funding to go round. How did we do it, back then? How did it last for so long?

We had a great squad of players. Repeatedly. We had coaches who pushed us to breaking and then reassembled the loose pieces. We were never happier than when we were emptying ourselves utterly. But, more than any of that, we just never went away. Some teams, you score a few early tries against them, you know they're going to fold. Not immediately, perhaps, but you can see the foundations are weak, and that the walls will come tumbling down before too long.

Wales? Other teams hated playing us, because you could try everything you wanted, and a lot of it might come off, but we never went away.

I was 27 years old now. I didn't know any other way. My dad had always said to me: 'You will always get out what you put in.' Whenever we took the field, the plays could be complex and the occasion enormous, but it was always simple to me. 'Right, I'm here, and we're going to keep going until the end.'

Keep going. Keep plugging away. You might think there's no glamour in plugging away. But oh, the glory and the holy moments that plugging away can bring you! Never go away. Never go away.

It was close against South Africa, in our semi-final in Yokohama. It was a semi-final. When are they ever romps?

Injuries were mounting for us, just as they had four years before. No Liam Williams, no Josh Navidi, no Foxy. I lasted until just before half-time, and then my hamstring blew, pretty spectacularly. I ripped it from top to bottom, in a very hamstring way; one minute I was sprinting, the next my leg didn't work and I was on the deck. There's seldom much warning, when you do your hamstring properly.

It was blow for blow, when I was on the pitch, and it was blow for blow as I watched, helplessly, on the bench. It was closer than the quarter-final against the Springboks at Twickenham four years before. It was Biggs and Handre Pollard swapping penalties, and it was Damien de Allende smashing through our covering defence to score their try, and us being brave from a scrum in front of their posts to go wide and put Jadsy in for ours. It was 16–16, deep into the match.

Of course we believed. For the last four games against South Africa, winning every one. For all the tight games we'd come through. Because we knew no other way.

This time, it went against us. This time it was the Springboks winning a penalty late on, and Pollard nailing it, because Pollard was always going to nail it. And you can't hide it, when it happens – not in your body language, when you're dragging yourself round the perimeter of the track to salute the fans, not in your words afterwards, not in the most honest place of all, the part of you that you go back to in your most testing moments. That beautiful, painful truth about elite sport, once again: it doesn't matter how it happens, it doesn't matter how big or small the margin, it doesn't matter how much you might want something else. It just is, and nothing's going to change it.

So you go out afterwards, on that night, in the days that follow. All this stuff has to come out somewhere – all the hard yards of pre-season, the camps, the air miles, the hits, the injuries, the sore bodies, the various sore parts of your body that have been sore all the time for months on end. You don't feel any of that, when you win. The magic cloak of victory. When you're on the wrong side of it, it's brutal and horrible and it doesn't want to go away.

We drank a fair amount. A lot of big men in a lot of very small Tokyo bars. I have a wonderful photo of Alun Wyn in a stars-and-stripes motorbike helmet, saluting an uncaring world with a vodka martini. I have memories of watching the Springboks hammer England in the final, and taking some parochial comforts from that. So physically and mentally shattered that none of us could be bothered pretending otherwise.

There was another bar I ended up in with Foxy, Ken Owens and Alun Wyn, and it was completely red shagpile – walls, ceiling, floor. I hadn't really processed it until I sat down and started feeling the chair and the wall. When you're in a bar and the chair is carpeted and the wall is carpeted and the ceiling is carpeted, then your world is probably upside-down enough, and it's probably time to go home.

But we weren't ready then, not quite yet. We never went away, remember?

FOURTEEN

PONT-Y-CLUN TO CARDIFF: CLOSING DOORS

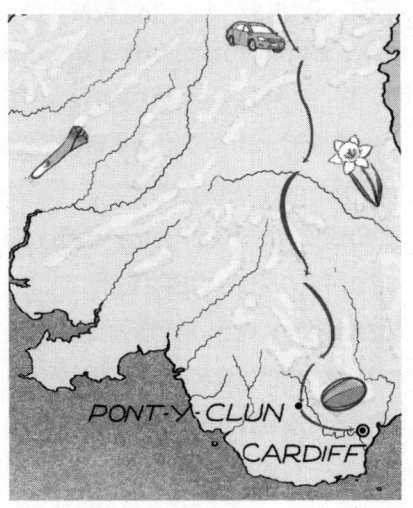

IN WHICH WE TALK ABOUT:

new brooms/a strange meeting/grey areas/'George, you big centurion, you ...'/brother/a lovely wingback chair/a deserted Stade de France/81 minutes and 22 seconds/anterior cruciate ligament/an unpleasant mistake/clunking noises/the return of Gats/hard work with hard work/Boffelli from well beyond halfway/a big decision/the last time

The end of one long regime, the start of a shorter one.

It wasn't just Warren Gatland we lost when he stepped away after that World Cup. Rob Howley had already gone; Shaun Edwards went too, the French having seen more than enough over the past decade to know who they wanted organising their defence. Wayne Pivac came in as head coach from the Scarlets, and the talk was of a new style – more expansive, less restrictive, more liberating.

There was much expectation of big ideas. The slightly confusing reality as a player was that nothing significant seemed to change when we were together. Maybe this was a good thing. We were coming off a Grand Slam, and a World Cup semi-final. We had a lot of experienced players going deep into the later part of their careers. The training week looked exactly the same. The training methods were the same.

Wayne still had an unreal squad at his disposal. Alun Wyn, Ken Owens. Taulupe, Foxy, Liam Williams, Gareth Davies. That was a huge asset to the new broom that brushed the same way as the old broom. Some of the boys got on well with him. The Scarlets lads knew how he worked. Like every coach, he had his favourites. For others, it would take longer to figure out what was going on.

If the messaging was similar, the delivery differed. We were used to simplicity and directness. 'Boys, this is what we're going to do. Sort it out.' Under Wayne, particularly with Stephen Jones as backs coach, it was always positive, just as it had been when I'd trained with Jonesy in my very first week with the senior Welsh squad back in the autumn of

2010. It was fewer direct orders and more questions – 'That was good, but could we do it another way?' 'Have you thought about trying this instead?

I could see how this was a good thing. Jonesy was instinctively positive. He had an appreciation of how intense it had been before. When you worked with him, you were under the same pressures to deliver, but it no longer felt like you were under the microscope every day. Rather than being hard on you all the time, there was a greater emphasis on enjoyment. Less focus from Wayne on rigid standards off the pitch; a willingness to let those who wanted to let their hair down do so. Wayne and Jonesy gave you the energy to enjoy what you were going through. The world of coaching was changing to match the changing world around it.

Wayne is a people person. He believes that when players are happy, they play their best. Collaboration can be preferable to conflict. Being positive was my natural way. I wanted to keep being that way. When I was left out of the starting XV for one game and Wayne told me to go back to the Ospreys (the region I had joined on leaving Northampton in 2018) because he wanted me firing, I got it. It made sense, and I bought into it and I went to see him to get the most out of it.

'Let's give me something tangible to work on, so I can come back to you on Monday and we can review it. And I'll sit down with the other coaches and review it with them too.'

Wayne agreed. 'Yeah, okay. Come and see me after training.'

So I went after training. I took my notepad and my pen. I asked him what he wanted me to focus on, as I would have done with Howlers, as I would have done with Shaun and

Gats. He said attack was a big focus. He asked me what I thought.

'Well, I know my own goals but this is something that you said to me that I need to set. So what's your opinion on what I need to do?'

I was thinking about Howlers telling me to keep making those support runs, because nine times the ball wouldn't come to me, but on the tenth, if you stopped, that was the one that would come your way.

'Oh yeah, you've got to just run hard.'

The old regime had been about pure detail. Percentages, stats, hard evidence. Metres made, speed of ball. Wayne's way was different. It was about feel. It was about the big picture rather than the individual paint strokes. I was still expecting the old ways from a new coach.

'Right, well how do you want to measure that? How do I give you a tangible measurement against that?'

'Oh, we'll know. I'll see your game and we'll know.'

I asked him what he wanted to look at in defence. I remembered Shaun drilling us on the rip before Scott Williams burgled Courtney Lawes at Twickenham in 2012.

He looked at me. 'Defensively? Well, what do you think?'

'Well, again it comes down to what you think, really.'

'Okay … make your hits.'

'Right … is it make all of my hits? Make half of my hits? It would be great to have something tangible.'

'No, make your hits.'

So I wrote down 'Defence.' Next to it I just put, 'Make my hits.'

I asked about counter-attack.

'Yep ... yep ... want to see you full of energy for this.'

'Okay. Anything we can measure, so I can make sure I do it?'

'No, just full of energy.'

He told me he wanted me back on the wing, having moved me to outside centre. Keen to make this work as well as possible, wanting to get it all spot on, I asked what he wanted to see from me there. He said he wanted me to make sure I caught all my high balls.

I wasn't trying to be difficult, or to undermine him. I was just accustomed to a different way of doing things. The way I had been schooled, I wanted more. I wanted to get right the things he was expecting from me.

'Right, to recap, you want me to ... attack: run hard.'

'Yep.'

'Defence: make my hits.'

'Yep.'

'Aerially, take all the high balls.'

'Yep.'

'And have good energy.'

'Yep.'

'Okay, and how am I going to measure this so then I know I've had a good game when I come back on Monday, and we sit down to review it?'

'Don't worry, I'll be watching the game and I'll know.'

I went back to the Ospreys. I started on the wing. After four minutes, we had an injury, so I had to move to centre. I scored a try.

I went back into Wales camp on the Monday morning. Wayne came bowling over.

'Yep, mate, you were outstanding.'

'Ah, it was good that I played both positions.'

'Both? Yeah, yeah, yeah, both.'

As much as the old guard had been brutal at times, they had been consistent. They were across everything. If you played in two positions for your region, they knew about it. They had driven standards, and we had responded to them. If you had messed up, they would tell you that you'd messed up. If you were shit, they would tell you that you were shit. There was no grey area.

This was softer. It was new. There was room for opinions and differences in them.

So there was a whole lot of change, with Covid thrown in there too. At times it seemed puzzling that we could carry on playing rugby in a pandemic, in a sport that involves more physical proximity than any other, a scrum as close to a mobile virus transmission unit as you could ever dream up. Even when the television directors realised how underwhelming it was in the complete absence of crowd noise, they would often pipe the fake cheers in at the wrong time. You'd score a try and the celebrations would follow three seconds later.

I was glad we could play. It just made the occasion of my 100th cap very different to how I might have imagined it. England in Cardiff in February 2021, in the Six Nations, to win the Triple Crown – it was the stuff of dreams, something I had once added to my list of goals, once all the ones on the old list from the back of my Llandovery door had been ticked off.

'Play for Wales 100 times.'

I even got interviewed for BBC Sport's coverage by Sam Warburton, although he had to be on his laptop in his kitchen and I was watching a socially distanced monitor in a deserted team hotel at the Vale. He started off with a howling line. 'George, you big centurion you, how are you?' I came back at him, because that's the way we always were – 'I'm not starting with that, Sam, that's rubbish ...'

You allow yourself a little daydream about how it might be, when you get close to a landmark like that. I imagined my family being pitch-side. I imagined all my mates from down the years on free tickets up in the stands. And then when it came down to it, I ran out of the tunnel and there was nobody there, and you realise you look an absolute idiot because you're clapping your own entry onto the field.

We beat England comfortably. We stuck 40 points on them. You wanted to celebrate it all with a Welsh crowd, but it was just red seats and the blue sky up above. The next day, the WRU kindly opened the stadium up again, so I could walk onto the pitch with Becky and carry our new arrival, Jac. Becky had given me a congratulatory card when I'd got home the previous night and I was ploughing into a pint and some Cadbury's, the rock 'n' roll celebrations of a pro rugby player. With it was a present: a tiny t-shirt with one word on it: 'Brother'. That was her rather lovely way of telling me that Jac was soon going to be joined by another new arrival. Take that, Covid.

I'd loved speaking to Sam, once he'd got the cheese out of the way. It was the nods I got from my peers that meant the most to me, after my family. When someone who has played alongside you, who has lived your life – when someone like Alun Wyn shakes your hand and gives you a brother hug and says, 'fucking hell, G, that's good' – it almost knocks you for six then, because they know. The sacrifices, the pain, the state of your body, the pressures.

Because being a rugby player in Wales is brutal, absolutely brutal; when it's good, it's good, and when it's bad, you're left in no doubt you're really fucking bad. My fear, I realised that week, had always been that I would fall short of my true potential. That I would fall short of expectations.

When I hit 100 caps, it felt like no-one could ever say that I wasn't a good player. No-one could ever say I didn't give my best.

You don't get to 100 caps by accident. You don't get to 100 caps because of injuries to others. You don't get to 100 caps because there is a coach who fancies you. And so, a few days later, I tried to enjoy the moment more than I might otherwise have allowed myself to. We were renting a house in Penarth at the time, right by the pier. I'd go out and swim in the sea for recovery, take Jac out for a walk in his buggy along the pier. It was a nice big place, but Mum and Dad were staying, and Jac was pulling things off the wall, and Mum was running around telling everyone to put a coaster under their mugs of tea, and Becky was clattering around, and the two dogs were jumping and barking and generally being too excitable for a house that wasn't theirs.

I went and sat in a lovely wingback chair in the front room, looking out to sea. Quite naturally I fell into a real slow rhythm of breathing, hearing the noises of family life behind me but looking out at a calm, flat day in Penarth. I've told you how I always talked to myself, in the hard times. How I asked myself those questions. 'You wanted this. You wanted this. Do you still want it?'

Now those thoughts turned round at me. 'You wanted it. And you did it. You did it.'

Through all the years of the hard regime of Gats, Howlers and Shaun, maybe I didn't allow myself to enjoy the successes as much as I could or should have done. It's not that they wouldn't have allowed me. It was just our mindset at the time. It was as if we were scared that enjoyment meant complacency. Like being satisfied meant losing our edge.

Here I was now, the sixth man in Welsh rugby history to play 100 times for his country. Alun Wyn. Gethin Jenkins. Stephen Jones. Gareth Thomas. Martyn Williams. I sat in that chair, and I breathed, and I allowed myself to take it in for the first time in 11 years.

I had wanted it. And I had done it.

We walked out at a deserted Stade de France four weeks later with a Grand Slam in our sights. There were almost 1,000 caps in our starting XV, the most experienced Welsh side of all time. That was what had taken us there.

We nearly made it all the way, too. A mad old game, four tries in the first 20 minutes, Romain Taofifenua and Antoine Dupont for France, Dan Biggar and Josh Navidi for us. It was

17–17 at half-time. After Josh Adams scored in the second half off a Tips grubber, we had a 10-point lead, and with 13 minutes to go Paul Willemse was red-carded for them and it seemed we were home.

But nearly is never there. Taulupe went to the bin. Fourteen men apiece, 10 minutes to go. Liam Williams got a yellow card for going off his feet at a ruck, and we were down to 13.

We held on until the 77th minute. Lungs screaming, legs in bits. Charles Ollivon smashed over. We exited, and we had the ball just short of halfway, and there were 80 seconds on the clock.

We got pinged again. Sealing off at a ruck.

France hitting us hard down the left, spreading it wide right. The clock in the red. Pick and go's, our defence stretching, stretching. Wave after wave coming at us.

There were 81 minutes and 22 seconds on the clock when they went wide left for the last time. You train for the worst, a lot of the time. And when I looked up, I saw the worst picture you could ever train for: a three on two, with about 35 metres of space outside them.

I had Tips inside me. Tomos Williams was on my right. And Gael Fickou played it brilliantly, because he dummied as if to come back inside, so I had to hold for him, and that left Tomos coming back to cover Arthur Vincent, and Brice Dulin outside him with all the time in the pandemic world to take the pass and go over in the corner.

Sometimes you just have to blank out the horrible times. Shake hands, walk off the pitch and try to think about something else. It's not easy, when you're sitting in a dressing-room with a group of broken men, in a city shut down and nowhere to run and hide or drink and fall.

Nothing you can say or do to make it better. All of it hanging. In a very Welsh way, just absolutely hanging.

The year wasn't done with dishing it out. In April, Ospreys were playing Cardiff. I'd played a lot of rugby by this point, and I was weary and bashed up. My body was giving me stern words; with selection for the British and Irish Lions tour of South Africa imminent, I was expecting our coach Toby Booth to give a few of the boys some time off, with little left for us to play for in the domestic season.

He did. I just wasn't one of them. He pulled me aside a few days before.

'Look, I need you to play.'

'Well, I'm a bit creaky – do you really need me?'

'Yeah, I need you.'

Me thinking: 'You don't need me. You've got all the academy boys screaming out for gametime and this is a prime opportunity to give them some. They'll be hissing. They're fresh.'

Toby again: 'I need you.'

It wasn't a very good game. The second half began. I gave chase to a nothing sort of kick – old habits, and all that. The ball bounced up. I re-gathered it, not realising the referee had already blown his whistle, eyes only for the defender coming up. I put my weight through my right leg to step left.

I'd heard the boys talk about ACL ruptures. How the pain comes in straightaway and goes from zero to 100. I got to 100 alright. But by the time I was carried back to the physio's room, I could feel almost nothing. I was at about 10.

For about a minute, I thought I'd been an absolute softy. I was ready to ask them to strap it up and get me back on. That was when our physio Chris Towers looked at me.

'G ... no.'

'What do you mean, "G ... no"?'

'I'm really sorry, but you've done your ACL.'

Of course you don't want to believe it. I asked him how he knew. He did the basic test. It instantly became blatantly obvious.

I burst into tears at that point. I wasn't expecting to get picked by Gats for the Lions tour, but I thought I'd done enough to put my name in the mixer. And in that one moment, it just all bubbled over and I just went. All of it, sweeping over me. Three Tests on the tour in 2013, that try in the first, the Folau tackle in the second, the way we won the third. Doing my hamstring in New Zealand in 2017. Not even getting on the plane, this time.

Anterior cruciate ligament rupture. You hear those four words, when you're 100 caps in, and it's hard not to think it might be the end. I wasn't a bashed-up old car, at 29 years old. But I was also a model with 300,000 miles on the clock. I had a full service history, all original parts, well looked after, but the mileage on the clock could not be ignored.

They gave me OxyContin, after the operation. Opioids were an unpleasant mistake. Once I'd nodded off on the sofa talking to my mother and come to, dribbling, four hours later without realising I'd even been asleep, I realised they weren't for me. Our doc at Ospreys put me on more suitable medication, and I started getting my head around the recovery.

It wasn't going to be big milestones all the time. It was going to be little milestones, week by week. It was going to be lying on the sofa in a knee-brace, not being able to play with my son. It was taking confidence from other players who had been through it and come back okay.

This is where elite sport does help you. Establish your goals, work towards them.

'Right, this week I'm going to try to get my knee to bend past 30 degrees.'

'This week, I'm going to make sure I can do a partial loading for five seconds.'

'Now, I've noticed my calf muscle is atrophying, so rather than doing 20 calf raises this set, I'm going to do 25.'

It wasn't a straight line to recovery. I suffered from persistent swelling around the knee, and had to go back in for a second procedure to tidy it up. That put me back another nine weeks. I knew that every day for the rest of my life I would have to do activation on it each morning, ice each evening, to keep it moving and keep it functioning.

I wasn't stupid. I had seen my dad be physical all his life, always motivated, running from our house to RAF Valley, doing a day's work, going to the gym, then running home again. I had watched him age and seen how his body changed and how his body moved. Why should I be immune to the same processes, when I had done it all for a living, rather than a fond hobby? Exercise is good for you, but only to a certain level. Sometimes I would try to give Becky a lie-in, so I'd take the boys downstairs, me carrying Tomi. Five steps in, my good knee would make a cracking noise. Jac would say,

'You okay, Daddy?' And I'd say, 'Yeah, I'm okay, I'm okay.' Five more steps in, and my ankle would start making clunking noises. 'What's that noise, daddy?' 'Ah, it's just my joints warming up for the day.'

I wanted to be able to run around with Jac, and with Tomi. I wanted to be able to play football with them, and go out on our bikes. I didn't want to have to take 25 minutes to do my activation and prehab beforehand.

But I never questioned if it was worth it, all this collateral damage. I daydreamed about an advance in medical science, where they could give you one jab and the fluid sped simultaneously to all your joints, and lubricated them and made them work beautifully and smoothly and pain-free again. I also knew there was no Control George, a second me who had stayed in Rhoscolyn and never begun this mad journey. A George who worked on the land, or in an office. Control George might have knackered knees from tramping round fields all day. He might have a bad back from sitting slumped in front of a computer. If you put two cards in front of me and told me they were my two options – card A, where I played rugby and struggled to get down the stairs, and card B, where I skipped down the stairs every morning but never ran out for my country, never scored a try that made 73,000 people scream the place down, never stood shoulder to shoulder with men like Sam and Foxy and Alun Wyn – I'm always picking A. I'm never not doing what I'm doing now.

Rehab? I could do that. It was familiar. I knew it would work. It was always worth it. Always.

*   *   *

It would be more than a year before I returned to the Welsh camp. Not long afterwards, I was followed by a familiar face. Wayne Pivac had won only three of his last 12 games in charge. Wales had lost at home to Italy and Georgia. With a World Cup coming around, the WRU turned to a man who had taken us to two semi-finals and a single point each time from the final itself. Gats was back.

A lot of it made sense. What didn't was how much had changed. Welsh regional rugby was in even more of a mess. Less money, fewer world-class players. The national squad was losing its icons at a startling rate. Alun Wyn and Ken Owens would retire from international rugby before the World Cup, Jonathan Davies and Josh Navidi too. Gats would naturally want to play the same physically dominant rugby that had worked so well for so long, but the firepower was no longer there. Shaun Edwards was with France. Robin McBryde had gone. Howlers was still serving time for his misdemeanours It was like *Anchorman 2*: a good idea, in isolation, but when you've been raised on on the original *Anchorman*, you think – was it really the best notion to try to do it all over again?

So it was a tough Six Nations for us, in the late winter and early spring of 2023. We finished second bottom in the table, our only win coming over Italy. Going to France for the World Cup that autumn, my knee felt manageable, and I was settled at outside centre, but I'd seen enough of this tournament to understand the pressures we were under. Gats was in charge, and we had historical success in our recent past, yet we were a fundamentally different group to those other years.

Only half our squad had been to a World Cup before. Some of the younger lads sometimes seemed unprepared for what it took to thrive there.

We had been pushed hard in pre-season, because that was the Gats way. It challenged me like never before, because my body was creaking now in a way it hadn't been in Japan or England or New Zealand. Some of the boys were naïve; they would ask you questions about what kit they should be wearing, and you wanted to remind them it was all in the schedule given out to us all, and they should relish the responsibility of looking after themselves. Some seemed worryingly impressed by what had happened before. They would ask about the toughest training camps we had ever done. You'd tell them about Spala, and Gdansk, and Switzerland, and Doha, and they would be astonished.

'No way you did that!'

'Yeah, you just get on with it ...'

There would be complaints from some about a session we were doing that was nowhere near as bad as what we had done before. You didn't want to sound like an old man who thought the past better than the future, but you'd also find yourself explaining that there was no point wasting your energy worrying about a session, because worrying wasn't going to do anything about it.

It was a new kind of mindset for us old guard to get our heads around. We had never queried what Gats and Shaun and Howlers had put us through. We had always been put to the sword, and we never questioned why we had to do an extra rep, or get up early for an extra session before breakfast. We did it because we were told, and we kept doing it because it worked. Some of the new crop were struggling to get it. They couldn't understand what was going on, and they couldn't process real hard work, because they'd never been exposed to it before.

Naturally, with that disconnect in daily view, it was seldom always plain sailing in camp. We got a serious amount of great work done, and it could be liberating, seeing expectations set lower than before. It also worried me. I had to do what I'd always done, and keep my own energy high, and shake everyone's hand each morning, and bring the positive vibes and the passion. We were here now. I'd done all the hard work. There was no point in moaning about it or going home. I might as well fly into it. Full-fat milk, every time.

It worked, up to a point. We had a brilliant tussle with Fiji – of course we did – and we got through it, squeaky though it might have been towards the end. We put 40 points on Eddie Jones' Australia, Gareth Anscombe pulling the strings. We started really well against Argentina in the quarter-finals, me making a half-break up the middle early on in the build-up to Dan Biggar's try, us 10–0 up after 20 minutes and still 10–6 up at half-time.

It's a beautiful stadium, the Stade Velodrome in Marseille. The sun was shining, and you could hear our supporters in the curved stands all around. But it was one of those games where neither team was firing. It got sloppy, and we started to struggle at the breakdown, and they kept kicking penalties, including a monster from well inside his own half from Emiliano Boffelli.

It wasn't that we weren't trying. Even with us not playing well, we were always in it. Tomos Williams made a great sniping break to put us back in front. But you could feel the momentum ebbing away from us, as if all the additional emotion we had gone through to get that far had taken too much of a toll, and as it became a caveman fight, blow for blow, their fitness and energy began to tell, at the exact point we had to step up and deliver.

We couldn't fire enough shots. They went over from close range to edge in front; Rio Dyer made a break and Louis Rees-Zammit almost went over in the corner for what would have been an unreal finish. Instead, Nicolas Sanchez picked off a pass as we tried to force it. A great read from Sanchez, and at that point, the game was gone. Absolutely gone.

We were physically and emotionally spent. Had we somehow wriggled through, could we have mustered anything more against the All Blacks in the semi-final? You'd hope, at that point, for that gameday, at that stage of a World Cup, you could go again. But it's a tough place to be. Argentina had beaten us by 12 points, and the All Blacks would go on to beat them by 38. I always believed in rugby miracles; I had been part of more than a few. Maybe that's why I sensed this might not be another.

I knew too it was my last World Cup. Defeat sat with me longer for that reason, more than any other. Less painful than the one-point semi-final against France as a 19-year-old, less painful than the one-point defeat against South Africa as a 27-year-old. Right there on the pain-ometer with the other quarter-final defeat, to Fourie du Preez's late try at Twickenham in October 2015.

I'd become quite good at dealing with sporting grief, after those bright days and dark nights. I had my own process and strategy. Each player is different; some boys can walk away the next day and be fine with it, some will fester for weeks. It took me a hell of a time to get over this one.

I had a beer with Gats, in the aftermath. An honest conversation, as many words that night as we had shared in discrete years in our past. I was out of contract with the Ospreys at the end of the season. At some point, probably soon, my time with Wales would have to come to an end too.

I had no offers to stay in Welsh rugby. I did to go to France, but if I went over there, it would be hard commuting back and forth to play for Wales. Gats was as forthright as ever: George, you have to look after your family now. Things here are tough.

I was long enough in the tooth to understand I was just another slab of meat in the machine. If you're a watcher of sport, there's sentiment left, right and centre. It's all about sentiment and emotion. Inside the machine, there is no sentiment. Loyalty is expected one way but never guaranteed the other. I looked at the offer to move to Aix and play for Provence for two years. I could take Becky and Jac and Tomi. We could begin another adventure as a family. I looked and I looked, and it all made sense.

I didn't think about my last game for Wales until it was right upon me. Saturday 16 March 2024, Italy at home. A Six Nations where we had played four and lost four, when I had been left out of the opening match against Scotland, brought back against England and Ireland and then dropped for the defeat by France. The 121st time I would run out to represent my country.

The week before was busy. I made my retirement announcement early and got all my media stuff done with it. I wanted to focus on the here and now. I wanted to focus on beating Italy.

We trained Tuesday. I spent Wednesday wrapped up in my family. Thursday, the last big day of training. So it was Friday, and the captain's run on the pitch at the Principality, when it arrived like a gut-buster.

The stadium was empty. Quiet. The sun was shining. The roof was open. Pigeons were flapping around. Becky and the boys were allowed into the stands. And once we had done our last few drills, and caught a few high balls, and the kickers had taken their tees off the field – then I just stood in the middle of the pitch, and it hit me like an absolute train.

'Enjoy it, because it goes so fast.' That's what Shane Williams had said to me after my first Test.

'Take in every minute, because it goes so fast.' That had been Stephen Jones, at the end of my first autumn series.

Here I was, 13 and a half years on, four Six Nations titles, four World Cups and two Grand Slams. Only Alun Wyn and Gethin with more caps, only Shane with more tries. And I stood there surrounded by all that pristine grass, and I realised my entire life had been about being in this place. A sad moment, because it was the last time; a happy one, because I'd actually managed to live my dream. When I had set out on this journey as a young man in the sleepiest corner of a distant island – here was exactly where I always wanted to be.

I could feel the sun on my back. I could hear the boys doing their last bit of prep away behind the posts. No other noise. I looked around, and peace came upon me.

I was able to take the kids into the changing-room afterwards. On gameday, the WRU were brilliant; they gave me a room and a box for my family, they helped me with the stupid amount of tickets that I had to find. I led the team out, and Italy were sensational. And then sport, which had given me so much, so many amazing highs and pleasures and experiences and formed me and shaped me and been this wonderful, wonderful thing in my life – sport decided to be true to itself, and deliver one final rabbit punch to the back of the head.

I ruptured my Achilles about two minutes from full-time. It felt like someone had shot me from the stands. I also knew there was no way in hell I was going to let them stretcher me off. Not now. Not in this game, in this moment. I would walk off this pitch, the final time I ever played for Wales. My arms might be heavy over the medics' shoulders, and I might not be able to put my right foot down, but I was getting myself over that whitewash.

I had to speak at the players' function afterwards. Standing there on crutches, looking for the light. Bringing the positive vibes, one more time: 'Well played, Italy, although you could have done me a favour today. Our lads – keep going. There are good times coming. The squad is here. Trust in yourself and trust in the system. Keep grafting and it'll come.'

Becky came with me. Jac and Tomi were running around my legs. My family and my kids are the most important things in the world. In this moment, I didn't want my boys to see I wasn't strong or bulletproof. I wanted them to think I was a superhero and I could take everything.

I didn't want them to see me cry. Not because I didn't want them to be okay with their emotions, or to be able to cry themselves. I wanted them to know things won't always go to plan, but that we'll get through it together.

I wanted them to see that rugby was the defining part of my life, and that I had loved it. I wanted them to look back and see nothing but my best all the time. I wanted them to see Daddy finishing rugby in a happy place, because it had given him so much.

That's all I wanted in that moment.

EPILOGUE

So now this journey of mine has taken me to a new place. The sun shines in Aix-en-Provence, a lot more than it does in Rhoscolyn. Jac and Tomi spend a lot of time running around outdoors. I rehabbed my Achilles, and now I'm running around again too, in the Pro D2.

I wonder, sometimes, what would happen if I could go back and talk now to the kid who grew up obsessed with the thrill of accelerating into open spaces, the boy who loved hearing everyone else dropping away far behind him. What I would say to the 16-year-old George in his first term at Llandovery College, homesick as hell and compensating by compiling a long list of rugby goals on the back of his bedroom door?

I know what 16-year-old George would think: who's this weird guy in a curry-stained tie? Why has he introduced himself as Future George? What are you doing on school property? Mr Banks? MR BANKS ...

Future George, once he'd validated his identity, and apologised for not signing in at the front office, would probably keep it disappointingly simple.

'Young homesick George, keep plugging away. Keep doing what you're doing. It's worth it. But for God's sake, make sure you enjoy it along the way.'

I'm not a man for regrets, at this stage in the journey. I've travelled too far, seen so many places. But that's my one, if I have one. Maybe I should have enjoyed it far more than I did.

I thought, if you wanted to be the best, you couldn't linger in the good times. You couldn't savour your achievements or you would lose your edge.

I realise now that the Grand Slam days only come around on rare and sacred occasions. Not many people get to go to the semi-finals of a World Cup. Not many people get to go on a British and Irish Lions tour. Not many people get to play for their country over 100 times.

I came from North Wales. A place like no other. No-one else for a long time had made it to Cardiff from there, so I always felt like the baton-holder. When I thought about all the people who helped me along the way – my family, my friends, my coaches, all the uncles and aunties who weren't my real uncles and aunties – I felt I had to do it right by those people, because no-one else had the opportunity. I was doing it for these people who put time and energy and love into my progress. That pressure to make them proud outweighed any idea of revelling in any of it – having a couple of beers, or going out, or not going full-fat milk in every single training session. Of looking around and saying, I'm doing alright, here.

I felt I had to set the standard. I had to set the tone. It was my family and my home and my legacy. I didn't want to be remembered as that guy people in sport talk about sometimes – 'Ah, he had all the attributes, all the skills. He had unreal fitness. Unreal competitor. But he just let himself down with his effort. He just didn't quite get it. He couldn't hold it all together.'

It's hard, sometimes, this life of triumph and despair. In elite sport, people equate satisfaction with going soft and losing your drive. It's a game that you play with yourself mentally all the time: how much is not enough, how much is too much? I'm not sure that I ever found out.

I saw a changing of the guard towards the end. How the younger generation are very happy to talk about that sort of thing, whereas we were the opposite. We were the ones, thanks to Gats and Shaun and Howlers, with a bit of a bastard in us for evermore. Never complaining, always pushing. 'Ah no, just do your job. Be quiet. Get on with it.' Would I change it? Probably not. Because that's what got me to where I am and got me fighting and hissing to where I needed to be.

Something else, when I think about my mum and dad, my brother Josh. When I think about Daf Robs and Ceitho, and Keith Withers and Barry Banks.

I didn't leave them, as my journey took me onwards. I carried them with me. I carried them all the time.

It was never just for me. It was for us.

So this generation of mine, the Alun Wyns and Sams and Foxys and Halfers and all the rest? Maybe we'll come full circle, as we age. We'll become excessively sentimental older men. We'll sit in the rugby club, dropping curry on our ties, and it'll all come out. We'll tell each other how much we love each other. We'll cry at the drop of a hat. We'll think of a training camp in Spala or Gdansk, and we won't even shiver that much.

Maybe. I'll report back and let you know, on that one.

ACKNOWLEDGEMENTS

It's so hard to know where to start, as so many people have helped me along the way. I'm sorry if I miss anyone, but you all know that you've had a huge impact on my life.

Thank you to my early coaches: Martin Williams, Iori Hughes, Steve Richards, Dafydd Myrddin, Keith Withers.

To Andy McCann, Christian Abt (or DHL, as I call him), George Wilson (or Lil G), David Luxton and Archie O'Reilly. And to all the team at HarperCollins: Jonathan Taylor, Tom Whiting, Adam Humphrey, Georgina Atsiaris.

To Adidas, for supporting me from the very start, and Gavin Murphy and the Team at Breitling.

My last acknowledgment goes to Tom Fordyce. A massive thank you for holding my hand throughout this process. Thank you for being very kind and patient trying to work out my spelling and grammar. I've loved every second of it.

PICTURE CREDITS